REPORT FROM
RED CHINA

HARRISON FORMAN

NEW YORK : HENRY HOLT AND COMPANY

Contents

PART I

The Border Region

iii

PART II

◇◇◇◇◇◇◇◇◇

The Front

PART I

✧✧✧✧✧✧✧✧✧✧

The Border Region

To

SANDRA *and* BRENDA LU

1

❖❖❖❖❖❖❖❖

Hush-Hush In Chungking

It was a curious anomaly. China was battling for survival against a strangling Japanese blockade. Yet half a million of the best troops in China were reportedly being used to blockade some of their own people, the Chinese Communists in the north—a blockade which recurrently threatened to explode into a bloody civil war.

We all knew about it, of course. It was an open secret—and for the resident foreign correspondents in Chungking it was the biggest hush-hush story in China. Not that any of us knew much of the truth of what was going on inside that blockade. None the less, we were never permitted to say a word about the Communists in any of our dispatches—except perhaps to quote the Generalissimo and other high government officials when they accused the Communists of "forcibly occupying national territory," of "assaulting National Government troops," or of "obstructing the prosecution of the war."

Such charges naturally only whetted our interest in the Communists. By and large we pressmen were neither Communists nor Communist-sympathizers. The Communists claimed to wield influence over something like ninety million people in north and central China—equivalent to nearly three-fourths of the population of America. This alone made them news. Yet during the past five

I

years the Government had not allowed a single newspaperman to go up there. At one time or another we had all filed applications for permission to visit the Communist-held areas. There were no flat refusals. One of us was told, "Later." Another, "Inconvenient at present." A third, "Unsettled conditions."

Just what was happening behind that blockade? Were these Communists really as bad as they were painted by the Government authorities? Were they treacherously attacking Central Government troops? Did they refuse to fight Japanese? Were they consorting with the puppets at Nanking? Were they oppressing the people? What connection did they have with Russian Communism, and what influence and direction—if any—was being exercised from Moscow? How were they managing to carry on behind the double blockade—a blockade by Japs on one side and Central Government troops on the other? What were the basic points of difference between the Kuomintang * and the Kungchantang,† and what were the possibilities of a peaceful settlement? Just what part do they, or can they, play in the war against Japan?

From the standpoint of straight news, these and many other pertinent questions required answers—answers based on observed and indisputable facts. But there seemed to be little chance that we should get such answers so long as that blockade continued.

Then one day last spring the Government Spokesman, in reply to a question asked at one of our regular weekly press conferences, officially denied the existence of a blockade of the Communist-controlled areas. We newsmen were quick to seize upon this opening. Jointly we drew up a petition addressed directly to the Generalissimo. It was signed by the resident correspondents of virtually the whole world. And at the next press conference we presented this formally and publicly to the Government Spokesman with the request that it be forwarded to the Generalissimo.

Much to our surprise, Chiang Kai-shek agreed to let us go—

* The Kuomintang Party, headed by Generalissimo Chiang Kai-shek, has assumed responsibility for the formation and operation of the National Government of China during the "Period of Tutelage" until the establishment of constitutional government which has been promised "within one year after the conclusion of the war."

† The Kungchantang is the Chinese Communist Party.

as guests of the Government—though it was some months before we eventually did get away.

It takes a week or more to go by truck or bus from Chungking to Paochi—except in case of breakdown. And trucks and buses operating in hinterland China always break down at some time or other for periods ranging from a few minutes to a few days. By air the trip to Paochi takes exactly two hours. A chartered flight in a big Douglas DC3 piloted by an American took our party of six foreign correspondents and fifteen Chinese on the first leg of our journey. We were officially known as the Press Party to the Northwest.

The walled city of Paochi (literally "Precious Chicken") is the terminus of the Belgian-built Lunghai Railway. It is a bustling little boomtown with a frontier atmosphere. From the airfield on the high plateau overlooking the city, Paochi, surrounded by yellowing fields of wheat, made a beautiful picture set squarely in the midst of the broad, fertile valley below. A bus took us down a switchback road, past rows of cave-homes gouged into the cliffside and through the city's main street lined with gawking citizens to a special train that awaited us. It was a modern deluxe Wagons-Lits sleeper, and the luxurious diner attached to it was spic and span, with perfectly clean linen, polished silver, and starched napkins decoratively fanned in sparkling water glasses. A vase of big red roses stood on every table.

As we waited for our train to get started, a freight train pulled in from the East. One of its boxcars, in sharp contrast to our luxurious accommodations, was packed with missionary refugees from the Honan fighting front to the east. There were fifty-four of them, of whom sixteen were children including three babies in arms. The car was almost filled with bedding, furniture, cribs, bicycles, and baggage of all kinds. Babies cried, children bawled, parents scolded, while others of the grownups crowded around us, all talking at once, each trying to tell us of his own harrowing escape from the advancing Japs. We listened until our engineer sounded his whistle and we boarded our train for a side-trip to the Foh Sing cotton mills near by.

Evacuated from Hankow just before the Japs captured the city in 1938, the Foh Sing mills, one of the largest in Free China, had moved to Paochi and set up its machinery in huge caves dug so deep into the cliffs that, though they had been repeatedly bombed, not so much as a spindle had been jarred. Four thousand people work in these caves, which are well lighted and well ventilated and look like freshly whitewashed subway tunnels.

It was nearly midnight when our special pulled into Sian. In the glow from its brilliantly lit, templelike railway station we were greeted by almost a hundred of the city's notables. After introductions and the usual exchanges of calling cards we were whisked off to the excellent Sian Guest House.

Sian is one of the largest cities in China. High in traditions and history, it was the cradle of Chinese civilization and the favorite capital of emperors down through the centuries. Its creneled city wall, built centuries ago, is the most perfectly preserved in all China. Of massive stone, fifteen feet high, it is constructed in the form of a huge rectangle, with imposing battlements spaced at regular intervals.

We spent four very interesting days in Sian. Though we were guests of the Generalissimo, the local government officials were not quite sure how to handle us. As official guests we were to be accorded all courtesies and assistance. As sharp-eyed newspapermen we might see undesired things or get wrong impressions. So, though all was smiles and *ke-chi* (politeness) in our formal relations, the Sian officials watched and recorded our every word and movement. We learned later that special ricksha-men, who insisted that we make use of their services, were assigned to the Guest House. When we refused to ride they followed us wherever we went. We mildly protested, and the ricksha-men quickly disappeared, to be succeeded by plainclothesmen who loafed about outside the Guest House door and followed us with bicycles in case we picked up cruising rickshas on the street. We took it all more or less goodnaturedly, laughing and joking with these men, whose interest in us worried us but little. We were unsure whether all this was done in obedience to orders from Chungking or at the command of the Sian Government which is notorious for its indifference to Chungking authority.

The second day, as I was entering the Guest House, a messenger handed me an envelope. The letter it contained was written in curious English, and I shall print it here word for word, withholding only the signature just in case the name signed was the fellow's right name:

Dear Mr. Forman:

We are deeply obliged to you and your friends and your countries for your help and sympathy with our self-defence war. With a desire of knowing the "Inside Northwestern China" now you arrive here.

When you ask to visit Yenan, this special and strange place, there brings about an unprecedented agitation among the Chungking authorities. As facing a calamity the Government officials, from Chungking to Sian, from Generalissimo Chiang to General Ho Ying-chin, Chang Tze-chung, Tai Li [the head of National Military Council secret police], Hsu En-tseng [head of Bureau of Investigation and Statistics— the Secret Service of Kuomintang], are wholly mobilized. In Shensi General Hu Tsung-nan [Commander of troops blockading Communists], Chu Shao-chou [Governor of Shensi] and many other important government officials are also busily and nervously mobilized. They prepare and discuss how to deceive you, to blockade you, and to watch you.

Now, I want to tell you some of these preparations and knacks by which they "welcome" you:

When Generalissimo Chiang promised you the visit General Tai Li flew Shensi with Chiang's instructions on February 14th. He took a conference instantly with General Hu Tsung-nan and gave instructions which order how to prepare and arrange in secret.

Generalissimo Chiang appropriates a fund of five million dollars for this "calamity" of your visit and three-fifths of this amount is used in secret service—"special arrangements," that is, blocked, deceit, surveillance, and "guide." Receiving the instructions from Generalissimo, General Hu Tsung-nan immediately convened the "special conference" discussing the problems and the methods of surveillance, hiding, blockade, isolating, camouflage, counterfeit, translation, guiding and following as you arrive at Sian. Many secret policemen are preparing in the disguise of translators, ushers, servants, and roomboys. To assure the fulfillment of these arrangements, "Sian Provisional Headquarters" were established. Its organization and role are as follows:

COMMANDING SYSTEM

Commander-in-Chief—General Lo Tze-kai [Hu Tsung-nan's chief of staff].

Vice-Commander—Ku Cheng-ting (Head of Shensi Provincial Kuomintang Headquarters, chief secretary of the so-called "Special Conference," and the leader in the joint action of Special Services in Sian. His responsibility is to draft the "Conversational Outline" and train the special agents disguised as representatives of the people, submitting and disclosing the faults of the Reds. These "representatives of the people" are all the officials or higher members of the Secret Service disguised, whom the foreigners living long in Sian are possibly well acknowledge).

DIVISION OF LABOR

a. In Paochi (when you land your plane), on the railroad between Paochi and Sian, and in Sian, all the units of special service work and act jointly under the Headquarters Command. Each unit must put in practice what they are appointed. While in Sian, Hu Kuo-cheng and his subordinates are principally responsible.

b. On the way to the Second War Zone (Ichuan and Kenanpo, headquarters for Marshal Yen Hsi-shan) and to Yenan, Li Yu-lung and his subordinates are principally responsible. While from Ichuan to Kenanpo, the Sian Kuomintang Secret Service are instructed to work jointly under the command of Chen Kien-chung who was specially appointed to the Bureau of Investigation and Statistics.

c. From Ichuan to the Red Region, and in the whole days you stay in Yenan, the translators and guiders, who are all high officials of the Secret Service and selected beforehand by Hu Tsung-nan's headquarters, are responsible. They are traveling companions of you to Yenan, and work jointly with Chungking Joint Staff in Yenan. They also are instructed to keep close connection with special service men in Yenan. Their mission is to watch you—especially when you contact the Communists. They will attentively listen to what you talk about and the materials attacking the Kuomintang which the Reds submit to you, and collect materials of the faults of the Reds which they will submit to you and thus make an unfavorable impression on you.

d. On the way returning to Sian from Yenan, Hu Tsung-nan's men are in charge.

NUMBER OF MEMBERS APPOINTED IN EACH UNIT

a. Tai Li's. The total number of persons mobilized, 392.

b. C. C. Clique. (That is, the Two Chens—Chen Kuo-fu and his brother, the ex-Minister of Education, Chen Li-fu.) The number is 413.

c. Hu Tsung-nan's. Total number is 400.

POINTS OF PREPARATIONS AGAINST THE JOURNALIST MISSION

a. Strictly limit the visit programme and the period of staying in Sian.

b. No freedom of action—limit and prevent you from "free visit" and occupy you whole days with fixed programme. Any person inquiring for or nearing to you, if not promised, must be followed and apprehended.

c. Isolate the foreign resident doctors, priests, and all other foreigners from you. Their houses are placed under secret guards and plain-clothesmen.

d. Any emigrant who can speak English is strictly forbidden to be translator or guider. All are examined and trained by the Provisional Headquarters beforehand.

e. Any interpreter in unions, administrative organs, school, and other places arranged to be visit must be selected and examined beforehand.

f. Any officer dispatched to talk with the Journalist Mission must comply with the "Conversational Outline" and must literally and metaphorically express the faults of the Reds.

g. Any secret police detective, if discloses the secret, must be put to death.

h. Same arrangement on the way north.

i. Frontier garrisons and the forts at Lochuan and other places opposite to the Reds must be concealed from view or demolished temporarily.

Dear Mr. Forman, I am a lodger and citizen of Sian, loving my country, loving the world, loving freedom, and loving what called Democracy. But I found that Sian, to my extreme disappointment, has no freedom, no Democracy, no patriotic sentiment under the tyranny and corruption of the Government authorities. I do not agree with what my Government has done, especially in the preparations for "greeting" you this time. So I must briefly write down the circumstances what I know as above. I resolutely believe that neither "Three People's Principles" nor Communism could control China, except the people themselves and Democracy. Anybody or any party who wants to have the whole power, and thus deprive the other of his rights and liberty, will sustain a crushing defeat. Our sacred mission is to create a world in which all men everywhere can be free. The cause of freedom shall not be trampled down nor the tide of world progress turned back by the criminal dictators. Please give me sympathy and listen to Chinese people's voice. At last, I must request you to pardon me my poor English. I am,

                    Yours faithfully,

                    (Signed) ―――――― ――――――

Though at first this letter seemed the work of some crackpot, it was too full of specific information to be ignored. Naturally I tried to check as much of it as possible. Without going into too much detail about it, I may say this: From what happened, and from what I was told by certain informed persons in Sian, I feel fairly certain the fellow knew what he was talking about.

We made four formal official calls, significantly in the order of their importance: Hu Tsung-nan's military headquarters first; then the Governor's residence; the Kuomintang Headquarters for Sian; and finally the Provisional People's Political Council. Luxury or comfort in the quarters and their appointments was scaled according to the importance of the office-holder, ranging from the exquisite palace where the Empress Dowager had stayed when she fled Peking during the Boxer Rebellion down to the simple stone floor, the paper windows, and the plain furniture of the fifteen-foot-square room where we were received by three bearded old representatives of the Provisional People's Political Council. They all looked extremely uncomfortable—fearful lest inadvertently they say something they were not supposed to say.

At Military Headquarters we were received by General Lo Tze-kai, chief of staff for General Hu Tsung-nan, for whom he said he spoke officially. Jack-booted and beautifully tailored, General Lo Tze-kai had accompanied the Generalissimo to the Cairo Conference. Though he greeted us cordially enough, we immediately sensed a latent hostility, as if he hated having been ordered to be nice to these foreigners who were meddling into affairs that were none of their business.

To our surprise, General Lo frankly admitted the existence of the blockade against the Communists, a blockade that he preferred to describe as "surrounding a Protective Area." He offered several reasons in justification of this action. First, he alleged, the Communists had failed to obey military orders. Their forces, nominally under direct authority of Yen Hsi-shan, commander of the Second War Zone, had refused to confine themselves to the areas to which they were assigned. In defiance of Marshal Yen's orders they had crossed to the east bank of the Yellow River and were illegally expanding the area under their control. Moreover, wherever they went they drove out the Government and Kuomintang authorities and substituted their own soviet system. As for contributing to the war effort, General Lo continued, their admitted policy was, "No hard fighting, and retreat when the enemy advances." This, he said, had been proven in Hopei and Shantung provinces where the Communists had deliberately moved out and allowed the Japanese to come in.

"The Communists haven't fought a single battle with the Japanese in the past six years," he charged. "Moreover, it's too much to hope they'll ever fight the Japanese. So you see, the 'blockade,' as you choose to call it, is not against the Communists but against the Japanese, who may decide to drive down through the unresisting Communist areas to attack Sian and China's back door."

It was certainly a novel explanation and one that did not credit us with much intelligence.

At the Governor's residence, Chu Shao-chou also admitted the existence of the blockade line, which he quaintly described as a "big ditch" set at intervals with "little houses," each garrisoned by "several dozens" of men. The "Protective Line," he alleged, was necessary to keep the Communists from illegal territorial expansion. They had been steadily expanding the area under their control until this area was already three times its size just prior to the outbreak of the war. This I knew to be definitely untrue, for I had visited the Communist areas some months before the war began in 1937, and the area then under Communist control was actually greater than it is today—the Government troops having steadily pressed them back since that time.

The Governor accused the Communists of murdering non-Communists, of treacherously setting upon Government troops when the latter were fighting the Japanese, and of trafficking in opium—one-third of the best land in the Border Region was planted with opium poppies, he said. These were serious charges; and, while I was not able to determine the truth or the falsity of the first two, this much I can say: In five months of travel in the Communist areas I found not the slightest trace of opium in any form.

Summarizing the situation, the Governor pointed out that, though Communist parties are permitted to exist in other countries, they are strictly political in nature. They have no armies of their own, no systems of law and taxation peculiar to them as parties. They do not issue their own decrees, nor print their own banknotes, nor generally consider themselves an independent state within a state. Obviously, these arguments were at least *prima facie* reasonable. But I felt that the problem could not be reduced to such simple terms; and before long, observation and experience were to compel me to see beyond the Governor's formulation.

2

Concentration Camp?

WE HAD heard of a special camp in Sian, a sort of political limbo for people who had come down from the Communist areas. Was it a concentration camp? The invariable answer was that it was merely a place where people came—voluntarily—to remold their ideology in preparation for a new life.

We asked to see it. The Sian officials hemmed and hawed for a couple of days, then consented.

The night before our visit, a "note" was added to our printed program for the next day. It read:

The Labor Training Camp [official name of the place] was established in the winter of 1939 by the National Military Council to give a short course in training to certain homeless youths who have fled to Sian from the Communist areas. Through labor service the youths are taught some productive technique or trade so that they may participate in the nation's wartime work. Departments of the camp include management class, chemical industry class, political class, and workshops. The policy of training, management, accommodations, food, and other conditions in the camp is the same as that found in training institutes conducted by the Government.

In our special deluxe buses we rode out through the West Gate one fine afternoon to a walled and guarded compound adjacent to the airfield. They were ready for us. Big posters in red and black were plastered on the walls, fastened to trees, and strung from building to building. They read (in English), "Welcome to the Press Party to the Northwest!" "We will Fight for Peace, Justice, and Democracy." "Down with Fascism!" English-speaking interpreters attached themselves to each of the foreigners in our party and stuck to us like leeches. The place was brushed and combed and the new whitewash in some places was not yet dry.

In the reception room we found a big wall-newspaper, again, for some unaccountable reason, in English. When we asked whether the students could read English, the answer was yes, that some of them could. The wall-newspaper—made up like any ordinary newspaper but with the copy in careful longhand writing instead of type—carried a story of a new American landing in the Solomons, a speech by Churchill, a feature about war production in America, and an "editorial" headlined, "A View to be Corrected" which I shall quote word for word:

The Northwest Youth Labor Camp is a special group in the special time. Everyone in this city, even in this province, is afraid of the Northwestern Youth Labor Camp. Anyone in this camp is regarded as a dangerous member. But in fact it is not really so. The Labor Camp consists of five battalions and one girl section: one thousand two hundred boys and twenty-five girls. Their daily routine is according to a constant routine which is military, political, and technical training. In the technical training there are such classes as Industrial Chemistry Class, Searching Class, Youth Class, and the like. In short, the Labor Camp is really a training unit like the Seventh Branch of the Central Military Academy and the Central Workman Training Corps, but not a dangerous association.

We began our tour of the camp. The quarters were not too bad, though crowded. Everything was spic and span. Blankets, sheets, and towels were brand-new. So were the uniforms. Heads were freshly shaven, showing light against sunburned faces. We peered into the classrooms. The students sat stiff-backed in their seats, paying no attention to us—so fascinated by the instructor's lecture on ancient history that not even our strange appearance could distract their attention for a moment.

We were led to a parade ground to watch the student sports.

One group of boys was playing volley ball. On the other side of the field, some girls in a circle were playing a sort of childish ring-around-a-rosy game. Would we like to talk to some of the students? We would. They took us over to the boys. As unobtrusively as possible I started over to the girls—whereupon several of the interpreters came after me, trying to persuade me to go back and join the collective interview. When I refused, they went with me—to "interpret."

The girls saw me coming, of course, but pretended to take no notice. I stood and watched them play for a few moments, and then asked the matron if I might talk to some of them. She smiled and consented. I picked the girls at random, asking first a few simple questions. Yes, every one of them insisted, she was there of her own free will. One went so far as to say she had come in answer to an advertisement in the local papers. Could they leave whenever they wished? Their answers struck me as evasive. One said, "I'm not yet physically fit." Another, "I want to finish my training course." A third, "I don't think I am sufficiently purified after my long and contaminating stay with the Communists."

The interpreters and the matron smiled benignly at these suspicious replies. Then I asked some personal questions. Twenty-four-year-old Miss Lo Chin-hsiu said she had been in the camp since she came out of the Communist areas in 1942. Why had she gone to Yenan in the first place? She had not gone there of her own free will, but had been forcibly taken there. Back in 1935 she had been living a quiet, peaceful life with her wealthy parents in Szechwan when the Reds swept through on their famous 8,000-mile Long March. The Reds had decapitated her parents, her uncle, and her brother, had thrown their heads down the family well—and had taken her with them to Yenan, where she had promptly entered the new Communist university. Some years later she had escaped because she had disliked her teachers, who were telling lies and cheating the youth.

Twenty-three-year-old Miss Fu Hsiu-ying said she also was the daughter of a rich family of Szechwan. The Reds had cut off the heads of her parents also and dragged her to Yenan. Yes, she had seen her parents murdered. She hadn't tried to escape during the

Long March. Not until a year after her arrival in Yenan had she found an opportunity to escape, and then she had come directly to the camp. Miss Fu Hsiu-ying was obviously confused in her dates. She had escaped from Yenan in 1938 (before the camp was established) and arrived at the camp in 1941. She finally said that because she was homeless she expected to stay in the camp at least three more years.

Miss Ho Ju-yung said she had served with the guerrillas in Honan Province since her escape from the Communists the year before. She had come to the camp because she felt she was not sufficiently grounded in Sun Yat-sen's Three People's Principles for effective work with the guerrillas. She hoped to return to the guerrillas after she finished her studies here, but she was not sure just when that would be.

I asked for the youngest of them. A chunky twenty-year-old stepped forward. She had been in the place since 1942, having voluntarily fled to this camp from the Communist areas. She admitted that in 1939 she had been influenced by Communist propaganda and had gone to Yenan to enter the Teachers Training College. There she had been sadly disillusioned. I asked her whether she would like me to take a message to any of her former teachers or friends. No; they were all bad ones up there. Besides, she could not remember any of their names.

The interpreters, who had begun to tug at my sleeve, now said that we were expected to join the others at tea. I started back with them. Passing one of the classrooms—the one where the students had been so fascinated with the lecture on ancient history—I observed that the class must now be in recess, for the instructor was not there and the students were chattering and gossiping, perhaps about us. I stepped in suddenly. For a moment they were flustered, then straightened up like good, disciplined students. I sat down and tried to draw them into conversation. With some hesitation they looked at the interpreters with me, and then gave such vague and obviously evasive answers that I shrugged my shoulders and left.

At tea we were entertained by the director of the camp and a dozen young people who were introduced as representative students. The director made a short speech in which he admitted that, while most of the students were there voluntarily, some were in confinement for "violation of military law."

These representative students were very friendly and did not at all mind answering questions. Indeed, they seemed anxious to be interviewed. Miss Tsao Ching had gone to Yenan with a group of her schoolmates in 1938. Through Communist propaganda distributed by agents in Chengchow, her home city, the girls had heard much of the good work being done in Yenan. On going to Yenan, she had spent four years studying nursing in one of the hospitals. But things were by no means as she had expected to find them. Communist propaganda had taught her to believe Yenan to be a place of high ideals and purpose; but she had found nothing of that in the four years she had spent there. It hurt her to see how callous the Communists were about the sick; they neglected them shamefully. They forced her to join the Communist Party, and she did not think that was proper. Finally, she made a daring escape over the mountains. At the border she was treated wonderfully by the Government soldiers, who told her so much about this preparative camp in Sian that she had asked permission to enter it. She had spent two years in the place already. How much longer would she need to prepare herself for a new life? She was not sure, but hoped it would not be much longer. She smiled at the director as she said this. He sat across the table, much interested in her story, listening as if he had never heard her tell it before.

Hsin Lo-fen looked like a bright young fellow. He was a radio operator. In Hongkong he had been influenced by Communist propaganda and at his own expense had traveled to Yenan so that he could fight the Japs. In Yenan they put him to work in a wireless station in General Wang Cheng's brigade. He said: "After three years of it I got thoroughly fed up with them up there. One day I asked Wang Cheng whether I could leave. Wang Cheng said he'd let me escape if I'd give him my wrist watch and gold collar-pin." That, Hsin insisted, was how he had got out of the Communist areas. He had come directly to this camp, of which he had heard a lot indirectly.

"Would you like me to report to the high military authorities in Yenan that General Wang Cheng had taken your wrist watch and gold collar-pin as a bribe to let you escape?"

"No. It wouldn't do any good anyway."

One of the students, Chow Wen-cheng, said he had been a major on the staff of General Ho Lung, with whom he had served five years.

"Once we were very close to the Japanese and expected to attack them," Chow went on, "in co-operation with Central Government troops under General Shih Yu-shan. This was in 1940, on the second of February, at a little place in Hopei called Weihsien. But, much to our surprise, Ho Lung gave the order to attack not the Japanese but the Central Government troops. After we killed about four or five hundred of them, the remnants of Shih Yu-shan's troops fled."

"And why did Ho Lung give such an order?" I asked.

"Because he wanted to expand the territory under his control, as do all Communists," he answered glibly.

Later, when I asked Ho Lung about this, he chuckled and replied: "Never heard of the fellow. Besides, neither I nor my troops have ever been at that place."

I think it entirely proper at this point to run ahead of my main narrative and report an interesting talk I had with two young fellows who came to see me in Yenan some months later. These were Wang Erh-ming and Lo Tso-ying, both in their early twenties. Both had been in the Sian Labor Camp at the time of our visit. They preferred not to talk about their escape for fear of implicating those who had helped them. But they had a convincing story to tell about the true conditions in the camp, and particularly about our visit.

First, they told how they came to be sent to the camp. In the spring of 1941 Wang, a radio operator in an anti-aircraft school in Sian, wrote a letter to a friend in which he referred to the new constitution of the Soviet Union. It was nothing of importance—merely something that had caught his interest mildly in a book he had picked up in a Sian bookshop. The letter was intercepted by the postal authorities and turned over to the military headquarters. In the meantime Wang had gone on special assignment to Tienshui on the Kansu-Shensi border.

Late one night two strangers with drawn pistols came to his quarters and forced him to accompany them. For two months they kept him in solitary confinement. No one questioned him; no one would or could tell him why he was being detained. Then they chained him and took him to Lanchow where he was placed in a "Political Prison." Two weeks later they brought him before a Colonel Chao, who asked him bluntly why he had been studying the new constitution of the Soviet Union. This was the first hint he had had as to why he was being held. Naturally he denied the charge of being a Communist spy; he had never been in the Communist areas and insisted that his only interest in the Soviet constitution was in learning something of what a constitution meant, since there had been much talk about a constitution for China when the Kuomintang Party's "Period of Tutelage" should be considered by that party to be at an end.

They whipped and tortured Wang in the effort to wrest a confession from him. This continued periodically until March 1944. Then he was manacled and sent down to Sian to the Labor Camp, with no information as to the length of his confinement. He did not press his captors on this because he feared they might put him back into solitary confinement.

Lo Tso-ying, my other visitor in Yenan, had been in the Manchurian army since he was a lad of thirteen. When the war broke out in 1937 he deserted and joined the Communist forces under Lin Piao. In 1940 he went to Sinkiang under army orders as attached to General Cheng, Lin Piao's chief of staff. General Cheng entered a hospital there for a course of treatment, Lo with him. On their return in October of that year the two were detained by the authorities in Sian, who refused to recognize their credentials and accused them of being spies of some sort because of the quality of the cloth of their new uniforms. In vain they explained that this was Russian cloth obtained in Sinkiang; they were not believed. For nearly three years he and General Cheng had been kept in solitary confinement. They were periodically tortured and brought before various officials who tried to make them confess to all manner of crimes. The General finally cracked and lost his reason, dying in prison. Young Lo was brought before a judge and sentenced to the Labor Camp for an indefinite term.

In the camp Wang and Lo were required to do some manual labor, though not overmuch. Discipline was strict, with severe corporal punishment for infractions. In their classes they studied the San Min Chu I, the Generalissimo's speeches, Chinese history, and the crimes of the "Traitor Party" and "Traitor Army"—as the Communist Party and its forces were invariably termed. Release from the camp could be obtained if one agreed to work against the Communist "traitors." Although the Communists were always referred to as "traitors," the students had been cautioned against using the epithet during our visit to the camp.

"We were certainly glad to get those new uniforms they issued us for your visit," chuckled Wang. "We needed them badly. They let us keep them; but the new blankets and other things which they borrowed from the Central Military Academy for the occasion were promptly collected and returned as soon as you left the compound."

The day before our coming the students were gathered in groups by their leaders, and spent several hours studying the proper answers to a mimeographed list of probable questions. We asked those questions and received the prepared replies, since the inmates had been warned that if any improper answers were given there would be serious consequences.

As Wang and Lo sat with me in Yenan, I thumbed back in my notebook. Did they know Miss Lo Chin-hsiu?

"She was supposed to say that her wealthy parents had been beheaded by the Communists. Is that what she told you?"

I smiled. "She did."

"Well, it's a pure lie," said Lo. "She was never in Szechwan where she said she was born; nor was she ever in the Communist areas where she said they dragged her on the Long March. She was just a loose woman around Sian who consorted with questionable characters. They accused her of having relations with the Communists—which was possibly untrue—and sentenced her to the camp. While she was not promised any better treatment or other reward for telling you that story, nevertheless she dared not refuse."

"Tsao Ching?" said Wang. "Oh, she's a bad one. I suppose she told you that sad story of her disillusionment in Yenan and of her daring escape across the mountains?" I nodded. "Huh! She escaped from the Communist areas all right—but she escaped with another woman's husband. They were both captured when they crossed the border and both were sent to camp. Her lover is still there, but he's lost all interest in her. And now she has her eye on one of the camp officials, hoping through his help to be able to get out."

Hsin Lo-fen? No, they didn't know him. Major Chow Wen-cheng? "Yes, of course," they said in unison. "The fellow who was to tell you he'd been on General Ho Lung's staff? Well, if he was ever a major in the Communist or any other army, then *we* were generals."

They gave me much other information, which I shall not set down here. They themselves had seen us only from a little distance. One of the boys of their group had planned to blurt out the truth regardless of the consequences; for his own protection he had had to be kept away from us. Only those who could be relied upon to tell the lies manufactured for them by the authorities were exposed to the correspondents. The others were carefully kept in the background.

3

Road to Kenanpo

A<small>T NOON</small> the next day we set out in our two deluxe Dodge buses for Lintung, a famous watering resort some seventeen miles east of Sian. It's a lovely place, surrounded by leafy aspens and bright flower gardens, and set back from the road among the hills. Seventeen centuries ago the Emperor Tang Ming Hwang built an exquisite palace here for Yang Kwei Fei, the most beautiful woman in Chinese history. So entranced was he with her charms that he neglected his court and empire to live with her and devote himself to her every whim and wish. A revolt, headed by his aide-de-camp, broke out; and, as the rebels demanded her life as the price of peace, Yang Kwei Fei was strangled.

Here it was that the Generalissimo had been resting at Christmas 1936—the date of the Sian coup d'état headed by the "Young Marshal" Chang Hsueh-liang and Governor Yang Hu-chen. Bullet holes in the walls and windows were still to be seen in the simply furnished room that had been occupied by the Generalissimo when the rebel troops came for him.

Our buses took us to Lintung station on the Lunghai where our special train was waiting for us on a siding. The big buses were loaded onto flatcars trailing our sleeper, and we set out for Tungkwan, a fortress city ninety miles east of Sian. Tungkwan is the key to the whole of China's Northwest. It is strategically located at the elbow of the Yellow River, and at the time of our visit was facing Japanese forces dug into the north bank of the river. The Japanese had been pinned down in their positions ever since reaching the place something over six years before.

After years of daily shelling from across the river, the walled city itself was in complete ruins. The Japs, indeed, had brought up some rather big guns only a few days before our coming, and were beginning to lob over shells, many of which proved to be duds. We examined a few of these.

Captain Chiang Wei-kuo, the Generalissimo's younger son, met us and acted as our guide and interpreter during our tour of the Tungkwan defences. Young Wei-kuo speaks good English. In 1939-40 he had been attached to an air training school in Texas. Prior to that he had been a private, and later a noncommissioned officer, in the German army. He was with his regiment when they were ordered to march into Czechoslovakia. After a short stay in Czechoslovakia with the German garrison stationed there, he was called back to China by the Generalissimo and commissioned in the Chinese army.

Wei-kuo is a slim, tightly built, enthusiastic young fellow. He wore a simple drab uniform that in no way differed from those worn by his brother officers of similar rank, with whom he seemed to be on the best of terms. Whenever a superior officer addressed him he snapped to rigid attention. At his waist he carried an American army service automatic. "Father gave it to me," he explained.

We were led down through a maze of candle-lit underground communication trenches, past smart troopers with coal-scuttle tin helmets who greeted us with *"Ko wei hsien sheng hao"*—"Greetings, gentlemen." We inspected machine-gun posts and peered through firing slits or through periscopes at the Japanese positions less than a thousand yards across the river. In the previous few months the Japanese had made nine serious attempts to cross the river at this point, but each time they were thrown back by intensive crossfire from the Tungkwan defences.

"In the last attempt I myself killed three Japs of which I'm certain," said Wei-kuo proudly.

At lunch, consisting of Chinese food served in foreign style,

General Hu Tsung-nan suddenly appeared looking like a little Napoleon in battle dress. There was some severe fighting at Linpao and he had left the battle front to pay us a very brief visit.

From Tungkwan our route lay along the west bank of the Yellow River. In many places the road was within rifle range of the Japs holding the east bank. The direct route to Yenan would be to go due north from Sian—a distance of something less than two hundred miles—passing through the blockade line at a point just above Lochuan. We were being taken on a circuitous route, it was explained, so that we might visit Marshal Yen Hsi-shan's headquarters at Kenanpo. We had no objections since the detour promised to prove of interest.

In ancient days Shensi Province was the heart of the Celestial Empire. The land was well wooded and richly productive. Great walled cities vied with one another in magnificence and there was peace and plenty for all. But with the passing centuries, weather changes caused successive droughts and famines, with consequent lawlessness. The population steadily decreased as families died off or moved away, so that north Shensi today is one of the poorest areas in all China.

As we rode north from Tungkwan our buses soon began to plow through sand-dune country much like the section of Indiana fronting Lake Michigan. In no time at all they bogged down and the countryside was scoured for men and animals to pull us out. We were then hauled for miles until a fairly solid roadbed was reached, and our buses could proceed under their own power once more.

Reminding us of the proximity of the enemy, or of the Communists, were scores of serviceable stone blockhouses lining the highway at intervals of several hundred yards. As we passed, each little garrison came out and presented arms in our honor.

We were met outside the picturesque walled city of Tali by a delegation of the city's notables headed by Chiang Chien-jen, a cousin of the Generalissimo, who was the special commissioner for the Tali district. In the magistrate's yamen, uniformed attendants whipped the dust from our shoulders and boots while hot water was brought in with cakes of genuine Palmolive soap for a wash.

We were then led to a parade ground to address a mass meeting of perhaps five thousand people.

At a banquet in our honor that night Commissioner Chiang described the short period, some ten years before, when Tali was occupied by the Communists. "There was complete social disorder during their stay," he said. "They plundered and burned and killed without reason. But they were finally driven out by the indignant masses and the people's organizations."

As we continued northward over the dusty rutted road, the way grew rougher and rougher. Presently it began to weave and twist through canyons and badlands cut and gouged with steep-walled gorges, awesome sinkholes, and yawning caves. The scene was relieved occasionally by a beautiful valley shut in by towering yellow loess cliffs.

When we arrived at Hoyang, most of the city's population seemed to be on hand to greet us. They lined the roadway for a mile or more from the city gate, waving British, American, Russian, and Chinese flags, shouting slogans and applauding as we marched down the line like conquering heroes. We were then formally received by the town's notables and quartered for the night in a temple seventeen centuries old.

The next day we rode through more badlands, at times sweeping to within a mile or so of the Yellow River, in full view and easy range of the Japanese artillery on the opposite bank. The reception for us at Hancheng was bigger than any we had been given before. Thousands of men, women, and children cheered and applauded along the roadway to the city gate. Directed by cheer leaders posted at twenty-yard intervals, they literally leaped into the air as they shouted. We might have been the liberators of a long-besieged city.

Within the city more thousands lined well-swept streets bedecked with United Nations flags. Red, green, and yellow banners with English slogans plastered the walls, trees, and telephone poles. Apparently an official holiday had been declared in our honor and the city's business was at a standstill. The slogans everywhere showed a suspicious similarity, as if they had been put up by a publicity agent riding ahead of us. Our quarters were the best we had had thus far, and the food was in keeping with them.

The stage to Ichuan took us over the Yellow Dragon Mountains with nearly two-mile-high elevations, steep grades, and magnificent scenery. Ichuan is barely ten miles from the border of the Communist-controlled areas, with which, we were told by the magistrate, there was regular trade. This trade, however, was restricted to salt and kerosene from the Communists, which was exchanged for cotton cloth and dyestuffs from Ichuan. From Ichuan we turned due east to the Yellow River crossing, which led to Marshal Yen Hsi-shan's domain. Our buses carried us until the road petered out altogether; then we mounted horses and rode down a narrow trail that snaked along razorback ridges. At last, almost without warning, we came out upon a promontory overlooking a deep, wide canyon with the Yellow River winding far below on its floor. It was a breath-taking landscape comparable in magnificence to the Grand Canyon.

It was long past noon when we led our nervous ponies across a rickety plank suspension bridge that seemed to be held together with little more than hope and a certain indifference to fate. It swayed unpleasantly as if it might collapse at any moment and hurl us all into the roaring rapids below. The knowledge that the Japanese were encamped down the river less than ten miles from this point hardly made things any better.

Once on the other bank we mounted again and rode up river for half a mile or so, then started up a steep, zigzag trail which only the goatlike China ponies would dare tackle with a rider in the saddle. As we climbed higher and higher they quickened their step. We knew we were approaching Kenanpo by the increasing frequency of immobile sentries who stood facing away from the trail, as if serving as watchers over our safety rather than as guards of honor. Squat, businesslike blockhouses spotted the surrounding landscape, reminding us that we were indeed close to the Japanese. Strangely, these sentries were armed not with the usual rifles but with Chinese-made tommy guns, to whose muzzles naked bayonets were fixed.

Presently we rounded an outjutting shoulder and caught our first view of Kenanpo perched atop a peaked cliff like some feudal fortress, boldly silhouetted and bathed in the brilliant afternoon sunshine. Fleecy white clouds scurried overhead, sharply outlined against a deep blue sky that contrasted brilliantly with the bright yellow loess of the mountainside. The great slope itself was pockmarked with hundreds of arched cave openings neatly spaced in tiers. Of these terraces as many as six and more were arranged one above the other—an almost unbelievable sight, like something out of a child's storybook.

4

Fortress Shangri-La

I SEEMED as if the whole ten thousand of Kenanpo's population turned out to greet us at the tunnel entrance to the city's civic center. They cheered and applauded us as we passed in review. Every man, woman, and child wore the same green cotton uniform—a simple, unadorned tunic and trousers; there was not a skirt in sight. Eager, smiling, well-fed faces regarded us curiously, for few foreigners ever get up to that out-of-the-way part of China.

Inside the caves where we were quartered, it was at least fifteen degrees cooler, which was most refreshing after the long ride in the hot sun. The caves were shaped like sections of a subway tunnel, with arched roofs, whitewashed walls and floors of baked brick. There was even electric light in our quarters, the current supplied by a fifteen-kilowatt generator that was driven by a 1931 Buick truck engine and fueled by charcoal gas.

Kenanpo is Marshal Yen Hsi-shan's wartime capital of what is left to China of Shansi, one of the country's most progressive provinces. At the time of our visit the city was barely three years old, having been built up from scratch, the site chosen principally because of its defensible position, flanked as it was by barren, rugged mountains.

As the "Model Governor" of Shansi for thirty-two years (since the age of twenty-nine), Japanese-trained Yen Hsi-shan has been credited with many progressive reforms, including the suppression of opium, the establishing of hospitals, the emancipation of women, the introduction of mass education, the growing of cotton, stock-breeding, water conservation and irrigation, and reforestation, as well as the opening of modern factories and steel mills, power stations, research laboratories, and the biggest arsenal in prewar China.

In 1929-30 Yen formed a coalition with the "Christian" General Feng Yu-hsiang, and together they fought Generalissimo Chiang Kai-shek. Following their defeat Yen fled to Dairen, Japanese port in Manchuria. Six months before the Japanese invasion of Manchuria, the chief of staff of the Kwantung Army, a former classmate of Yen's at the Tokyo Military Academy, told Yen in confidence Japan's plans for the conquest of Manchuria. Yen pretended sympathy until one day he was offered the post as head of the projected puppet state of Manchukuo—whereupon he fled to China, reported this to the Generalissimo, and resumed the governorship of Shansi.

During his year's sojourn in Dairen, Yen worked out his revolutionary "New Economic System." He spent the following years perfecting his theory, which he was unable to put to the test until September 1943 (less than a year before our visit). Sitting on a narrow sawhorse-bench in a simple cave, sipping a sweet, warmed wine, smoking British cigarettes smuggled in from Shanghai, we listened to the aging, kindly-voiced Marshal explain his paternalistic "New Economic System" which governs their way of life for the million inhabitants of Shansi remaining under Yen's rule.

"Under the economic system of our present society," Yen began, "labor is not exerted for the sake exclusively of production, nor is distribution in accordance with the amount of labor exerted. As a result various vices arise between man and man and between community and community. The causes of such vices may be reduced to two: First, money based on metal. Second, private ownership of capital.

"Under the system of money based on metal such as gold and silver, commodities must first be measured in terms of these metals before they can be exchanged for other commodities. As a result, men no longer labor for commodities but for gold and silver; which, because these are easily hoardable, may themselves be used for speculation, thus disturbing the balance of otherwise stable commodity values and interfering with the free exchange of such commodities according to normal needs.

"Private ownership of capital forces those who labor without capital to depend upon someone else's capital in order to produce. This is exploitation of labor, which leads to dissatisfaction and disturbances."

For money based on metal Yen has substituted his "Co-operative Certificates," which form the bloodstream for Yen Hsi-shan's whole "New Economic System." "Co-operative Certificates" are issued by Yen's provincial government, he said, with the authorization of the Central Government at Chungking. In appearance these "Co-operative Certificates" are similar to the national legal tender; however, they are not currency but receipts for produce which the producer delivers to the Yen Hsi-shan's provincial Union Co-operative. The certificates may in turn be used for obtaining by purchase or exchange other things turned in by other producers. Hence, this may be considered as bartering through the medium of the government-controlled co-operative. The certificates, said Yen, are issued by the provincial government only to the actual amount of the people's production—at the rate of ten certificate dollars for the produce of a man's full day's labor, whether he produces vegetables, wheat, shoes, or umbrellas—and have an artificial exchange value [1944] against national currency of one certificate dollar for six national dollars.

"There's no danger of an overissue of certificate dollars," Yen insisted, "since the outstanding issue is backed by actual commodities still unconsumed; and when certificates are turned in for consumable goods these certificates are immediately destroyed by the authorities and new certificates are issued to a producer bringing in new produce."

Since certificates are issued only against actual commodities produced locally, Yen pointed out that inflation outside his controlled areas should and did have no effect upon the cost of living within these areas. That, at least, was the theory.

"And when commodities within these areas are finally and totally controlled and self-sufficiency is achieved, there will be no necessity for an exchange value against national currency or any other money based upon metal. This will be so because internal economy will be entirely controlled by a balanced exchange of commodities based upon units of labor required to produce them, rather than by artificial values subject to speculation, as well as fluctuation according to supply and demand."

"Could your 'Co-operative Certificate' system be applied internationally?" I asked.

"Of course. It both can and should be adopted internationally. For without money based upon hoardable gold and silver to be utilized as a means to hold the economic reins of the world, nations will be forced to exchange one commodity for another based upon the labor unit, thus removing the evil of economic conflict, which is the major cause of war."

His answer to private ownership of capital, then, is a system of distribution according to labor. Under this system capital employed in production is owned and furnished by the public (i.e., the government or some other public institution), and goods produced by the laborer go to him for the support of himself and family after deductions for taxes, assessments, etc. The city and the village are units of economic administration. Distribution of land is controlled by the village and land is allotted to the farmers for cultivation according to each individual's capacity for production. Factories and shops are operated by local or provincial governments, so that farmers and workers are all assured of work according to their actual needs. They share their products according to the amount of labor exerted by each. The capitalistic or merchant class is completely eliminated, and neither free trade nor individualistic merchandising enterprise is permitted to exist.

This, to my mind, had a greater resemblance to Communism than did the system the Chinese Communists were alleged to practice in their blockaded areas adjacent to Yen Hsi-shan's territory. I expressed this thought to the Marshal. In reply he frankly admitted a parallelism of political aims between his system and the

Communism of Karl Marx. In fact, he claimed to have improved on Marx.

"The brain of Marx was equivalent to an eye with a microscope," Yen elaborated, "because Marx could see things others couldn't. But Marx made some great mistakes in carrying out his theories. According to Marx, excepting the prescribed part that is deducted for a worker's needs, all the rest of a worker's production must go to the state. Consequently, no worker is willing to work efficiently and energetically. My way is just the opposite; namely, with the exception of the part a worker must give to the state, all the rest of his production is for himself. This encourages every worker to do his best. Simply put, Marx's Communist principle is based upon distribution according to needs; my system is based upon distribution according to labor, which allows everyone to have what should be his but not what belongs to others."

It all sounded quite utopian. It was, of course, much too soon to assess the success or failure of Yen's "New Economic System" since it had been in operation less than a year. But, from what I could see of the Marshal's twentieth-century Shangri-La, things seemed to be going pretty well, if the well-clad, well-fed, and apparently contented people I saw in Kenanpo provided any criterion. To be sure, in the five days we spent with Yen Hsi-shan I saw no more than the city of Kenanpo. Whether the system was working as well in the rural areas, and whether the people on the farms outside Kenanpo were accepting the system unresistingly, I had no way of knowing.

By comparison with many other places I have seen in China, the people of Kenanpo were well housed. Their cave dwellings might appear primitive, but they are the most practical form of house construction in that barren, inhospitable country. Wood and stone for building material are scarce, whereas caves can easily be bored into the friable loess cliffsides, providing snug waterproof and bombproof homes that are cool in summer and warm in winter.

A typical cave home consists of two or more interlocking, tunnellike rooms perhaps fifteen to twenty feet deep, ten to fifteen feet wide, and ten to fifteen feet to the top of the arched ceiling. On one side of an arched entrance there may be a mud cookstove set into a niche, while on the other may be a dozen or more tiny niches each barely large enough for one of a flock of clucking hens. A tethered milk goat in a corner stares blankly at you. Inside, a long earthen platform (the typical Chinese *kang*), which serves as a bed, lines one side of the tunnel. Earthen stools, a table, and the usual little knickknacks complete the furniture. Visiting numerous cave homes picked at random, I noted their surprising neatness, their cleanliness, and their well-stocked larders, whose contents included stores of grain, mushrooms, garlic, a pile of coal, and a stack of firewood. Up and down the dusty interlacing trails flap-eared donkeys trudged phlegmatically while children, attracted by the foreigner's strange long nose and his queer dress, interrupted their shuttlecock play to gather around. They joined me as I stood watching a caravan of chanting coolies plodding up a mountain trail. These men were carrying up a dismembered motor truck from the road's end just across the river. It would be put together again for use on the highway east from Kenanpo.

I visited some of the co-operative shops and watched people exchange cotton or wool yarn for cloth. Often they did not bother with "Co-operative Certificates" since prices were fixed and so much yarn could easily be exchanged for so much cloth. The few factories in Kenanpo were small, but appeared to be well run. They were clean and airy, and working conditions seemed on the whole quite superior to those I had seen in most other parts of China.

Wherever one went one saw portraits of Marshal Yen, but never any of the Generalissimo or even of Sun Yat-sen. There were no Kuomintang flags to be seen, and from what some of the officials said I gathered that Yen Hsi-shan's acknowledgment of the Kuomintang's authority in Government affairs was purely for the sake of convenience. One of his high officials admitted to me that Yen's soldiery had frequent clashes with Central Government troops under Hu Tsung-nan. Yen's men were also continually involved in skirmishes with the Communists, one side invariably accusing the other of being the aggressor. Resisting pressure from three sides—from Japan, Central Forces, and Communists—fence-sitter Yen somehow manages to hold his own. The Japs seem not to press too hard, and there is more than a suspicion that they regard Yen as a possible successor to the Generalissimo, should Chiang Kai-shek be defeated. He is thought of not necessarily as a puppet, but rather as a compromise, between the extremes of treason at Nanking and national resistance at Chungking.

Lending some support to these suspicions was Yen's admission to us that on two separate occasions he had had direct and personal contact with the enemy, when peace proposals had been discussed. The Marshal, of course, explained that the meetings were unproductive since he deemed the Japanese proposals unacceptable. The fact remains, however, that he—an officer in the National Army of China and, as Governor of a province, the servant of the people—had had contact with the enemy without authority or instructions from his acknowledged superiors.

We asked him: "Have the Japanese attempted to make peace with you or to enlist your co-operation? If so, how many times and where?" It was a bold, almost an accusing, question. You would not have blamed him if he'd become angry at this suggestion of treason, but he replied quite frankly.

"Yes. Twice. The first time was about the middle of May 1940. The Japanese commander at Linfen, who had been my classmate at the Tokyo Military Academy, sent a student of mine with the following message: 'It is really unfortunate for us Asiatic people to kill one another. What effective means do you have in mind for restoring peace and good relations between us?' I replied: 'Since Japan has been fighting purely for her own necessities, she has not gained sympathy from the other peoples of Asia. If Japan were to fight for the necessities of the Asiatic peoples as a whole, it would surely be easy to restore peace and good relations.'" The second contact was in April 1942. "The Japanese commander Iwamatsu came to Anping, a village in Chihhsien, to have a personal talk with me. I told him the same thing I told the other one. The result was an unhappy ending."

The Marshal, who believes that China's material resources are sufficient to carry on a long war, trades heavily upon his avowed loyalty to the Central Government. "What we are doing here," he says, "is a forecast of the Central Government's social policies. They correspond completely to Doctor Sun Yat-sen's Principle of the People's Livelihood, with the only difference that I've developed it into something more concrete and practical."

Production of commodities is planned, he continued, to produce what is needed. Moreover, their movement and distribution is controlled.

"My New Economic System is militant in character," the Marshal emphasized, "and compulsory labor is its basis. If a man doesn't work he doesn't eat. That is our slogan. And we have severe penalties for idlers. Producers alone may consume."

He means what he says, too. All private enterprise in the areas under his jurisdiction have already been liquidated. Private capital and ownership of property has already been absorbed into public co-operatives. Merchants were allowed to sell their stock on hand at regulated prices; then the merchants themselves were registered and transformed into workers. They were permitted to seek employment independently, or receive employment through the provincial government. All together, four thousand merchants are today in productive enterprises making paper, towels, blankets, brushes, baskets, ink—products which a year before were imported by these same merchants from adjacent Jap-occupied territory. Other merchants are engaged as metal-workers, shoemakers, or skilled laborers, according to their special qualifications. Still others have become farmers.

Under Yen's "New Economic System," compulsory labor is planned on a twelve-hour basis. Work is classified into two kinds: First, work for national defense, such as digging ditches, repairing roads, the construction of fortifications, transportation of the wounded, munitions, and so forth. Secondly, work for personal livelihood, which includes farming and factory labor for personal needs. Because of the difference in people's trades, the number of working hours required of people in different categories is as follows: The laboring citizen must work eight hours daily for personal needs and four hours for national defense. Civil servants, schoolteachers, and soldiers must work four hours daily for personal needs; they may, for example, spin cotton on an old-fashioned wooden wheel, or cultivate a little vegetable patch—the Marshal himself raises tomatoes. Besides this, these groups labor eight hours for national defense in their proper callings. Lastly, students in college are required to spend at least two hours daily at production for personal needs, while high school students must spend four.

"All able-bodied civilians are compelled to take an active part in productive labor," says Yen. "Those who refuse are punished. They must work collectively and must exercise vigilance one over the other in order to accomplish their collective work." Evidently, Yen's system incorporates a considerable element of regimentation.

But the very heart of Yen Hsi-shan's "New Economic System" is his revolutionary "Soldier-Farmer Union." The aim of the Soldier-Farmer Union, according to the Marshal, is to increase the number of land cultivators as well as to produce more soldiers, so that the urgent wartime problems of the supply of men and food may be solved. In essence this union works as follows: Every able-bodied man of military age between the ages of seventeen and forty-eight must join Soldier-Farmer Mutual Help Associations in units of three. To each in turn will fall a term of military service; the other two meanwhile will remain in the village and jointly cultivate the land allotted to all three, thus contributing to the support of the absent soldier's family and dependents.

"Under my Soldier-Farmer Mutual Help Association, a man of military age willingly enters military service with his mind at ease because he is assured of his family's livelihood back home," the Marshal asserts. "Moreover, under this system not only are the evils of escaping military service eliminated, but military morale is actually raised. This is reflected in stronger national defense."

On November 11th of every year, Conscription Day, all the land is redistributed according to the individual adult male's capacity to cultivate. The provincial government has not actually confiscated landlords' land, the Marshal insists, but has merely urged the landlords to sell at fixed rates all land that they themselves cannot personally cultivate. Where a landlord has refused to sell, the government has taken his surplus land and parceled it out to tenants who pay the landlord five per cent of the land-yield for rent; thus, while the landlord still retains title to the land, its actual disposition and control is in the hands of the provincial government. The Kenanpo administration may deny the land to those who refuse to work or who commit one of the four major crimes—opium-smoking, gambling, theft, deceit. Soldiers who desert or are dishonorably discharged from the army may also be deprived of their land. Citizens' conduct is thus automatically controlled, for crimes against the society are punishable by depriving a man of his right to work and thereby of his livelihood. Through his Soldier-Farmer Union, then, Marshal Yen hopes eventually to abolish crime and imprisonment altogether.

Meanwhile, the Marshal readily admits that strong measures are necessary to cope with inertia and resistance. The slogan, "If one doesn't work, he doesn't eat," means also, "If anyone doesn't do as I think is best for him to do, I shall punish him severely." The mildest characterization, therefore, which one can apply to the Marshal's utopian experiment is that it is a benevolent dictatorship.

One last peculiar feature is worthy of mention. For his government functionaries, Marshal Yen has founded what is called the "People's Revolutionary League." He himself is president of the League, which in 1944 had a membership totaling 110,783. Organically, it considers itself a satellite of the Kuomintang—"though its moral regulations are much more strict," I was told. Honesty is a prime virtue, and every official must take a solemn oath on assuming office to commit suicide by poison or hanging if found guilty of smoking opium, gambling, taking graft, or deceiving his superiors." According to General Yang Ai-yuan, the Marshal's deputy commander, over a dozen wayward officials had already committed suicide in the presence of their fellow League members.

5

❖❖❖❖❖❖❖

I Enter Red China

Iᴛ ᴡᴀs late afternoon as we slithered down the stony, ankle-twisting mountain trail to the ferry landing. We waited about an hour for saddle-weary stragglers to come in, and then boarded the two flat-bottomed open boats for the wild dash across the swift current of the Yellow River. So tired were we from the long day's ride under a blistering sun that we hardly realized we were at last inside Communist China. After the lavish celebrations and receptions given us all along the line, our entrance into Communist China—through its side door—was something of an anticlimax. Three taciturn officials from the tiny ferry-landing village of Liang Sui An met us and put us up in a farm-yard which we shared with annoyed chickens, pigs, cows, and mournfully braying mules.

Morning brought an officer with three orderlies to greet us officially. We did not know it at the time, but they had been riding continuously for two days and nights over the mountains from Yenan, yet they looked as fresh as though they had spent the night in the adjoining farmhouse. All wore the same blue uniform and soft service cap with no insignia of rank other than a plain patch of red on the collar tab. The orderlies looked like Hollywood bandits with big Mauser pistols swinging at their hips, rifles on their shoulders, and Japanese Samurai swords slung carelessly over their backs.

It was evident that they worshipped their officer, yet they never saluted him and were plainly quite at ease with him.

At first meeting the officer appeared to have no very striking characteristics. He spoke little and he was without visible pretensions. It was not until some time later that we learned that thirty-seven-year-old Wang Cheng was one of the most famous generals in the Communists' ranks, a veteran of seventeen years' fighting in civil wars and against the Japanese, with seven wounds scarring his short, wiry, small-boned frame. Gray and neutral though he had seemed at first, Wang Cheng grew on us as we rode westward toward Yenan. As we all put aside our early reserve we found him to be easy-mannered, and boyish in his curiosity about our cameras, typewriters, and other fancy gadgets. He smiled toothily and puffed incessantly at a battered foreign-style pipe whose broken stem was bandaged like the big toe of his sockless, rope-sandaled foot. He carried a pair of powerful Japanese binoculars over his shoulder. "Took them from a Jap officer in a little scrap," the General said offhandedly. That was quite "a little scrap," I learned later. With fifteen hundred men he lay in ambush for a convoy of Japs moving along a highway in Inner Mongolia. As the Jap column of a thousand men with five tanks and forty-five trucks hit the mined section of the road, Wang Cheng led his men in for the kill. The Japs radioed for help and fifteen bombers came over, dropping tear and sneezing gas. Wang Cheng and his men, having no gas masks, were forced to retreat—though not before they had killed and wounded over 700 of the enemy, suffering 360 casualties themselves.

The binoculars were given him by an officer they had taken prisoner in that battle. Since it is not the policy of the Communists' Army to keep prisoners who ask to be sent back to their units, the officer was turned loose, and the binoculars had been his parting gift to General Wang Cheng. The officer was shot by his superiors upon his return to his unit for having disgraced the Japanese Army by allowing himself to be captured.

"We captured a Jap major-general once," Wang Cheng continued. "He didn't want to go back to certain execution, so we took him along with us. The Japs heard about it, though, and sent bombers to hunt us down. They located us finally in a little village which they plastered with bombs and at last he was killed."

The terrain grew rougher and rougher as we rode westward. But the landscape, which looked like a patchwork quilt of wheat, millet, cotton, and corn fields clinging perilously to precipitous mountain slopes, spoke clearly of the people's industry and determination.

"Most of this land was barren wasteland for centuries," said the General with a sweep of his arm. "It has been brought under cultivation only within the past two or three years—mostly by troopers of my brigade," he added half-apologetically. We perked up our ears. This sounded like a story. We urged him to tell us about it.

Returning from a long period of campaigning in North China three years before, Wang Cheng had been ordered to turn his brigade of ten thousand veteran Jap-fighters into farmers. They were to raise their own food, provide their own clothing, and become wholly self-sufficient and independent of both the government and the people. To this end he was allotted a wild wasteland of barren hills and valleys in the Nanniwan district and was provided meanwhile with a minimum of rations.

"First we dug caves into the loess cliffs for quarters," the General went on, "since winter was coming on and we had to hurry. Then we stacked our rifles while we cut down trees, fashioned crude tools, burnt stumps, cleared the land, and plowed the soil. In ancient abandoned temples near by we found temple bells, urns, and idols which we melted and hammered into plowshares.

"Since I know nothing of farming, I called upon my men to volunteer their experience and knowledge. Together we worked out a plan of production for cereals, vegetables, poultry, pigs for meat, sheep for wool, cotton for cloth. To pay for necessary seed and livestock to start us off, we lumbered cedar and pine logs from the mountains for sale in Yenan. A book on diet and feeding that we had captured from the Japs, and which for some reason I'd kept as a souvenir, now proved valuable. It introduced me to the mysteries of calories and vitamins and proteins—a sort of knowledge that was especially important for the health of my men. For we had received no medicines from the outside since the Kuomintang threw a military and economic blockade around our Border Region in 1939, and I was bound to try to improve nutrition in order to keep my men fit." He paused for a while, puffing vigorously at his wheezing pipe. "I'm not boring you with this story, am I?" he asked somewhat diffidently.

"No. No. Go on," I urged.

"Well, it was a heartbreaking struggle for the first year. We encountered many unforeseen obstacles and suffered many moments of discouragement. But Mao Tze-tung had told us it was imperative —a matter of life and death for the whole blockaded Border Region—that we should become self-sufficing. Everyone—man, woman, child, soldier, student, official—had to participate in production. I explained all this to my men. I told them it was up to them. They must not fail our leader—they must not fail themselves.

"It was a tough year, that first one. We worked hard, ate little, and patched our uniforms until they were hardly recognizable as uniforms. But the enthusiasm of my men was more than I could have hoped for. And last year we were able to raise enough to fill all our food requirements. Moreover, we harvested enough cotton and obtained enough wool from our flocks to clothe comfortably every single man in my brigade."

"You include, of course, the cost of spinning, weaving, and tailoring?" I asked.

"Cost? Hell, no! My troopers learned to spin and weave on machines they made themselves. They tailored their uniforms on sewing machines we captured from the Japanese. You'll see all this when we get to Nanniwan," he promised.

Nanniwan was a little off the direct route to Yenan, and from what Wang Cheng had told us we knew it would be well worth the detour.

As we approached the Nanniwan district we passed soldiers working in the fields, in groups of a dozen or more. They chanted as they wielded their picks, hoes, and shovels; their stacked rifles, machine guns, grenade-throwers, and trench mortars stood near by, stacked in orderly military fashion. Nearly all these arms were of Japanese manufacture and had been captured in battle. They were mute testimony that these laborers were first and last fighting men, not farmers.

The cliffsides were spotted with neat rows of caves, each about twenty-five feet deep and fifteen feet wide. The furniture in them was all soldier-made, crude but serviceable. Each cave quartered eight men. At brigade headquarters we visited a primitive press for extracting vegetable oils, and a small mill where paper was being made from a local grass-weed. There we saw also veteran soldiers spinning thread, weaving cloth, and tailoring uniforms.

We spent the night in General Wang's guest house, a neat Japanese-type bungalow.

"And why select the Japanese for your architectural style?" I asked.

"Oh—Japanese, is it?" Wang Cheng replied, mildly surprised. "I didn't know that. I asked Okada to build me a foreign-style house. It's just been completed."

"Okada? Who is he?"

"Okada is a former Japanese prisoner. He's an engineer, and was building blockhouses along the Tungpu Railway when we captured him three years ago. He's since joined the Japanese People's Emancipation League and is now attached to my brigade. Question him yourself if you wish."

Thirty-one-year-old Yoshio Okada was a pleasant-faced, intelligent fellow. He was dressed in a Communists' Eighth Route Army uniform and seemed perfectly at ease. It was obvious that he was well liked by the troopers, who crowded around as we talked to him through a Chinese interpreter who looked more Japanese than Okada-san himself. He told us his story. How he was captured in a surprise attack on a dark night, and how he expected to be tortured and killed; to his surprise he had been treated extremely well by his captors, who even offered to send him back to his unit. This he had refused because he knew of others who had returned and who had been secretly shot by the gendarmerie. He had entered the Japanese Workers' and Peasants' School in Yenan and after a year's training there he had joined the Paluchun (Eighth Route Army) in May 1942.

"And now he's one of our Labor Heroes," added Wang Cheng. Okada-san smiled with embarrassment. They had made him a

Labor Hero for inventing a suction water-pump which in principle resembled those in use on American farms.

After our evening meal we joined a gathering in an amphitheater under a full moon. A troupe of soldiers and their wives were about to perform a modernized native dance to illustrate their pride in the Nanniwan achievement. Before a wind-blown backdrop bearing huge pen-portraits of Roosevelt, Churchill, Stalin, and Generalissimo Chiang Kai-shek, an orchestra squatted and played soft melodious music on a queer mixture of ancient and modern instruments. The dancers sang in clear, confident voices.

"The Border Region is a paradise for the poor and the oppressed. There are no rascals or loafers here. Everyone works; everyone loves to work; everyone has land to cultivate—even the soldiers who, instead of being a burden upon the people, actually help them."

A vagrant entered—a loafer just arrived in the Border Region. "I have no food, no land, no family," he sang. From one side of the imaginary stage the vagrant watched a group of soldiers enter with picks and hoes over their shoulders. They were just returning from the fields. A woman made her entrance from the other side. "Come into my home and let me prepare a meal for you," she said. The soldiers thanked her but refused, at which she was annoyed. "What will my neighbors think of me when they hear you've passed by and I haven't fed you?" The soldiers laughed. "Many thanks, but we have our own food and will not take food from the people."

As they went out they saw the loafer. "You are a stranger? Have you eaten? If not, come with us." The vagrant looked amazed. "So this is the Paluchun," he said as he went out with them.

It was propaganda, of course—good propaganda. We naturally suspected that it had been put on for our benefit. Yet it must be borne in mind that these actors were playing roles that they truly performed in real life.

Meanwhile Wang Cheng was moving restlessly about from one place to another. Wholly at ease with his men he sat with them. They paid no attention to him as they watched the play. As I watched the General, an orderly approached and whispered something in his ear. He lifted his head sharply and a broad grin cracked his face from ear to ear. Then he jumped to a table top and shouted for attention. A telephone call from Yenan had given news of the long-awaited landing in France. The Allies had landed in Normandy! There was a spontaneous cheer, and the audience shouted lustily: "Success to the Allies!" "Victory for the United Nations!" "Down with the Fascist Aggressors!"

In the morning we went out to visit the 718th Battalion of Wang Cheng's 359th Brigade. The battalion commander, thirty-three-year-old Ho Lin, was a short, stocky fighting man. "There was nothing in this valley when I brought my 443 men here three years ago," he began. "In the first year we cleared enough land and raised enough food for about one-third of our needs. Last year we increased our production to meet practically all of them. And this year we expect to have a comfortable surplus and be well on our way to our goal of producing one year's reserve with two years' effort."

Ho Lin was proud of his battalion's livestock. They had a cow for every ten men, a pig for every three, as well as a sheep or goat to each man. Each company had over a hundred chickens in addition to a warren of rabbits. Already he had been able to increase meat rations for his men from the minimum standard of two pounds per month to over six pounds. In addition, he had been able to provide them with almost unlimited amounts of vegetables of many varieties.

His men lined up for inspection. I had been long in China and had seen much of the Chinese Army. These were about the best-nourished troops I had yet seen. Ho Lin's men never forget that they are soldiers, not farmers. In the winter months and during the summer months between planting and harvesting, these troopers receive intensive military training. Company Commander Ku Chen-chow gave us a summarized account of the activities of his men as typical of the others. Last winter they studied the short-distance attack. On a simulated battlefield equipped with ditches, low walls, dummies, and every sort of obstacle, the men were given intensive training in bayonet fighting, grenade throwing, and preliminary field engineering work, besides thorough training in the use of the rifle under all possible conditions. He was proud of his company's record on the rifle-range: only three out of 372 shots fired at a meter-sized objective at a hundred-meter range failed to hit the target. The average distance for throwing the heavy two-pound potato-masher grenade was forty meters. In addition to all this, the troopers were taught to read and write, were given lectures on current national and international affairs, and themselves formed dramatic groups for entertainment and recreation.

At the headquarters of the 719th Regiment we heard the same story of agricultural and educational achievement. Somehow this unit had also found time to build a huge auditorium of heavy stones and massive log beams brought down from the mountains miles away. Capable of seating 1,400 people, it had been erected in 27 days by a single company of volunteers.

The regiment was commanded by Chang Chung-han, a tall, intelligent, quiet-spoken fellow, son of a wealthy landlord of Hopei province. When the Japs came to Hopei in 1938 young Chang organized and financed a company of guerrillas to resist the enemy. By the time the Paluchun regulars entered the province, Chang's guerrilla band numbered over 4,000. Chang asked the Paluchun for special military training for his men, and later, by election, they joined the Paluchun ranks.

We visited the brigade hospital with wards in a series of caves dug into the cliffside. It was a saddening experience. Though the doctors and nurses were giving the soldier patients the best possible attention, they had little or nothing in the way of medicines for treatment. The dispensary was lined with neat rows of bottles for Western medicines, labeled in Latin; all the bottles were empty. The surgeons' instruments were made of scrap steel, mostly from Japanese bomb fragments. They were crude, but it was the best that could be got.

I was talking to a wounded soldier in one of the wards when I heard a commotion outside. I never did find out who or what started it all, but there was Wang Cheng blazing away at the Chinese reporters in our party:

"The calculated brutality of the Kuomintang in blockading shipments of medicines for our hospitals—medicines donated by foreign friends abroad for our fighters battling a common enemy—is a crime against the very gods. If there is a God, or even Chinese pagan gods, they must know and be shocked by this spectacle of utter shamelessness."

Sharp-tongued Chen Chia-kang, Chou En-lai's brainy secretary, echoed Wang Cheng. "I accuse the Kuomintang of deliberately holding and subsequently confiscating four truckloads of medicines donated by the British Red Cross which were never allowed to proceed beyond Sian en route to the Border Region!"

The Chinese pressmen stood silent, with impassive expressions.

Excitable Ma Han-ping, Wang Cheng's secretary, joined in. "Whom are we fighting, I ask? The Japanese? My best friend received a slight wound in the hand in battle—a slight wound, but for lack of antiseptics he developed blood-poisoning and died. And yet four truckloads of precious medical supplies for us were confiscated by the Kuomintang at Sian. Murderers, I call them! They murdered my friend!"

Irish-American Father Shanahan of our party tried to keep the situation from getting entirely out of hand. He said that Chinese troops elsewhere, on other China fronts, were suffering the same lack of medicines. He did not know whether it was due to negligence—deliberate or otherwise—or whether it was because there were insufficient supplies to go around. He promised, however, that we would do what we could to bring the sad state of affairs we had witnessed at this hospital to the attention of the Chungking authorities. The rest of us, including the Chinese pressmen, readily agreed to this, and the troubled waters were eventually calmed.

Before we left Nanniwan, Wang Cheng summed up some of the highlights of his work. He was particularly proud of the results achieved in the field of education. Thirty per cent of the time allotted to military training is devoted to cultural and political work. As a result of daily classes in reading and writing, over eighty per cent of the troopers are able to read ordinary newspapers, while the remaining twenty per cent, mostly new recruits, know at least from one hundred to five hundred Chinese characters, enough to read a special simplified Chinese warfront newspaper.

There is a close link between political and cultural education. The soldiers are taught a brief history of Japanese aggression, which is traced from early days through the Sino-Japanese War of 1894-95 to the present. A good deal of this is given them through the medium of the drama. A conscious effort is made to engender a deep-seated hatred for the Japanese.

"So that the men will have tangible evidence of the Japs' bestiality, we take them to destroyed villages, let them talk to the people who've suffered at the hands of the enemy. From a village on the Shansi-Charhar border a raiding party of Japs carried off truckloads of women whom they violated unspeakably. Many were killed for resisting; others, horribly mutilated. Some became permanently deranged. Of those who straggled back to the village many committed suicide. We allowed our soldiers to talk to the husbands, brothers, and fathers, and to those of the women who would speak through their shame."

Skill and ability is singled out, encouraged, with special honors and material awards for achievement. Thus, Labor Heroes are selected, praised, rewarded, and honored to encourage others to emulate them. This gives the soldier an incentive, improves and transforms the monotony of a soldier's life into something rich and good. It gives him, moreover, an awareness and social consciousness.

"We've talked of social security for our soldiers for many years," Wang Cheng continued. "But it wasn't until last year that we set up soldiers' co-operatives which enable my men to take the surplus earned from their labor on the land and invest it in a profitable enterprise which will provide them with some degree of financial security against old age or discharge to civilian life after the war."

The old saying that "to be a soldier is to be a monk" does not apply to Wang Cheng's men. Both Mao Tze-tung and Chu Teh told him to encourage marriages among his men, and to help them build homes and a future. Over four hundred of his men are married, producing about a hundred babies a year. Wang Cheng himself married in 1937. His wife is a girl from Manchuria, a graduate in chemistry from Peiping University. She has given him three husky sons of whom he is rightly proud.

6

✧✧✧✧✧✧✧

Yenan

THE bomb-proof cave-city of
Yenan today stands as a magnificent symbol of the tenacity and
determination of the Border Region people. The city itself is over
three thousand years old. In ancient days it stood as one of the most
important bastions against invasion by barbarian hordes from the
North. Yenan flourished down through the centuries until the
Great Mohammedan Rebellion of nearly a century ago, which re-
sulted in the laying waste of vast areas and the slaughter of millions
of Chinese throughout the Northwest. Yenan's massive city walls
remained intact, however, and the city was rebuilt. It grew steadily
until in 1938 and 1939 the Japanese, expressing their notorious hate
for the Chinese Communists, by repeated bombings pulverized the
city. When they had finished with it, old Yenan was a mere rubble
heap.

But the destruction of the city's buildings drove away neither the
Communist government nor the people. These merely went outside
the city and dug deep into the thousand-foot loess cliffsides flanking
Yenan valley, so that Yenan today is truly a cave-city, bomb-proof
against blockbusters. The cave homes in rows of arched openings
separated from one another by flying buttresses, march in imposing
tiers which climb the cliffsides. Steep paths zigzag from one tier
to the next, connecting the lowest with the highest tiers. Before
each cave opening is a tiny leveled patch notched into the cliffside

46

for a chicken-coop, a pig-pen, a vegetable garden, or a children's
playground, with perhaps a string of laundry flapping in the hot,
dry sunshine. In the valley below, women may be seen laundering
on the bank of the muddy Yen River. Horses, mules, grunting pigs,
and heavily laden high-wheeled carts roll up yellow dust clouds,
while pedestrians and horsemen wear gauze masks to filter the
dust from the air.

We were put up in the Yenan Guest House, with a comfortable
cave room assigned to each of us—quarters much better than our
Press Hostel in Chungking. Among the first people we met were
two foreigners—Michael Lindsay and Ma Hai-teh. Lindsay is a tall,
baldish, bespectacled Britisher in his middle thirties. A graduate
of Oxford in 1931 (his father is Master of Balliol), Lindsay took a
post in China as a tutor in Yenching University at Peiping. For a
short period in 1940 he was British Press Attaché in Chungking.
The work was uncongenial to him, however, and he returned to
Yenching. On Pearl Harbor day he made a dash from Peiping and
escaped to the Communist guerrillas operating in the hills near by.
Though a professor in history and English at Yenching, Lindsay's
hobby had long been radio, and the Communists persuaded him to
stay with them to build and repair their equipment and train opera-
tors and technicians. He stayed in the front lines for over two and
a half years, playing hide-and-seek with the Japs, who were especially interested in capturing or killing him. He had arrived in
Yenan the week before we reached the city.

Ma Hai-teh is as American as Lindsay is British. Born in Buffalo,
educated in North Carolina and Switzerland (where he received
his medical degree), Ma Hai-teh has been seven years with the
Communists. He has taken the Chinese name of Ma Hai-teh (he
refuses to disclose his American name) so that he may more completely submerge himself in the medical service of the Chinese
Communist armies. Also in his middle thirties, he is full of boyish
good humor and enthusiasm, and will unhesitatingly drop everything to act as interpreter. He is an enthusiastic supporter of the
Chinese Communists.

"One of the things I like most about this place," says Ma Hai-teh,
"is that there is absolutely no professional jealousy here. This is

due in large measure to the fact that there is no financial incentive, no rivalry for special honors or favors. All of us work together like members of a big family, and satisfactions and disappointments are mutually shared. This restores medicine to its proper role, which is that of a science in the service of mankind."

Ma Hai-teh told me of a new disease which has puzzled him and his Chinese colleagues. For want of a better name they have called it Limping Sickness. The disease has a definite standardized clinical entity, but they have been unable to find any record of it in medical history. It is indigenous to an area of about thirty-six hundred square miles straddling the Yellow River due east from Yenan.

"Its victims resemble each other as if turned out on a mass assembly line," he explained. "The principal apparent deformity results from a swelling of the head of the tibia and stiffening of the knee joint, causing the characteristic limp. The disease is an inhibition of growth in certain bones from the age of puberty to the age of about twenty-one or twenty-two when all bone growth ceases. The bone shows an excess growth of bony tissues, especially around the joints where pressure is applied. There's a lipping of joint surfaces and a shortening of the bones of the leg, forearm, fingers, and toes—sometimes to a half or two-thirds of their normal length in proportion to the body."

The disease affected all boys and girls within the age-spread, not only among the native inhabitants but also among immigrants into the region. Though the disease does not entirely cripple its victims, it greatly lowers physique and working power: those affected cannot carry heavy loads or walk distances, and their stubby fingers require special, thinner-handled farm implements.

"For lack of necessary equipment for chemical and biochemical analysis and X-ray to study the bones during the changing period, we have been unable to determine the specific cause of the disease. Our research has been terribly hampered, too, because of a lack of utilizable calcium and the vitamins connected with bone growths. We suspect the water," he continued. "The trees in that area have a high phosphorus content, and wood glows under water at night. Since the water which the peasants use drains this region, we assume this disturbs the calcium-phosphorus balance in the blood, and this may account for the deformity of the bones."

Diet has already been definitely eliminated as the cause of the disease. Moreover, it is not a wartime affliction, since it has a long local history. Meanwhile, there was little that could be done after the disease had once taken hold. They were attacking the problem at the source by persuading the natives to send their children away during the susceptible age-spread. The peasantry were showing some opposition to this because they were reluctant to be separated from their children so long.

"However, the youngsters whom we have been able to move out of the area have thus far shown no signs of the disease—thus proving that it is not hereditary and that it is definitely due to some local factor," he concluded.

Some days after I cabled the story of this mysterious new disease, a flood of cablegrams came in from various organizations in America asking for further particulars about the new Limping Sickness. There was not much that Ma Hai-teh and his associates could add to the story as he had given it to me. What was needed —and needed badly—was an X-ray machine. And while there were several organizations, including the American Red Cross, prepared to supply such equipment to the Eighth Route Army, the Kuomintang blockade of this area prevented such equipment from being shipped up to Yenan.

Some months later, however, this problem was solved. The American Army Air Force had established a temporary post in Yenan with regular plane transport with Chungking, and the American Red Cross was then able to fly an X-ray machine to Yenan, together with several tons of medical supplies for the Eighth Route Army. The full equipment had not yet arrived by the time I left Yenan, so that is was too early to find out what more had been learned of the Limping Sickness.

Ma Hai-teh is attached to the Bethune International Peace Hospital located on the outskirts of Yenan. The hospital, located in a series of caves, was established and named for Doctor Norman Bethune, Surgeon-General for the Royal Canadian Flying Corps during World War I, who died in 1939 in the service of the Chinese

Communist armies. It is sponsored by Madame Sun Yat-sen and supported partly by contributions from abroad. The Bethune International Peace Hospital is something unique—not only for what it does, but for what it does without. Because of blockade by the Japanese and the Central Government troops, it had received no medical supplies from abroad during the past three years except for the small quantity of drugs we brought through for it in our baggage from Chungking.

The hospital staff were a bright-eyed, intelligent lot. Lack of proper equipment and supplies had not daunted them—really it had spurred them to ingenious improvisations and tolerable substitutes. Chinese herbs, medicines, and chemicals were being scientifically tested. Many had been found to be not merely suitable as substitutes for Western medicines, but indeed to have qualities definitely superior to these. Their dwindling stock of remaining Western drugs was hoarded in a single drawer, and their precious few sulfa pills were dispensed, in case of extreme urgency, only after consultation by the whole medical staff.

Rope-sandaled, Western-trained Chinese doctors and nurses worked in cave laboratories making slides from broken windowpane glass for the hospital's single and very ancient microscope. Eye-undines were made from tiny teapots with string wicks in their spouts. Eye-droppers were fabricated from a piece of rubber hose plugged at one end. Cultures were incubated in a rack placed next to the smokestack of the kitchen stove. The little glass tubes in which the last of their stock of Western-made catgut had been packed now served as test tubes. The needle end of a broken glass syringe was plugged up and the result was a graduated medicine glass. Their surgical-intrument sterilizer had been evolved from a gasoline container. The instruments themselves had mostly been captured from the Japanese, as was the collapsible metal operating table in the simply furnished operating room. For blood-sedimentation tests they placed two plain glass tubes in a rack with the millimeter scale taken from the edging of an ordinary stencil paper pasted alongside. Home-made plaster-of-paris was stored in airproofed earthen crocks. Medical cotton was made from locally grown cotton, while gauze was manufactured from thread spun by the doctors and nurses themselves on ancient wooden spinning-wheels. The staff members also planted and tended their own vege-table gardens, hauled their own water from the river in the valley far below, and did all their own laundering.

For lack of anesthetics and such essentials as glucose, they were obliged to perform many transfusions, the blood donors usually being the staff members. There was not a single watch or clock in the whole hospital, and time was told by incense punks which burned for exactly one hour, or by water falling drop by drop into a bottle, with a watching attendant to clang a bell to note the pass-ing hours.

"What we miss most here is recent medical journals or mono-graphs on new developments in war surgery which would keep us abreast of medical progress," said Dr. Chow Pei-chi. Dr. Chow was trained by German doctors in a military hospital in Kwangsi. The whitewashed walls of his bare cave-laboratory were hung with pen-portraits of Louis Pasteur, Robert Koch, and others whose pictures he had found in old medical magazines.

Across the valley from the hospital was the Yenan Medical Col-lege. Its dean was Wang Ping, a fine, intelligent, serious-minded doctor. At the time of our visit there were 210 medical students in the college, of whom 54 were women. The textbooks were all hand-written translations from Japanese, American, British, and German works. On the walls were medical charts, mostly copies hand-drawn by the students themselves, though there were also a few profes-sional lithographed examples. The eye-clinic had good eye-testing instruments captured from the Japanese. The same lack of surgical and other material hampered the college. Its staff could diagnose but not prescribe; not even spectacles were to be obtained. They used ordinary manicure scissors for iridectomy operations, while the optical lamp was made of a Standard Oil Company oil lamp with a tin hood made from a German die-can, lined with tinfoil from Japanese cigarettes. For lack of formalin, cadavers were pickled in *by-gar*, a potent Chinese whiskey, while waiting to be cut up by anatomy classes.

From January to June all students had to put in at least three hours daily spinning thread or at some other form of production.

Boys and girls alike, they sat in orderly rows before their spin-ning-wheels in a huge auditorium. When my visit was over and Wang Ping and his associates asked me for criticisms and sugges-tions (everyone in the Border Region asks, almost demands, that you give criticisms and suggestions on any and all occasions), I told them frankly that I thought it a waste of time to make these students spend three hours daily at spinning. Time and brains were too scarce and precious to be wasted on such work, no matter what they say about its serving as a good example for others.

"Those three hours daily put into more study, or at least into reading in your meager library, would be much more valuable to your cause and your problems than the example they set for lazy peasants by spinning thread," I said. "It is sheer waste and ineffi-ciency."

That they take criticisms seriously was proven later when, after a medical conference in Yenan, this question was brought up and the order given to cancel the three hours' daily production require-ment.

7

Is This Communism?

A<small>T THIS</small> point it would be well to review briefly the events that preceded the present developments in the Shan-Kan-King (Shensi-Kansu-Ninghsia) Border Region.

In the decades between the Chinese Revolution in 1911 and the coming of the Red Army in 1935, North Shensi was one of the most oppressed districts in the country. Its barren, mountainous, sparsely populated area was harassed by banditry. It was a region of opium-growing, and suffered from maladministration and crushing taxation ruthlessly imposed by local warlords.

Worst of the local warlords was Chin Yu-hsiu, known as the "Local Emperor," a gentleman with eleven concubines, who owned most of the best land, which was worked by virtual slave labor. He imposed more than forty different kinds of taxes upon the miserable population, who, moreover had to support not only his army but the private mercenaries in the service of big landlords.

Meanwhile, as far back as 1921 and 1922, Communist Party workers had begun establishing secret Communist cells in North Shensi. These were organized by graduates of Peiping University who came to Yulin, Suiteh, and Yenan as teachers. Later, these co-operated with the developing revolutionary Kuomintang Party under the leadership of Dr. Sun Yat-sen. They helped the Kuomintang to organize peasants' unions and workers' unions. They directed their efforts towards securing reductions of rent and interest and towards arming the people against the scandalously oppressive warlords. When the Kuomintang-Communist break came in April 1927, the North Shensi Reds were hounded and massacred by the Kuomintang along with other Communists throughout the country. Over ten thousand were killed in North Shensi.

However, two local youngsters, Kao Kang and Liu Tze-tan, began to organize the scattered remnants of the leaderless Communists and with the support of the farmers and villagers were able to confine the Kuomintang forces to the larger cities. By the next year, 1928, they felt themselves strong enough to begin military action against the Kuomintang forces in an effort to drive them out of Shensi altogether. With a brigade of armed peasants, workers, and students, they attempted to capture the towns of Weinan and Hwaying on the direct line from Tungkwan to Sian. The expedition failed miserably when the Kuomintang sent four battalions of regulars to engage the rebels. Not only were the Communists poorly armed, but they lacked military experience and, moreover, made the fatal mistake of trying to stand up against the regulars in positional battle, with the result that they were defeated and dispersed.

Two years later, when the Kuomintang garrison in Yenan revolted, the Communists rallied again and joined them, and in doing so won stronger support from the restless masses. Partisan warfare against the Kuomintang authority was organized on an increasing scale. Their slogans at the time were. "We demand equality in land holdings"—"Those who till the land should own it"—"Down with extortionate taxes"—"Down with greedy officials and rotten gentry"—"We demand the right of the people to elect their own governments"—"Oppose Japanese imperialism."

When the Japanese began their invasion of Manchuria and North China in the next year, the rebels decided to change their name from the Democratic Partisan Troops to the Northwest Anti-Japanese Allied Army. They announced and insisted that henceforth they wanted to fight the Japanese and not the Kuomintang, though the policy of the Kuomintang was one of appeasement of the encroaching Japanese.

Thus it was that the Communists prepared North Shensi as an anti-Japanese base. In October 1935, Mao Tze-tung and the vanguard of the Chinese Communist Armies arrived in Shensi, and were followed, in November 1936, by Chu Teh and the rest of the troops, after their incredible 8000-mile Long March from Kiangsi. The Shensi Communists were then absorbed and Kao Kang made chairman of the Communist Party's Northwest Bureau, which today includes the Shansi-Suiyuan Anti-Japanese Base in addition to the Shan-Kan-Ning Border Region. The Communists then settled down to put their new home in order.

Meanwhile, they called upon the Kuomintang and the people of China to stop civil war and form a united front against Japanese aggression. When the Generalissimo was detained at Sian some months later by rebellious Government troops at Christmas 1936, the Communists proved their sincerity. Despite their long and bitter military struggle with Chiang, and putting aside their memories of thousands of their party who had been executed by the Kuomintang, the Communists now quickly stepped in and urged Chiang's captors to release him in the interests of the larger struggle against the invader. As a matter of plain fact, it was largely Communist influence which set Chiang Kai-shek at liberty. Shortly thereafter, with the intention of cementing co-operation between the Kungchantang (Communist Party) and the Kuomintang in an anti-Japanese united front, the Communists put forward their now-famous "Five Suggestions" and "Four Guarantees."

With the outbreak of the war with Japan in July, these "Suggestions" and "Guarantees" were accepted and implemented in an Agreement with the Government signed on September 22, 1937, wherein the Communists, among other things, voluntarily undertook to change the name of their Soviet base in North Shensi to the Shan-Kan-Ning Border Region, to stop the confiscation of land, and to establish democratic rule through universal suffrage. They agreed also to change the name of the Red Army to the National Revolutionary Army and to make active preparations for sustained combat against the Japanese under the leadership of the National Government and Generalissimo Chiang-Kai-shek.

During the 333rd meeting of the Executive Yuan, the Com-

munists insist, the Generalissimo confirmed the agreements made
with them concerning the name and the geographical extension of
the Border Region. It was to have an area of about 130,000 square
kilometers. Within this region were recognized to be some two
million inhabitants. Unfortunately, misunderstandings arose between the Kungchantang and the Kuomintang, and two years
after the outbreak of the war with Japan the Border Region was
surrounded by several hundred thousand of the Government's
crack troops. The Communists assert that a blockade line, fortified
with over 10,000 blockhouses, was constructed and is at present in
existence. The gradual tightening of this blockade has reduced
the Border Region's area to about 90,000 square kilometers with a
population of 1,500,000 plus about 80,000 garrison troops and government personnel.

The political evolution of the Border Region from the Communism of the civil war days into a representative democracy is
perhaps the most significant feature of the Region's history. In
1938 the Border Region government began to carry out general elections through direct and secret ballot without distinction of class,
party, clique, religious belief, property ownership, sex, or nationality. In the spring of 1939 the first congress of the Border Region's
People's Political Council convened. In 1941, electoral procedure
was revised to conform to the new "one-to-three" system—a plan
whereby the Communists limited themselves to the acceptance of
only one-third of the elective government posts, leaving the other
two-thirds for non-Communists of all classes and nationalities
(meaning Mongols, Mohammedans, etc.) "who are anti-Japanese
and democratic." If the results of an election brought in more than
one-third Communists, they would voluntarily relinquish the con-
ceded posts. Since that time this principle has been strictly observed.
Of the eighteen members in the Border Region Government today,
for example, only six are Communists. It is a principle of the Communist Party that non-Communists in the Government shall have
both post and power, and that Communist members must submit
to majority rule.

In the winter of 1941 the elections for the Second Convention of
the People's Political Council were held. The Communist candi-

dates offered a platform which had been drawn up by the Border Region Political Bureau of their party. They declared this platform, on the basis of which they appealed for votes, to be grounded upon the Three People's Principles and the Testament of Dr. Sun Yat-sen. Because the platform expresses the spirit and intentions of the Communists and because later, in program form, it was adopted by the People's Political Council. I consider the high points of this election manifesto well worth quoting:

"If Communists are elected to the administration," the brief preamble concludes—

"1) They will resolutely seek to unite all social strata, all anti-Japanese parties and groups in the Border Region. They will seek fully to develop man-power and material, financial, and intellectual resources in defence of the Border Region, Northwest China, and the whole of China, with the firm intention of driving out the Japanese imperialists.

"2) They will persistently urge unity with friendly parties [the Kuomintang], friendly armies [Central Troops], and all loyal people outside the Border Region, and they will as persistently oppose capitulatory, divisive, and retrogressive acts.

"3) They will seek to enhance the fighting capacity of the armed forces of the Border Region, to insure their material provision, and to improve the recruiting and mobilization system of other military services. They will endeavor to strengthen solidarity between the army and the people, and at the same time they will work to strengthen the organization and training of the Self-Defence Corps and Youth Vanguards, and to perfect their leadership.

"4) They will support preferential treatment for dependents of anti-Japanese soldiers of the Eighth Route Army and the Kuomintang Central Troops with the object of providing them with material security and moral support.

"5) Our Party is willing to form an electoral bloc with all political parties and all public organizations, and establish definitely the practice that Communists shall occupy only one-third of the list of candidates nominated, so as to enable all parties, groups, and non-partisan people to participate in activities of the people's representative organs and direction of the administrative affairs of the Border Region. If a Communist is elected as the head of a certain administrative institution, he will insure that two-thirds of his co-workers be non-Communists. Communists in administrative posts will co-operate in a democratic manner with non-Communists. They will give due regard to non-Communist opinion, and they will not adopt domineering monopolistic attitudes.

"6) The Communist Party desires to safeguard civil, political, and property rights equally with the rights of freedom of speech, press, assembly, organization, belief, residence, and movement of all anti-Japanese people, including landlords, capitalists, peasants, workers, etc. The Communists believe that—with the exception of the Judiciary and Public Safety Institutions, which are entitled to carry out their legally designated functions—no institution, army unit, or organization should have the right to bring charges against any person. The people should have the right to bring charges against any public functionary guilty of illegal acts.

"7) The Communists desire to improve the judiciary system and abolish corporal punishment of prisoners, and they urge that more importance be attached to evidence than to affidavit. With regard to traitors, except those hopelessly unchangeable, a policy of magnanimity should be adopted towards them, irrespective of their past history. Efforts should be made to instruct and convert them. They should not be manhandled and coerced into testifying against themselves or into writing statements of repentance. With regard to such elements as renegades and anti-Communists who plot wrecking activities in the Border Region, they should be treated similarly.

"8) The Communists will urge the strict enforcement of the principle of clean and honest government and severe punishment of any functionary guilty of graft or embezzlement. They will oppose jobbery. If a Communist violates the laws, the Party is of the opinion that he should be subjected to a severe penalty. At the same time, we believe that the salary system should be based on the principle of economy and frugality. The necessary material needs of all functionaries and their dependents should be satisfied, and an adequate cultural and recreative life must be guaranteed them.

"9) Communist representatives will urge measures intended to develop agricultural production and to mobilize the masses for their spring sowing and autumn harvesting, and help poor peasants to overcome difficulties in securing plowing animals, farm implements, fertilizers, and seeds. They will propose that a further 600,000 *mou* [six *mou* equal one English acre] of untilled land be cultivated in the present year in order to increase the supply of food crops by 400,000 piculs [one picul equals 133 pounds]. Migration of people to the Border Region will be encouraged.

"10) The Communists declare their belief that in the districts where land has been distributed, the right of private ownership of land should be guaranteed to all peasants who have acquired land. In other districts where land has not been distributed (such as Suiteh, Fuhsien, and Chinyang), the right of ownership of land should be guaranteed to the present landlords, and the right to recover debts should be guaranteed to creditors. The Party declares that the rates of rent and interest must be reduced. Tenants should pay a certain amount of rent to the landlords, and debtors should pay a certain amount of interest to creditors. The Government should regulate the relationship between landlords and tenants and between creditors and debtors.

"11) The Communist representatives will propose measures designed to develop industrial production and trade, encourage private enterprise, and protect private property. They believe the Border Region should welcome investments from outside and abroad, foster free trade, and oppose monopoly and manipulations. At the same time it should develop the co-operatives and promote the development of handicraft industry.

"12) The People's Political Council should regulate the relationship between employers and employees, put into practice a ten-hour working day, raise labor productivity, foster labor discipline, and adequately improve the livelihood of the workers.

"13) The People's Political Council should devise a rational system of taxation. With the exception of the poorest section of the people, who should be exempted from taxation, a progressive tax system—in which the rate of taxation varies in accordance with the amount of property or income of the tax-payer—should be enforced, so that the costs of the anti-Japanese War are equitably borne, and by the great majority of the population. At the same time the organization of financial institutions should be improved, financial relations regulated, national currency protected. Notes issued by the Border Region Bank should be consolidated so as to facilitate the development of a healthy economy and finance.

"14) The Communists advocate that the PPC should continue the policy of eliminating illiteracy. It should foster the teaching of Latinized Chinese [i.e., Chinese with the substitution of Latin orthography for the old characters], perfect the regular educational system, put into practice universal public education, improve the livelihood of primary school teachers, and provide supplementary education for adults. It should devise legislation to strengthen the education of cadres, spread the circulation of popular books and periodicals, encourage free study, etc.

"15) The People's Political Council should broaden health administration, improve medical facilities, and welcome medical personnel, so as to mitigate the suffering of the people from epidemics. At the same time it should give medical relief to refugees migrating into the Border Region.

"16) In accordance with the principle of equality between man and woman the administration should seek to enhance the social standing of woman politically, economically, and culturally and should fully strive to develop the active initiative of woman in economy. It should protect working women, pregnant women, and children, and enforce a monogamous marriage system based upon mutual consent.

"17) In accordance with the principle of equality between nationalities, the People's Political Council should insure to Mongolians and Mohammedans equal political, economic, and cultural rights with the Chinese people. It should establish self-governing areas for the Mongolian and Mohammedan people, and it should respect their religious faiths, customs, and habits.

"18) The Administration should welcome overseas Chinese into the Border Region to study, to participate in anti-Japanese work, or to build up enterprises.

"19) The People's Political Council should provide vagrants with opportunity to work on the farm, secure jobs, and receive education. It should seek to correct the bad habits of functionaries and others in discriminating against vagrants. It should pursue a policy of winning over, uniting and educating Hweimin [organizations with superstitious and semifeudal practices and purposes].

"20) The Administration should advocate magnanimity towards prisoners of the Japanese and Puppet Armies, should accommodate and extend hospitality to any of them who desire to participate in our war of resistance, and should release those who do not wish to remain. They should not, without exception, be killed, or tortured, humiliated, or coerced into signing statements of repentance. Similar lenient treatment should be adopted without exception towards those who, after being released, join the enemy and are again recaptured by our army. This should be the practice regardless of how many times such people may have been released or captured. Similar treatment should be adopted towards the members of any armed forces within the country who are taken prisoner during their attacks against the Eighth Route Army or any other anti-Japanese army.

"21) The Administration should permit foreigners to come to the Border Region for touring, participating in anti-Japanese work, or engaging in industrial, cultural, and missionary activities under the condition of respecting China's sovereignty and observing the decrees of the Government. Every possible protection should be extended by the Border Region Government to those foreigners of any nationality who are persecuted by any government on account of their revolutionary activities."

Whatever may be thought of these proposals, two things seem clear to me: they represent an all-inclusive and reasonably consistent effort to deal with the situation in which the Border Region finds itself, and constitute a program that is far removed from Communism, at least as we have come to understand the word.

8

✧✧✧✧✧✧✧✧

A Mixed Economy

COLLECTIVISM, a basic principle in Soviet Communism, does not exist in the Border Region today, except in the modified democratic form of labor exchange brigades and co-operatives. With personal property as a foundation, and voluntary consent as a principle, co-operative effort in a number of forms has been utilized to organize a scattered, individualistic, and backward rural economy. Over a hundred thousand agricultural workers (about one-quarter of the total agricultural labor power) have been organized into exchange brigades and hired-labor groups. Two hundred thousand have been organized within consumption, transportation, production, and credit co-operatives. Over 137,000 women have been organized into spinning co-operatives.

The labor exchange system has proven its worth in increased production. In one respect it is akin to the Soviet Union's collective farming, though in the Border Region each farmer retains ownership of his own patch of land. It more closely resembles, perhaps, our harvest combines for farmers in America. Practically it works this way: A group of eight, ten, or a dozen neighbor farmers get together and exchange their labor power by working together on one man's field today, the next man's field tomorrow, and so on till all have been cultivated. Plowing, sowing, weeding, and harvesting are all done co-operatively. Should one man have more land than his neighbor, the scale is balanced by a supplementary contribution of, say, a son's manpower, or an extra portion of food contributed to the pool. No one is under compulsion to join a labor exchange brigade, but few refuse since the scheme has proven itself profitable. Wives also participate in the labor exchange by taking turns in preparing the group's meals. In this way, the other wives are given time in which to engage in co-operative spinning and weaving.

The first to start a labor exchange brigade, and prove its worth, was Wu Man-yu. When, back in 1939, he and a group of his neighbors demonstrated that collective effort was more efficient than the old system, hitherto hesitant peasants throughout the Border Region quickly took up the idea. The slogan of the labor exchangers today is: "Keep Pace with Wu Man-yu." Today Wu Man-yu is the Border Region's Labor Hero Number One. There are 180 such Labor Heroes in agricultural, industrial, army, cultural, and transportation fields. Wu Man-yu was the first to achieve this honor, which the Border Region Government conferred upon him in 1942. His portrait is hung prominently in galleries, homes, and public places alongside those of Mao Tze-tung, Chu Teh, and other high political and military figures.

Wu is sixtyish, strong-bodied, red-faced, with merry eyes and a friendly smile, a wispy white mustache, and a shiny bald head. He can neither read nor write, but he has an extraordinary knowledge of farming methods, together with a great ability to improvise and adapt. They made him a Labor Hero because he was able to cultivate three times as much land and raise three times as many crops as an average farmer. As a Labor Hero, Wu Man-yu, and others like him, are not only held in high esteem by the people but are invited to attend all public and state functions, at which they occupy seats of honor along with the highest government and military officials.

"Mao Tze-tung himself came and called upon me several times and invited me to his home for dinner," he said proudly; "and actually shook my hand," he added, showing me his calloused palm. Not so many years ago, before the coming of the Red

Army, Wu Man-yu came to Yenan as a destitute refugee from a famine-stricken area.

"I had to sell my three-year-old daughter for six pounds of corn to feed the rest of my family until I was able to cut enough firewood in the hills to buy more food and farm tools to till the acre of poor land that I rented," he continued. When the landlord had him thrown into jail for failure to pay his rent, his wife starved to death. The Communists came shortly afterward and divided up the landlord's land and Wu Man-yu got "one hill" as his portion. (The Border Region, by the way, today subsidizes refugees with land, farm implements, and food until they are able to become self-supporting.)

With this modest start Wu Man-yu in the past eight years has built up a farm of over sixty-five acres, all of which he has reclaimed from uncultivated wasteland. Moreover, he has a flock of forty sheep and goats, four oxen, one horse, four beehives, and "I don't know how many chickens," he concluded. He has invested thousands of dollars of his savings in a farmers' retail co-operative. Frequently the army, in its self-subsistence campaign, calls upon him to teach the soldiers his techniques.

At his invitation I went out to visit his farm, located in a fold in the hills not far from Yenan. He must have forgotten that he had invited me, or perhaps he had thought I would not take his invitation seriously. At any rate, he was away on a mountain slope cutting firewood when I arrived. His surprise and pleasure at seeing me were evident. It was just as well, and I preferred it that way, so that what I might see would not have been specially prepared for my coming.

He slung a big load of firewood over his shoulder and we walked on towards his home, a series of three large and several smaller caves gouged into a cliffside overlooking his hillside fields. The clearing before the cave was alive with romping children, grunting pigs, squawking chickens, and barking dogs. A brace of fat oxen eyed the scene phlegmatically. The children all wore good cloth shoes—a sure sign of prosperity anywhere in China—and looked happy, lively, and well-fed. The little girls wore small bangles and earrings of a metal which might have been silver.

The womenfolk—his daughters and daughters-in-law—were so very shy that they dashed into the caves at my unexpected arrival For peasant folk they were extremely well dressed with good-quality cotton clothes, surprisingly clean.

The caves were of the conventional type, quite roomy, with arched roofs and whitewashed walls. On the *kang,* the broad earthen platform filling one end of the room which serves as a bed in Chinese peasant homes, were good cotton-padded quilts and homespun wool blankets. On one wall were strung a half-dozen red silk banners inscribed with black characters, tokens of appreciation presented to him on various occasions. On the wall behind the *kang* hung three glass-framed certificates of appreciation from Mao Tze-tung, his most prized possession.

He was the friendliest fellow, simple and earnest, but he hardly knew what I expected of him. I told him that I was merely interested in seeing how he lived and in talking with members of his family. The menfolk were off in the fields with labor exchanges and he took me outside to point out the little groups of men at work high up on the hillsides all around. The womenfolk quickly lost their shyness in their curiosity and left their spinning and weaving to come over and chat.

There were eleven members in the immediate family, plus four hired men, the latter being refugees from the Honan famine. Altogether he owned about seven hundred *mou* of land. However, he could at most cultivate only about five hundred of them, even with his ambitious Production Plan for next year, and so he had given the other two hundred *mou* of land to refugees to break, and so to establish themselves.

The labor exchangers, coming in for lunch, sat down to a good meal of meat, vegetables, bread, eggs, and honey, all produced on Wu's farm. Wang Cheng had given him the beehives as a reward for teaching his troopers how to cultivate more efficiently.

He was quite amused to watch me photograph this and that, and then before I left he asked if I wanted to take a picture of him with his new ox, the one they had presented to him at the last Labor Heroes' Convention. He was very proud of that new ox.

Against bad times he had stored up enough reserves to feed his entire family for a year and a half. "And, if this year's crop comes up to my expectations, I shall have an additional three years' reserve," he said. Everyone in the Border Region is urged to draw up his Production Plan for himself and members of his family, and Wu Man-yu had already prepared his. He would open an additional 120 *mou* of wasteland and increase his year's production from eighty piculs of grain to 120 piculs. As for distribution of labor power in his family: "Three other grownups and I will join a labor exchange with my neighbors. My twelve-year-old grandson will be a goatherd. Of the three women, two will cook and take care of the pigs. The third will devote all her time to spinning. Except for the acreage planted to millet [a hardy grain], the wheat and other fields will be turned at least twice. Four bags of manure will be spread on each *mou* of land. Wasteland will be weeded twice. For myself, one part of my time I shall give to leading a labor exchange, and another part I shall devote to training cadres in our local Self-Defense Corps and also take a census in our district in accordance with the Government's wishes. I shall give five piculs of grain to refugee immigrants coming to our hamlet and invest more money in our farmers' retail co-operative. I am going to invest a mule in a co-operative for the transport of salt."

Is it any wonder, then, that the slogan of the Labor Heroes is "Keep Pace with Wu Man-yu"? While the Government sets a goal for the people to achieve—the laying aside of one year's reserve with three years' labor—Wu Man-yu and the Labor Heroes set a minimum goal for themselves of bringing in two years' crop with only one year's labor.

The Production Movement to make the Border Region self-sufficient began as a reaction to the imposition of the blockade in 1939-40. By 1942 it had been taken up on a large scale, and today it has spread throughout North China to other Anti-Japanese Bases under Communist direction. Everyone, from the lowliest farmer to the highest Government official, draws up his Production Plan, outlining what he hopes to achieve in agricultural production for the year. (Mao Tze-tung raises American onions in his little vegetable patch. Chu Teh plants lettuce and cabbage).

The enthusiasm with which the people have co-operated with

the Production Movement has exceeded the expectations of even the most optimistic of its promoters. They like to tell you about the effort made by the family of Li Lai-chen.

Li Lai-chen lives with his three sons, three daughters-in-law, and one grandson in the Hsiang-yuen district of the Taiheng mountains in Shansi Province. Because of recurrent Japanese mopping-up campaigns, crop failures, and consequent apathy, the Li family became poorer and poorer. When there was no longer enough food for all to eat, or clothes to wear, they began to blame each other. At last they demanded of father Li that he should divide up their land so that, having sold his portion, each might go his own way. But the ties of family are still precious in China; so old Li called a family meeting to examine their problem and devise ways to meet the situation.

First they held an election, and Li was elected Family Leader—a post for which tradition would have designated him. The eldest son was elected Leader of the Male Minor Group, and his wife was chosen to head the corresponding group of females. At regular meetings the spirit of criticism and self-criticism was fostered and encouraged. Each pointed out the others' defects as well as his own, with recommendations for correction and improvement which all discussed frankly. The Production Plan drawn up by old Li was argued over for a whole month before it was unanimously passed with amendments agreeable to all.

Among the menfolk the eldest son, being the strongest, was required to spend only half his time in the fields, and the other half as a hired laborer to bring in the extra cash needed for the purchase of things not produced on their farm. Li and the second son were evaluated at half-labor power each, putting in their full time on the farm. To the third son was assigned the care of the family's animals, which he was to utilize in a transportation co-operative—again to earn additional cash.

The women also arranged a division of labor. The old mother was asked to take care of the grandson and to devote herself to spinning and weaving. The three daughters-in-law divided their time between household care and a spinning-and-weaving co-operative.

The family adhered strictly to a budget. In the family Production Plan each member had a specific part to contribute. Since the jointly owned 32 *mou* of land were expected to yield 30 piculs of grain, the eldest son (who spent only half his time on the farm) had to earn the equivalent of 2.8 piculs of grain in cash. The youngest son (who spent no time on the farm) guaranteed to earn the equivalent of 10 piculs of grain through his transportation co-operative. The three daughters-in-law each guaranteed to spin and weave, monthly, two catties of cloth for clothes. (A catty equals one and a third pounds.) A profit-sharing and rewarding system was established. For those who exceeded their allotted contribution to the Production Plan, the surplus was to be divided into ten parts—eight to go to the family as a whole, and two parts to the individual as a bonus. Money saved by a thrifty member was to be divided in exactly the same way. Those who helped others, in addition to meeting their own planned contribution, were to be rewarded suitably in accordance with recommendations made and passed at a family meeting.

The Li Production Plan proved so successful that other families in their village soon followed their example, giving up the feudal, patriarchal system for Li's democratic method. The movement spread, and before long Li was elected a Labor Hero.

In some degree everyone participates in the Production Movement. Students, functionaries, factory workers—everyone owns a spinning-wheel or a patch of land, if only to spin a few ounces of cotton or to raise a few pounds of vegetables. Even the room-boy for my cavelike quarters spent his spare moments at a spinning-wheel or in tending his tiny vegetable garden outside my door.

There are Labor Heroes in every field. During a visit to a spinning and weaving mill I talked with Li Chih-hwa, the blacksmith Labor Hero—a tall, quiet-spoken, intelligent man. They had made him a Labor Hero for doubling his work output by keeping two forges going at the same time, thus avoiding the waste of time entailed by waiting for metal to heat up between spells of pounding and shaping. An apprentice stood by each forge as the metal was being reheated, while Li Chih-hwa moved back and forth from the one anvil to the other, devoting his full energies to the working of the metal. During the little spare time he has available, he teaches his apprentices three new Chinese characters daily. These he writes on a little blackboard set atop the two forges. As I talked with him, his three apprentices smiled broadly behind his back and stuck up their thumbs, meaning "He's tops!"

The fireman Labor Hero is Tung Yu-hsin. He works for the *Giefang Rhbao* (Chiehfang Jihpao), the Communists' official newspaper. Tung was a Manchurian Puppet soldier captured by the Paluchun back in 1938, who decided to remain with the Communists after being offered his freedom; and now he tends the fires that boil water for the newspaper's staff of 500 workers. By a simple reduction in the size of the fire-hole, and by improving the air-draft of the stove, he was able to reduce daily coal consumption from 325 catties to 25 catties. For this he had been elected a Labor Hero and generously rewarded.

Li Wei, the soldier Labor Hero, is one of Wang Cheng's squad leaders. He had a sad tale to tell me of his life before he joined the army. His father, a hired laborer, was so badly treated by his employer that he died while Li Wei was still a boy. His mother tried to get a living by begging, but eventually she married again, and Li Wei was given to a distant relative to work as a goatherd with no pay and little food. When the Eighth Route Army came to his Shansi home in 1939, he promptly joined them. He worked hard, was exemplary in his behavior, and was promoted to squad leader. When Wang Cheng brought his brigade to Nanniwan, Li Wei started the "cultivate one *mou* a day" movement, himself setting a goal for his fellows by cultivating almost two *mou* a day, and often pitching in to help a lagging member in order to maintain the squad's high average.

Li Wei is the true peasant type: slow of speech but inherently friendly and hospitable. He was proud of the spic-and-span cave in which he and his buddies lived. "When he joined the army he could neither read nor write," said one of them, adding proudly, "now his articles, which are posted in our company's wall-newspaper, are among the best written and are read by all of us."

There are women Labor Heroes, too, such as Kuo Feng-ying, a sturdy, self-possessed woman of thirty-six. She was married at fifteen and led a hard life until, when she was twenty-four, her husband died, leaving her only nine *mou* of land, a picul of black beans for food reserves, and the care of two children, aged nine and seven. Kuo Feng-ying did not sit down to bewail her fate, nor did she become dependent on others. She unbound her feet, put cotton into the tips of her shoes for support, and diligently set out to get the utmost from her tiny patch of land. By dint of sheer hard work she gradually prospered. Last year, when she harvested a bumper crop, her neighbors called a meeting and recommended her as their representative to the Labor Heroes' Convention, at which she was elected a National Labor Hero.

The Labor Heroes they are most proud of are the ex-*erh liu tze* Labor Heroes. The worst thing you can call one in the Border Region today is an *erh liu tze*—a loafer. In their struggle for self-sufficiency—almost a matter of life and death—these blockaded people have little patience with *erh liu tze*. Loafers were not merely parasites. Their wayward habits, their laziness, gambling, cheating, lying, and stealing are sources of demoralization for others, and they have no place in the vigorous society for which the Communists are striving.

Of an estimated 70,000 loafers in the Border Region when the Communists arrived in 1935, all but 9,554 were reformed by the beginning of 1943, and these were particularly hardened cases. But the Government was determined to solve the problem completely. An intensive reform campaign was instituted; and by the beginning of 1944 all but 3,967 loafers were reformed, these diehards resisting all pressure directed against them. When pleas, bribes, even threats, proved of no avail, the people decided to take the law more or less into their own hands: every loafer had to wear a big white badge inscribed *"erh liu tze"*—to be jeered at, hooted, and incessantly humiliated in the campaign to shame him into reform.

The Government, meanwhile, was employing subtler methods. At a recent convention for Labor Heroes, five hardened loafers were chosen by the Government and invited to attend. Suspecting that they were in for some sort of punishment or public humiliation, these five at first declined—only to yield when their neighbors insisted. On their arrival at Yenan the five loafers were astonished to find themselves accorded the same courtesies extended to the Heroes. As they entered the big auditorium they were applauded loudly and ushered to the platform to be seated with the honored guests. They were served with wine, cakes, and sweetmeats, and were called on to participate in all discussions on an equal footing with the Labor Heroes. By the end of the convention, all five announced their determination to reform—whereupon they were vigorously acclaimed by the Labor Heroes and offered liberal advice and assistance in drawing up their own Production Plans. The Government, on its part, offered them grants of land and loaned them farm implements, seeds, and animals. By this time the five loafers declared, "If we fail in this reform, we shall no longer consider ourselves human beings!"

Meanwhile, Yenan's Municipal Government had called a simultaneous convention of the Yenan district's sixty-three loafers. Throughout the five-day convention they were lectured by officials and educators as well as by Party and Government leaders. The five reformed loafers were called over to address their recalcitrant fellows, telling them what they had seen and how well they had been treated, and vowing their resolve to reform. On the final day of the Loafers' Convention they were addressed by Liu Shen-hai, who, previously to his conversion two years before, had been perhaps the most notorious *erh liu tze* in the Border Region. Today he is a Labor Hero. He told his story to the convention: His wife and four children had left him because of his laziness, shiftlessness, and gambling. He had decided to reform. Starting with one donkey, he had worked hard at salt transportation. Today, he already owned six donkeys, a mule, three cows, and eighty-one sheep, and had 150 *mou* of land under cultivation. His family had returned to him, and they were now well fed, well clad, and happy. His example had prompted two other loafers in his village to reform, and he had helped them get started toward self-sufficiency.

During his speech to the loafers, Liu Shen-hai became so enthusiastic that he challenged Wu Man-yu to a production race for next year. "I never dreamed that a confirmed old *erh liu tze* like myself could achieve such high honors as have been given me," he concluded. He was referring to the fact that the people of his own village had chosen him as their local Labor Hero, while at the national assembly held some time before this Loafers' Convention he was elected a National Labor Hero. Yenan Municipality's initiative, by the way, reformed a fair number of the sixty-three diehards, though some remained obdurate. But the convention was far from being a failure, for it also fixed it clearly and finally in the public mind that Yenan is a community of workers. I imagine that the proposers of the Kuomintang blockade hardly had this end in mind, but they have certainly enabled the Yenan administration to tap yet further sources of popular regeneration.

9

The Drive for Production

THE Production Movement is not for civilians alone; the army also participates—which is perhaps the unique feature of the Paluchun, something that obtains in no other army in the world on such a scale (so far as I know), and is certainly the most important factor contributing to the amazing cooperation between army and people. The visitor to the Paluchun cannot doubt that it is this confraternity with the people that enables the Paluchun to support the incredible ardors of a war which it must wage with captured or improvised arms. For, since the imposition of the economic and military blockade in 1939, the Paluchun—containing 570,000 regulars (as of October 1944)—has received not a single round of ammunition, not a single dollar for wages, not a single ration of food, from the Central Authorites in Chungking. The blockaded, war-harassed people of North China would have been terribly hard-pressed to sustain the Paluchun; and the Eighth Route Army therefore joined in the Production Movement. An army that so helps itself will surely obtain the warm support of a people, and this in turn will build army morale.

I have written about Wang Cheng and his 359th Brigade, but that brigade is only one of five garrisoning the Border Region. And this prompts me to set down a curious and suggestive point. Talking to a group of officers one night, I hazarded the thought that perhaps the 50,000 soldier-farmer Paluchun Troops stationed

73

in the Border Region areas adjacent to Kuomintang China might not be enough to stand up against Hu Tsung-nan's 500,000 Central Troops in the event Chungking should open a new "squeeze." Without a moment's hesitation they spoke in unison: "Ko-la! Ko-la! [Plenty! Plenty!]" There was no boast in that. They were perfectly matter-of-fact about it. "You forget," they added, "that we have the people with us."

Some significant facts and figures on the Paluchun's production effort may be interesting. In 1939 the Border Region garrison opened 25,136 *mou* of land and harvested a total of 2,590 piculs of grain. By 1943 they had reclaimed and cultivated 215,000 *mou*—having thus added to cultivation an area equal to a third of the total land cultivated in 1936, when the bulk of the Red Army arrived in North Shensi. By the end of 1943, it had harvested 31,000 piculs of grain. At the close of 1944 it hopes to have 842,034 *mou* under the plow, and expects to produce 120,393 piculs, about four times as much as in 1943.

In addition to millet, almost the only crop in former years, the army raised wheat, rice, beans, corn, soya beans, barley, flax, oats, rye, cotton, and a wide variety of garden vegetables. Considering the notorious poverty of the Shensi soil, this range of crops was itself notable; so, too, was the volume of the new crops. Excluding grains, but including vegetables, uniforms, paper, and about everything else for the army's supply, the Border Region garrison in 1943 achieved 79.5% self-sufficiency; the remaining 20.5% was supplied by the Border Region Government.

Taking as a base (100%) the level of living in December 1939, the army's standard of living dropped to 88% by 1940, and to 84.2% by 1941—all as a definite consequence of the blockade. By 1942, when the Production Program was beginning to get under way, the standard of living had risen to 96.3%; and by 1943 it had risen to 125.5%—or 25.5% higher than the 1939 level. In 1943 a soldier's standard equipment was: two summer uniforms, one winter uniform, one-quarter padded cotton overcoat (i.e., one coat had to last him four years), and one-half padded cotton quilt. As footwear he received two pairs of summer cloth slippers, one pair of heavy cloth winter shoes, and one pair of rope sandals. In addition, his "GI" included one-half puttees, one-third bandolier, one-third rice-bag, two towels, and three catties of wool—from the last of which he would be able, after spinning it into yarn, to make a muffler or some extra socks. In Wang Cheng's brigade, last year, every man was issued an all-wool uniform, the result of the brigade's own wool production. All this may seem very little in comparison with our own army's equipment—and little it is. Yet the greater part of it was produced by the soldiers themselves, in circumstances that might well appal a Western quartermaster.

Some idea of the severity of conditions, not only in the Border Region but throughount China, may be got from this: that the Paluchun soldier's monthly allowance of meat was four pounds and nine ounces per month—which, though considerably more than the Kuomintang troops are given, is approximately only a fourth or a fifth of the quantity of flesh food consumed in wartime by a working-class American, who has other rich sources of protein to draw upon, besides. But the comparison, suggestive though it is, is not a totally just one. The important fact is that the Eighth Route Army man lives very well according to Chinese standards, and he knows it. It is all the more encouraging to him that he himself is a major factor in production. His meat ration is balanced with a vegetable allowance of about 48 pounds, and 60 pounds of millet, which means two pounds of cereals per day and one and a half pounds of vegetables. Oil, seasonings, and fuel are also provided, the fuel being good anthracite coal. Obviously, this diet is difficult to keep in balance, even allowing for the fact that for a great part of the year the vegetables are fresh.

It is interesting to compare the soldier's food allowance with the rations received by a typical worker in one of the small arsenals operated in Yenan. A worker whom I questioned told me that he received a monthly food allowance (in kind or cash at the current market rate) of 40 pounds of millet and 20 pounds of wheat, with four pounds of meat. In cereals, then, he probably had a slight advantage over the soldier, while he was at a small disadvantage in the matter of meat, and in vegetables received only a little more than three-quarters of the soldier's ration. His wife and children also had an allowance calculated according to the same norms. It is noteworthy that, for the purpose of rationing, the Yenan child becomes an adult at the age of seven. It must also be remembered that a midday meal, principally of vegetables, millet, and bread, was provided by the factory itself. Wages and clothing were also received by the arsenal worker, the former being set in terms of millet prices so that they would not be affected by market fluctuations. Actually, the worker receives either the grain itself, or money. In the case of this factory, of course, there are no capitalists; but there are differences in the wage scale. Comparing the salaries of foremen and departmental chiefs with the wages of skilled workers and apprentices, the ratio was approximately 4—3—2. The army has also established co-operatives in which the soldier may invest the extra sums he may have earned by taking part in the production scheme. It is almost impossible to present an exact comparison of the sums invested, in terms of American money.

The Border Region has its own currency unit, the *pienpi*—considered illegal by Chungking but none the less enjoying the full confidence of the people in the region governed by Yenan. The Yenan *pienpi* may possibly be counted as one eighth of a Chungking dollar, which in 1944 was itself a fortieth part of an American dollar. But the scale of values cannot possibly be compared, since the inflation of currency and prices in Kuomintang China is tremendous, and the exchange rate for American dollars is pegged at an artificial and quite absurd figure. It must be borne in mind that the Border Region authorities have been much more successful in preventing inflation, with all that this implies for the normality of exchange. Nevertheless, though the figures will mean little to the American reader, it is worth while to review the financial position of what is by far the best brigade in terms of co-operative investments. Wang Cheng, with an eye to postwar financial independence for his men, was the outstanding organizer of army co-operatives; 60% of them were run by his brigade, every soldier of which belonged to at least one such enterprise. In 1943 the average investment of a Wang Cheng brigadier was 4,158 *pienpi*, the total of investments being nearly fifty million *pienpi*. Besides this sum, made up of individual investments against which the soldier held his own receipts, the brigade had collective investments of some twenty-nine million *pienpi*.

The articles and materials directly produced by the Paluchun range from clothes to arms, from metal tools to lumber. Even parts for Singer sewing-machines (immensely important in the Border Region as elsewhere in China) are turned out by uniformed workers. Cylinder heads and piston rings are essential in a country where breakdowns are common. Steel articles and weapons, by the way, are made on the "labor exchange" plan: the army at the front tears up the railway tracks in areas under Japanese occupation and despatches them to the "rear," where the army in production converts them into weapons. But these are only the more dramatic instances of production effort. Glance over the issue lists of any army depot in the world, and the multiplicity of articles in use will remind you of a Chicago mail-order catalogue. The Paluchun's demands are far smaller than the American army's; yet, such as they are, they are chiefly supplied by the army itself. Do some new quarters or factory buildings have to be put up? Or is a news-sheet to be smuggled into a Jap-controlled region? The bricks and lime for the buildings will as often as not have been made by the garrison's colleagues in arms; and the ink and paper also.

To an American accustomed to think of prodigious indices of production, to whom the use of tools is second nature or better, and whose inventiveness is encouraged by the very momentum of his industrial civilization, these Eighth Route Army achievements may seem limited. But China is not the U.S.A., and Chinese civilization is an agrarian one, in which the old slow rhythms are still regnant for the most part. The Chinese craftsman is a superb and industrious worker, particularly when he is using his own tools of traditional type upon jobs thoroughly explored by generations of workmen before him. Even the rural craftsman is a skilled and responsible worker in his own trade. But these crafts and trades are rarely concerned with the production of the articles required by modern warfare. The Paluchun and administration leaders, then, faced a tremendous problem, for whose solution—knowledge being scarce—great enthusiasm and endless patience were required. A bayonet that folds back on the rifle, and can be instantly and silently pulled into action position, may seem a trifling instance of ingenuity to an American factory manager; but to the Yenan peasant-soldiery it was a solid achievement.

All these articles—buttons, ceramics, ammunition, spark plugs, batteries, wire, shoes, toothbrushes, and soap—are produced in factories hardly worthy of the name and, it must be confessed, in quantities hardly worthy of notice if the American scale of reference be used. But when the Red Army reached North Shensi there was no industry at all. By 1937, when the war with Japan officially began, it had established a small arsenal, a uniform factory, and a printing shop, with a total of 270 workers. By the end of 1939 there were 700 industrial workers. Today the Border Region counts 12,000 factory workers on full-time jobs, with the possibility of future increases that are large in terms of a region upon which the modern epoch is only just making its first impact as a consequence of the Communist effort.

The Government, of course, has joined the army in encouraging industrial development. It should be noted that the Yenan administration in no way limits itself to setting up state enterprises. To encourage private enterprise and co-operatives alike, the Government will place orders substantial enough to guarantee a fair profit; or it will provide working capital for a co-operative. Soap, matches, paper, chemicals, glass, and porcelain ware are thus produced. In May 1943 the first iron foundry was opened; that its production is not great is due principally to the fact that the workers and directors know very little about running an iron foundry. They frankly admit this—but it does not keep them from trying. Iron is essential, and what little they can produce, however inefficiently, is of vital importance. The foundry has two small and three comparatively large furnaces and about 200 workers employed in shifts. Some thousand soldiers dig ore in the mines, which are about ten miles distant from the foundry.

The army is also opening more and more coal mines in the Border Region. Long mule-trains move over the roads, loaded with solid chunks of good anthracite. Although lack of proper mining equipment and transportation facilities necessarily limits production, it is steadily growing.

I spent some time visiting factories in the Yenan area. The arsenal nestles half-hidden in the foothills at five or six hours' horseback ride from Yenan. It was originally established for the purpose of manufacturing agricultural implements; but when the blockade against the Border Region was established and civil war threatened, the plant was hurriedly converted to the making of hand grenades and the repairing of damaged weapons. The factory then had only two lathes, one casting machine, and a single experienced gunsmith. Other machines were added, most of them made laboriously by the arsenal workers themselves. Today the establishment specializes in the manufacture of cartridges and grenade-throwers. The metal is obtained from steel rails and other war booty, as well as from such diverse sources as scrapped temple bells, caldrons, flatirons, and old shell cases. Power is supplied by a 1933 Soviet Zis truck engine and a 1929 Chevrolet truck motor. These units, fueled with charcoal gas, are coupled to nineteen overhead pulleys on a single overhead shaft.

The workers' contributions to the arsenal's wall-newspaper varied from technical advice to political pep talks and scraps of local news. One item described a new American method of milling. Another cautioned hygiene in food and drink in hot weather: "Don't eat uncooked food or drink cold, unboiled water"—adding, perhaps facetiously, "Don't gorge on meat." They worked a ten-hour shift, with a half-hour lunch period.

I talked with the factory's Chih Tao Yuan—literally Point-Way Representative, or political commissar—about the workers' off-duty activities. "Point-Way Representatives" are something between efficiency experts and father-confessors. It is their job to devise ways to cut corners in production, and to them the workers bring their complaints and suggestions. Workers are permitted, even urged, to unionize. In this arsenal 178 of the 331 workers were members of the trade union. As dues, the union members paid one per cent of their wages, half of which went directly to the union office, the other half being used for buying periodicals, getting up theatricals, and the like. A clubroom for all workers was provided by the factory. There was a schoolroom, too, with teachers and textbooks for the two-hour classes held regularly after the evening meal. Attendance was more or less compulsory, in the sense that fellow workers brought a great deal of moral pressure to bear on *erh liu tze* who were reluctant to attend.

In a co-operative spinning and weaving mill, I found exhibited considerable native ingenuity in compensating for the lack of proper machines. The improvised machines made by the co-operators were of rough construction, but they worked. For lack of long leather belts to run the bobbin machines, the workers had devised a belt of tightly woven wool, hardened and strengthened with pine resin and beeswax; it served the purpose well. The inventor had got the idea for this by observing that the peasants used waxed wool belts on their hand-operated spinning-wheels. When applied on a larger scale to the factory's motor-run machines, the wax melted in the heat generated by the speed; so they added pine resin for hardening.

Essential springs were made of coiled telephone wire looted from the Japanese. This was hardened and tempered by heating in a crucible with charcoal and old bones to a temperature of 700-800° Centigrade. The shop foreman who had improvised this was justly proud. He demonstrated the superiority of his telephone-wire spring which, dropped from the same height, bounced higher than did an imported sample.

This mill had two sources of power. The first was a blindfolded mule harnessed to a huge wooden cogwheel meshed with a whole series of lesser wheels, belts, rollers, and pulleys. As the mule walked in a circle, the system developed enough power to operate a number of machines. The mule, I was told, worked the same number of hours as a millhand, with a half-hour off for lunch. The second source of power was a great water-wheel. The spill from this wheel was utilized to irrigate the vegetable gardens that the millhands had planted nearby. Since these gardens produced more than the workers could consume, the surplus was sold to provide funds for the co-operative purchase, at prices as much as 40 and 50 per cent below the market level, of those articles of food not supplied in their allowances.

Because the locally issued *pienpi* has been declared illegal by the National Government, it is not accepted or allowed to circulate outside the Border Region. The Kuomintang—particularly the Chief of the General Staff, Ho Ying-chin—says that one of the principal reasons why the Eighth Route Army was outlawed, and no money provided to pay its wages, was that the Border Region Government had begun to issue illegal currency. Ho Ying-chin says he has evidence that the Communists in the Border Region have been issuing *pienpi* since 1938. I discussed this with Nan Han-chen, Chief of the Financial Department in Yenan, together with other responsible Government officials, and they vigorously denied Ho Ying-chin's charge. "Actually, we began issuing banknotes *only* after payments to our troops were stopped and an economic and military blockade was imposed upon the Border Region," they maintained. Some small-denomination notes have been issued and were in circulation prior to this break with the Kuomintang; but these were issued only in denominations up to seventy-five cents because there was a dearth of small change. Moreover, they pointed out, these were issued not by the Border Region Government as an official bank issue, but by the Kwang Wha Trading Company, a semiofficial mercantile establishment—and issued clearly not as money but as coupons, much like streetcar tokens. The total issue never exceeded 1,000 *fapi* (say $25 American), in denominations from one cent to seventy-five cents. Regular *pienpi* banknotes were not issued until after the New Fourth Army incident in January 1941; to be exact, the first issue to the public was made on February 18, 1941. "If Ho Ying-chin claims to possess banknotes issued by us before that time," said Lo Man, General Secretary of the Border Region Government, "they must also have been distributed to the people here and still be in their possession. We ask you to make a diligent search for such banknotes to satisfy yourself and answer General Ho Ying-chin." I did so, and was never able to turn up a single banknote dated before 1941.

So then, because *pienpi* is illegal and unacceptable outside the Border Region, it cannot be used to purchase vitally needed things which might be smuggled through the blockade. But the Border Region does possess two things vitally needed by the Big Rear (as the people of Yenan call Kuomintang China): salt and petroleum. These two products are exported from the Border

Region and are allowed to pass freely through the blockade line, there being exchanged for cloth and whatever else the authorities outside the Border Region see fit to allow the merchant-muleteers to take back with them. As for salt, the Border Region contains some of the best salt-producing areas in the whole of China, but production is perforce limited to the immediate needs of the region, plus what little the Big Rear reluctantly accepts.

As for oil, at Yenchang—about halfway between Yenan and the Yellow River—the Border Region Government works a comparatively small oil field. This was originally discovered, surveyed, and brought in by a Japanese engineer back in 1906. He drilled four wells, two of which produced oil; but by 1910 he grew discouraged by the meager output and the handicaps imposed on him by the Manchu Government, and abandoned the project. For a few years the government of the new Republic of China tried to run them, but in 1914 turned them over to the American Socony-Vacuum Oil Company, which operated them under contract with the Chinese Government. Socony imported a lot of drilling and refining equipment and dug five new wells. But, when these proved unprofitable (owing chiefly to lack of transport, there being no roads or railroads for many miles around), Socony, too, washed its hands of the project and withdrew, leaving all its equipment behind. From 1916 until the coming of the Red Army vanguard in 1935 the Chinese Government made halfhearted efforts to operate the wells, but never made them a paying proposition.

Today the Communists are working hard to develop this oil field, realizing that—regardless of how unprofitable it may prove in producing oil, with its byproducts of gasoline, kerosene, and candles—it is nevertheless a precious medium of "foreign exchange." The effort might still be described as "uneconomical," though in the situation in which the blockaded region finds itself the ordinary criteria are invalid. The administration frankly admit that they have no one who really knows anything about scientific oil-drilling. Some of the old workmen are still on the job. Of these, Chen Tsunhsia, who manages the fields, confesses that he is no oil engineer, but merely a man with some years of practical experience in working in the oil fields under foreign supervision. The few steel drilling bits left by Socony are almost at the limit of their usefulness. The worn-out pistons in the suction pump have been covered with cloth and leather to prevent leakage. For lack of steel, sheets of slate, quarried from the river bank, are used for lining the oil-storage tanks. As a matter of fact, improvisation and substitution are the rule here, also. The steam engine is the one installed by the Japanese engineer in 1906; the unit brought in by Socony is unusable for lack of spare parts. The kerosene and crude oil are transported from the oil fields in bamboo-and-lime casks loaded on mules and donkeys. The candles made from the byproducts are of a fairly high quality, much better than any obtainable in Chung-king or other places in the Big Rear. The gasoline is mostly kept, for running the twenty-odd dilapidated trucks which operate in Yenan and its immediate vicinity.

The workers I talked to seemed to be well content with the returns on their labors. Several old-timers, who had been there for many years, working under successive employers, were very enthusiastic about today's working conditions. Their hours were shorter, they were treated like human beings, and they had their own union, their own clubroom, and a voice in the direction of affairs. One of them, who spoke some English, was a Singapore-born Chinese who had been a sailor for many years before he drifted up to the Yenchang oil fields. "This is much better than sailoring ever was," he said reflectively. Life is difficult in the Border Region, as throughout China, but in his satisfaction I heard the voice of hope—and I believe I heard confidence.

Certainly there was confidence in the tone of white-haired old Lin Chu-han, Chairman of the Border Region Government, when he gave me an over-all picture of the Region's production for 1943. Here are its highlights. The yearly food consumption being estimated at 1,620,000 piculs, the total production for 1943 of 1,840,000 piculs provided a surplus of 220,000 piculs—which means that there was more than enough for everyone if it was equitably distributed. This production of foodstuffs could be broken down into: 24.5% millet; 21.5% wheat; 14% yellow millet; 11.2% beans; 7.1% buckwheat; 6.4% kaoliang; 5.1% flax; 3.7% corn; 3.2% potatoes; 1.4% cotton; and 2.2% vegetables and miscellaneous grains.

The production of salt—the Border Region's chief export, as has been said—reached 600,000 animal loads in 1943. It was transported by co-operatives, which had increased the number of animals at work to ten times the 1942 number. There was distinct progress, too, in other lines such as stock-raising, handicrafts, and industries. Over 137,600 women had taken up spinning, most of them being associated with spinning co-operatives. Every factory had increased its production over 1942 by 100% to 400%, while reducing production costs 20% to 30%.

"Even Taoist monks, blind men, and old women," said Lin Chu-han, "were swept into the surging tide of production. One Taoist monk named Chang Feng-ming, of the Ching Kang Temple, was so fired by the people's enthusiasm for reclaiming wasteland that he cut off his Taoist pigtail and turned farmer. In Ching Yang hsien, a blind man of fifty-seven persuaded his grandson to lead him to the fields every day, and managed to reclaim and cultivate four and a half *mou* of wasteland. And in Chi Tan hsien there was an old woman who during the autumn harvest rose every morning with the rooster's crow and wakened her neighbors to join her in the fields at the first light of dawn. It would be hard to find examples like this elsewhere in China, or, indeed, in the world.

Lin went on to attribute this enthusiasm to the active leadership and encouragement that the people got from the Party and the Government. First, the rent reductions sponsored by the Government had lightened the tenant farmers' burden and inspired them to work harder in order to live up to their side of the bargain, which insured to the landlords the payment of the reduced rents. Moreover, the Government lent the farmers money so that they might buy oxen and better farm implements. It encouraged cotton-planting by tax-exempting cotton crops for three years and by accepting cotton as a substitute for grain in the future payment of the grain tax.

The Border Region's manpower has been increased through a policy of preferential treatment for refugee immigrants, which has attracted thousands of famine refugees from Honan. They were given land and helped to establish themselves as self-sufficient producers. The labor exchange system was encouraged in order to increase efficiency in production. Already 24% of the Region's 338,760 agricultural laborers had voluntarily organized themselves into labor exchanges, and it was expected that this figure would be almost doubled by the end of 1944.

But the most significant progress registered in the Production Movement was the participation of army, Government, and Party workers. These would ordinarily be parasitic elements on the Region's economy; but, now that they are already producing 64% of their own food and clothing, and are fast approaching complete self-sufficiency, the tax burden on the people has been correspondingly lightened.

"The army's production record alone," said Lin Chu-han, "is hardly short of miraculous. Is it any wonder, then, that the people say, 'Never before in history has there been such an army as our Paluchun, which can fight, produce, and live harmoniously with the people'? In production as in fighting, our troops are zealous and full of creative ability. During the reclamation period last spring, they went up to the hills before dawn, remaining there until after dark, refusing to rest for even a moment beyond the minimum time for meals. And this compelled their commanders to institute a new rule forbidding them to start work before the time fixed or to continue beyond the stated period.

"And that's not all. The commanders themselves work quite as hard as the men do. During the last planting season, Regimental Commander Chen Chung-yao hurt his hand badly; but he nevertheless insisted on working right through the season. Political Commissar Tze Chi, who had lost his right arm in battle and so could not hold a plow, boiled the drinking water and cooked the food for the soldiers working in the fields. Our army is indeed an army to be proud of, our troops the true sons of the Chinese people!"

10

Medicine versus Witchcraft

MOST of Yenan University's thirteen hundred students are married. However, school regulations forbid husbands and wives to live together, except on Saturday nights when special "Guest Caves" are made available by the school authorities.

"Keeping them apart during the week not only enables boys and girls to study better, with fewer distractions, but at the same time sweetens love between married couples," I was told by Chow Yang, the president of the university. When I questioned the students about this rule they would not discuss it.

Children live in the women's dormitories with their mothers, who form labor exchange brigades through which the mothers take their turns, by groups, in caring for the children. This seemed to work out satisfactorily and everyone appeared quite happy about it. The girls apparently felt that they might have their cake and eat it too—that is to say, they could have a husband and a family, and still obtain an education. The education they got at Yenta (the popular name for Yenan University) was wholly a practical one, so that Yenta is hardly a university in the Western sense.

"The principal characteristic of our new educational program," Chow Yang explained, "is that it is based firmly upon practical realities. Until last year we modelled our curriculi upon those of foreign institutions, placing too much emphasis upon such studies as the classics, philosophy, and abstract sciences. We paid too much respect to foreign forms in literature and art and neglected native Chinese forms. As a result, our students left Yenta wholly unfit to meet the urgent demands of wartime environment.

"Today our students spend at least three months of the year obtaining practical experience—the equivalent of your laboratory work. A student in banking works in a bank. A student of law is attached to a law court. A student of practical science gains appropriate experience in a factory. A student of administration takes employment in a Government office."

Students also participate in the Production Movement. Last year they were already 60% self-sufficient in food, having cultivated and harvested their own fields of wheat, millet and vegetables and raised their own meat on the hoof.

Connected with Yenta is the Lu Hsun College of Arts and Literature, popularly called Lu I. There are about three hundred students of music and drama at Lu I, which occupies an abandoned Catholic church about three miles from the city. The church proper is used as an auditorium for student meetings, dramatic performances, and such, while the old converts' resident quarters have been turned into dormitories. The boys and girls are chiefly from the frontline areas. After two years they are sent back to the various fronts to organize dramatic plays, musical entertainments, and the like. The sexes were dressed alike, in simple trousers and belted blouse. Their interest in one another seemed to be confined to that required for enthusiastic co-operation in their studies.

The place was a bedlam. A high soprano practiced scales while a drummer rapped out an intricate figure. A few yards away a student with the face of an esthete seemed quite undisturbed as he played his battered 'cello. In a dormitory cell a lusty-voiced girl from Honan sang a plaintive folksong to the accompaniment of a dozen Chinese fiddles played by her roommates. In the courtyard three plays were being rehearsed—war plays whose simple plots were based upon true incidents such as an heroic deed or a Japanese atrocity. They were simply but powerfully told, and told in a language understandable by the peasant and the soldier about whom they were written, and for whom they were to be performed. Later these same students would troupe from village to village, performing for the *laopaishing*—the peasantry.

I attended a concert given by the music students of Lu I. Seven home-made violins, a much-worn piano, and the 'cello opened the program by playing the national anthems of China, the United States, Great Britain, and Soviet Russia. A chorus of seventy-five boys and girls marched on to the stage and gave an excellent performance of Shostakovitch's *Song of the United Nations*. This was followed by other British, American, and Russian songs, sung in harmony and with great feeling. A tenor attempted a selection from *Madame Butterfly,* but he was as off-key as the piano itself; and other soloists tried nobly to sing Western music in key, failing miserably. But the chorus was invariably a success, especially in modern war songs such as the newly written cantata *Song of the Yellow River Boatmen*. The hit of the evening was made by two fellows who sang local folk songs in the broad Shensi dialect, which differs as much from Mandarin or Cantonese as Gaelic does from English.

The Communists take their culture seriously. Artists, writers, musicians, educators, dramatists, and newspapermen meet regularly, to discuss their problems frankly and criticize each other and their work. There were about forty present at the meeting I attended. Most of them came from Shanghai which, before the war, was the cultural center of China. But the Westernized, highly sophisticated art and literature of Shanghai were as far from the peasant folk lore of hinterland China as James Joyce is from Confucius. Under war conditions, away from Shanghai, the literati resembled fish out of water. It was almost impossible for them not to look down upon the ignorant peasants, the workers and soldiers, who retorted by rejecting them. Without a public, they wrote, painted, and made music for themselves, ignoring the common folk below their cultural and intellectual level. If the peasant failed to appreciate good literature and art, that was his misfortune. Art could not debase itself by talking down to the masses.

Far-seeing Mao Tze-tung observed this and decided that it was no good. Calling a meeting of all cultural workers, he flayed them for their high and mighty airs, warned them of retrogression and decay if they persisted. They must adjust themselves to new conditions, a new society—a society unlike the feudal Shanghai aristocracy of intellectuals, students, and wealthy patrons, but a new democratic society created by and for the peasant, the worker, and the soldier.

"For this you must go to the people, must strive to understand them before you can ever hope to have them understand you," he continued. "You must study their dialects as mediums of expression. You must study their sentiments, their local customs and habits for content. You must learn to love them for what they are, not for what you think they should be."

This was wartime, he pointed out, and it was the duty of the cultural worker to contribute his talents to the war effort. For this he must not try to introduce new and bewildering forms of expression but must work with the familiar forms accepted by the people themselves. The people's traditional music, art, literature, and drama must serve as basic molds for new wartime content. New forms must be rooted in these and evolve from them.

Yenan's literati took Mao Tze-tung's words to heart with amazingly good results. The evolution of the *Yang Ko* is a good case in point. The Yang Ko—literally "Planting Song"—is indigenous to North China, particularly Shensi and Shansi provinces. Its origins date back to the Sung Dynasty, a thousand years ago. The traditional Yang Ko was performed chiefly at New Year's and on other festival days; though it was not limited to holidays and might be performed to celebrate any important occasion. Singing a lively tune at the tops of their voices, the villagers danced in a circle with a vigorous congalike step. The modern adaptation of the Yang Ko differs considerably. For example, in January 1943, Yang Kos were performed in nearly every village simultaneously to celebrate both the abolition of Western extraterritoriality and the victory at Stalingrad. Artists, musicians, and dramatists prepared little skits, musical numbers, and decorative art work, which, to their surprise, the people readily incorporated into their Yang Kos. From this start, the Yang Ko today has evolved a number of complicated forms. Today a Yang Ko may be exclusively an operetta or a musical comedy or a straight drama with the lines sung in verse in the Yang Ko musical cadence.

I have seen dozens of these Yang Ko dramas and they never failed to fascinate me. They were so utterly different from anything to be found anywhere else in China. Mostly they dealt with war topics: the story of a village traitor, the heroism of a soldier's wife, the atrocities of the Japanese in their mopping-up campaigns. It required effort to accustom myself to the versification and the singing delivery of the lines, but the dramatic skill of the performances very soon captured me. So that they might be given in the smallest village, the plays were written and the actors trained to perform almost without a single prop or stage effect. Besides war topics there is much treatment of domestic problems—particularly the problem of adjustment to those innovations which the Communists were attempting to make. Such new-fangled modernisms as sanitation, child care, animal breeding, and crop rotation clashed with deep-rooted traditions and superstitions. This conflict was taken as a rich source of Yang Ko themes.

For example, I witnessed a Yang Ko that struck at the "witch-doctors" or "wizards." The first scene opened with a young girl, the daughter-in-law of the family, seated at a spinning-wheel. The mother entered and scolded the girl for having drunk cold water from the well. (The first propaganda touch: all drinking water should be boiled.) The girl admitted she had done wrong to drink unboiled water, and continued to spin. Presently she became sick and began to retch, whereupon her parents put her to bed and ignited incense punks before the family idol. The son came in from the fields and expressed anxiety about his sick wife, who continued to retch offstage.

"I'm going to call the Government's doctor at the village clinic," he announced. But his mother and father objected: "No, go for the village wizard." "He's an old faker," said the modern-minded son. They replied: "But he's been attending local people here for seventeen years, and knows us and our ills much better than the doctor with his new and strange ideas." Reluctantly, the son agreed to fetch the wizard.

The next scene showed the wizard at home. He looked like

an old tramp. He sang his lines: "This business of digging in the ground is the bunk! No farmer's life for me, no matter how much pressure they put on me to participate in the Production Movement. As long as people believe that I can kick devils out of them, I'm okay!"

He sipped tea as he continued to muse. "I have just heard that my colleague in the next village has killed a young boy. Bungler! He's spoiling the profession."

The son came in. Though obviously little impressed by the wizard, he asked him to treat his wife. The wizard shook his head dubiously. "I'm a very busy man. But then, your parents are old friends of mine." With this he agreed to accompany the son. "Things are looking up," he said in an aside, and the audience laughed.

The following scene showed the parents getting more and more worried as the girl continued to retch offstage, and at its close the son entered with the wizard. The wizard sat down grandly.

"Yes, yes, I know," he said pompously as they told him of the girl's symptoms. "She has the Zz-zz sickness. It's in her blood. Bad!"

He began to pull his witch-doctor props out of a gunny sack and set them up on a table. The audience laughed—they had seen these things before. The wizard then stripped to the waist and draped himself with a red sash. On his head he put a black turban with paper ornaments. Then he took up a jangling trident and began a dance something like an Indian war-dance, stopping now and then to make cabalistic designs on the floor. The family watched him with awe as he worked himself up to a frenzy. At every spell of retching from the girl offstage, he quickened his pace. Finally he went to the adjoining room to look at the patient, jangling his ear-splitting trident.

Within a moment he was back with the assertion that the window in that room was in the wrong place. "Bring her out here!" The family obeyed, the girl appearing on a pallet. The wizard then tied her fingers with a thread which he attached to his trident. He shouted to the devils, "Get out! Get out! Get out!" The girl screamed with pain. "Bad!" he muttered. "Bad! The devils want her badly. And they're very, very strong. I'm not sure I can successfully fight them and drive them out of her." The family pleaded with him to do his best; they would absolve him of all blame if he were to fail and she died. The girl says, "Mother, please send him away. I was actually beginning to feel better before he came." At this, the wizard began to shout: "That's the devils talking! They want to take her away immediately." And he jangled his trident, screaming frenzied curses at the devils. Then he took a rope and began to strangle her. "Get out! Get out of here!" The girl fainted and he loosened it.

"If she dies you'll answer to me," said the son warningly as he dashed out to find the Government's local medical inspector.

The audience began to hoot and howl. "Throw him out! Beat him up!" they yelled between catcalls and curses.

Meanwhile, having circled the pallet three times, the wizard announced, "She'll be better in three days."

He began hurriedly to pack his witch-doctor props and pocketed his fee of $8,000 plus a bag of millet and a square of figured silk, hoping to be off before the doctor should arrive.

The son, with the doctor and the village head, entered as the wizard was leaving. The others detained him while the doctor approached the patient. Quietly taking her pulse, he looked under her eyelids. The audience watched him, awed and hushed. They winced perceptibly as he jabbed a hypodermic needle into her arm.

The son could contain himself no longer. "What is it? Will she live?"

The doctor smiled. "Nothing very serious, though you should have called me sooner. She's merely pregnant—three months."

"Pregnant!" They all looked at him, amazed. How did he know such things merely by looking at her? The doctor quietly explained the symptoms. "She must have drunk some cold water or something that made her sick and vomit."

"Yes! She told me she had drunk cold water," the mother cried.

The girl regained consciousness. "Oh, I'm feeling much better already," she said; "but my fingers hurt." They had been cut by the wizard's cords. The doctor applied some iodine and ordered them to take her to the other room for rest.

Then they went to work on the wizard, calling him a lazy, good-for-nothing scamp. He tried to bluff his way out. "I've been ordered by the gods to drive the devils out of people."

"Oh ho! Ordered by the gods, were you? And how do you drive out the devils?"

"I absorb them."

"Absorb them, eh?" (The audience laughed.) "And just how do you absorb them?"

The wizard looked uncomfortable. "They grab me by the sleeve, and then—and then—well, I absorb them."

"Well, you just go ahead and set up your doodads and show me how you absorb the devils."

"I—I—haven't time. I've got to hurry back and attend to my fields."

"Don't worry about your fields now; just you go ahead and show us how you absorb devils."

Reluctantly, the wizard set up his props and began to put on his show. The others chuckled and the audience howled. Finally, he stopped. Taking the village head aside he whispered: "Why go on? You know as well as I do that there are—no devils. Let me go and I'll promise to quit wizardry."

The others overheard and, to his surprise, intsead of being enraged, offered to help him reform. They would lend him farm tools and help him to break the soil of his farm. The son offered to sponsor his entry into the local labor exchange brigade.

And so the play ended with a song and a dance. An old ex-wizard then entered and made a short speech: The play was based upon his own experience; at the time of his reform he had presented his props to the Government for exhibition—they were the very articles we had seen on the stage. He would be glad to talk to anyone who wanted more information about wizards and their quackery.

For two reasons I have thought it worth while to tell the story of this play. First, it is an example of what the Communist cultural workers have been doing with the Yang Ko, its traditional values being retained by having all the dialogue in verse and all the lines sung, not spoken, in a simple seven-beat cadence. In the second place, it gives a good idea of the problem of superstition.

Also rooted in the original Yang Ko of the peasantry is the "Living Newspaper," a rather special form of Yang Ko drama, not yet a year old. As the name suggests, it has a message to transmit. It is a far cry from the stilted, formalized Chinese drama of long beards, falsetto voices, and exaggerated dialogue. The Communists' Living Newspaper is vivid and actual, designed primarily to bring the news of the day to the illiterate masses, to enlarge their vision, and to make them conscious of the greater world in which circumstances have made them an integral part. In some respects the Living Newspaper might be compared to some of our popular radio programs, such as "The March of Time" or "Five-Star Final." Performances are given in the open with no stage and the minimum of props. Plentifully seasoned with lusty burlesque and humor, they are certainly to the liking of the fascinated spectators. A mixture of Western and Chinese instruments provides an orchestral accompaniment, skilfully employed to accentuate dialogue and to heighten dramatic suspense. Living Newspaper performances are full of propaganda, but propaganda specifically calculated to encourage the people and mobilize their resistance to Japan. For example, the performance entitled *Second Front,* given just three days after Eisenhower's landing in France, opened with Tojo brandishing a broken, blood-tipped sword. He staggered about the scene trying to console a caricatured Hitler who moaned about his failure in Russia. Hitler was very much worried over the imminent opening of a second front in France.

"Help me by attacking Siberia," begged the weeping Hitler.

"I wish I could—but my head is splitting already, trying to hold those island-jumping Americans in the Pacific," Tojo replied. (The audience howled and jeered.) "But here's a secret weapon for you," and he showed Hitler a sheaf of yellow papers bearing cabalistic designs. As he mumbled some mystic mumbo-jumbo over these, Hitler looked on foolishly. "*Now* you should have no fear of the Americans and the British," he assured Hitler as he handed the papers over.

"Then why," demanded Hitler, "why haven't you used it against these same Americans and British in the Pacific?"

"Oh—it won't work against an enemy at sea," Tojo stammered lamely as he made his exit.

Goebbels hobbled in, with a bandaged clubfoot. Hitler ordered him to blow his propaganda trumpet so as to frighten Eisenhower into giving up the projected landing. Goebbels was ludicrously dubious, admitting his failure against the Russians.

In the next scene five sad-faced sandwich-men entered with big placards reading collectively, "The Invincible Atlantic Fortified Wall," whereupon Hitler began to make one of his notorious speeches at them in which Goebbels joined. (All this, as the basic Yang Ko dictated, was done in measured verse, sung to a simple tune.)

Goebbels then blew his propaganda trumpet, as Hitler sprinkled bits of Tojo's yellow paper on the heads of the skeptical "Atlantic Fortified Wall."

Drums rolled and the battle began. Without a single prop the performers gave a most graphic illusion of every phase of a landing operation. First, the naval bombardment. Groups of sailors formed a big ellipse, suggesting a battleship's hull. Inside, teams of sailors with outstretched arms represented the big turret guns. Then smaller ellipses, symbolizing the landing craft—with soldiers jumping over imaginary gunwales, wading through imaginary surf, setting up invisible machine-guns. I shall not attempt to describe the innumerable details of this remarkable pantomime of a landing, but I must point out that it was all derived from radio broadcasts picked up during the past few days. At no time had the performers received photographs or even magazines from the outside picturing such elaborate operations.

Next, men wearing leather helmets (the air force) flitted about with arms outstretched. They circled the two cities of Bayeux and Caen, represented by two standards, zooming and diving like fighter planes. These were followed by heavy bombers—three men in a triangle with a fourth lying horizontally on their shoulders flailing his arms like a propeller.

Eisenhower appeared—tall, slim, and sallow-faced. Someone had said he looked like that, but there was no picture of him available in the Border Region. Eisenhower now led the co-ordinated attack against the wavering "Invincible Atlantic Fortified Wall" behind which Hitler and Goebbels cowered. Eventually the wall collapsed in a crescendo of drum-beating, and Hitler and Goebbels fled. Bayeux and Caen were captured.

The finale was a victory celebration. The ensemble of fifty or more lustily sang Shostakovitch's *Song of the United Nations* as they danced around huge flags of China, America, Britain, and the Soviet. Each girl flag-bearer was in national dress. The girls' Western costumes—of America, Britain, and the Soviet—were characteristically stuffed out with padded breasts; they also wore long artificial noses, the more clearly to indicate the Occidental roles they were playing.

Yang Ko dramas and Living Newspapers are performed irregularly. But Saturday night dancing—modern dancing—is a social event in which almost everyone participates. Lacking dance halls with polished floors, and dance bands with polished hair, the Saturday night affairs have much of the character of a rural barn dance.

Typical of these Saturday night dances was the one given in the apple orchard at military headquarters. Soft lights from candles or pressure lamps, covered with red, blue, green, and yellow paper and hung from spreading branches, flooded the plain earthen dance floor. It was not a good floor to dance on, to be sure; but since every man, woman, and child wore ordinary cloth slippers or rope sandals no one cared. The girls all wore a pajamalike belted blouse and slacks, skirts being impracticable for this rough frontier life. Moreover, to assert their emancipated status the girls did most of the choosing of partners; there was no hesitation or embarrassment over this. The orchestra was composed of a weird blend of ancient Chinese fiddles, modern violins, mouth organs, native banjos, a Cantonese zither, a musical saw, and a missionary-type pedal organ. The music? They played sentimental Chinese ballads, French minuets, and Viennese waltzes such as *The Blue Danube*. Occasionally the orchestra gave out with something really hot and modern—like *Jingle Bells,* or *Yankee Doodle*—in honor of their foreign guests.

But don't think that worried them. They danced foxtrots, waltzes, and onesteps with total indifference to what the orchestra might be playing. And all enjoyed themselves immensely.

On any evening you might see bushy-haired, shirtsleeved Mao Tze-tung, venerated leader of ninety millions under the Communists' protection, having a grand time dancing a fast onestep with a cute co-ed from Yenta, while a truck-driver might be swinging buxom Madame Chu Teh. Roly-poly Chu Teh himself, commander-in-chief of over half a million Jap-killers, who looks like a fatherly old cowpuncher, was having the time of his life dancing with a bright young thing one-half his size and one-third his age. Battle-scarred generals Lin Piao, Nieh Yung-chien, Yeh Chien-ying, and a dozen others—for each of whom the Japanese would gladly sacrifice a full division of crack troops—would be seen flitting about like jitterbugging college kids.

It didn't matter what the orchestra played. No one paid much attention anyway, so long as it kept good time and good rhythm. When the orchestra ran out of "popular" tunes, it delved into its concert repertoire, playing operatic selections from *Rigoletto, Aida,* and *Carmen,* jazzed up to quite passable dance pieces.

Every now and then they would play a Yang Ko tune, and everyone would join the conga-skipping circle with a lively hesitating step. The Yang Ko tunes were so catchy that I swear the saddle-horses hitched on the outskirts of that apple-orchard ballroom just couldn't resist adding their whinnies to the choruses, which everybody sang.

11

‹‹‹‹‹‹‹‹

Village Democracy

I N A LITTLE village two hours' walk from Yenan an election was being held, at which the representatives to the local People's Political Council were to be chosen. The Election Committee of eleven sat in a clearing examining the voters' qualifications. The Committee was composed of one rich peasant, one middle-class peasant, three poor peasants, two hired workers, three women, and the primary school teacher.

Of the 620 prospective voters, whose names were posted on a bulletin board, only three were declared unqualified. One of these was feeble-minded and the other two were not yet eighteen years old, the minimum age for voters.

One by one, the candidates got up and explained their platforms. This one said he stood for the achievement without delay of Mao Tze-tung's recently announced eleven-point goal. That program ran as follows: 1. Every family should have one year's reserve of grain against bad times. 2. Every village should have a spinning and weaving machine. 3. Every village should have a blacksmith. 4. Every *hsiang* should have one day and one night school run by the people, one group for studying Chinese characters, one newspaper-reading group, one blackboard newspaper, and one Yang Ko dramatic corps. 5. Everyone should strive to learn one thousand Chinese characters. 6. There should be a medical co-operative in every subdistrict, a doctor in every *hsiang*, and a midwife in every village. 7. Every *hsiang* should have a mutual aid or relief granary for storing grain raised by the common efforts of the villagers. 8. There should be a peddler for every *hsiang* [to sell daily necessities]. 9. Every family should own an ox and at least one pig. 10. Every family should plant a hundred trees and care for them. 11. Every village should have at least one well, and every household a latrine.

The next candidate said he agreed that Chairman Mao's eleven-point program should be given their full support, and thought they should set about immediately to do something about it. They should inform the Yenan *hsien* government that they were prepared to offer labor power for well-digging, the building of a schoolhouse, the reclamation of wasteland for the mutual aid granary, and so on.

A third candidate agreed with the programs of both his predecessors, but added that he thought his fellow villagers ought to put special emphasis on education. This was a new world they were living in—a world that reached beyond their little village limits, and they and their children should prepare themselves for greater responsibilities.

Other candidates expressed their views. I got the feeling, listening to them, that they meant to do something about these things. But it must have seemed strange to the old folks, who remembered the days of virtual slavery. For the most part they sat there with impassive expressions on their seamed faces. Nevertheless, I could almost read their thoughts: a mixture of bewilderment, disbelief, and gratitude to a government that really seemed to interest itself in the welfare of the common people.

There was nothing unique about this election; it was like all those that are participated in throughout the fifteen anti-Japanese democratic bases throughout north and central China, by the ninety millions under the protection of the Communist Eighth Route and the New Fourth Armies. Even in the so-called "occupied" areas, the people hold elections, mostly in secret but often quite openly, sometimes almost within rifle range of the Japanese blockhouses.

To watch this Communist-led democracy in action, I attended a meeting of the Border Region's Government in joint session with the standing committee of the Border Region's People's Political Council. All twenty-four members present had been elected by popular vote, including the eight who were members of the Communist Party. The youngest was thirty-one, the oldest eighty-one. Since the Chairman of the Government, Lin Chu-han, was in Chungking at the time as the Party representative in the negotiations for a settlement of differences with the Kuomintang and the National Government, the Vice-Chairman, Li Ting-ming, a non-Communist, presided. Members present included a peasant, a merchant, a big landlord, a tenant farmer, an intellectual, an educator, a doctor, an army officer, a cultural worker, a shop clerk, and a Moslem.

The meeting was held in the drafty, high-roofed Government Auditorium. Sparrows chattered noisily around their nests in the massive, rough-hewn rafters overhead. On the whitewashed brick walls rows of portraits of the honored Labor Heroes stared down on the shaven heads of the bearded legislators. Huge fifteen-foot portraits of Mao Tze-tung and Chu Teh flanked the auditorium's stage, while overhead small United Nations flags were festooned from one corner to the other of the hall.

Only a few spectators watched the session. The legislators sat at the lower end of the auditorium near the stage, at a table to which some rough benches had been temporarily moved. It was a warm day. The majority of the members were in their shirtsleeves, though each still wore the floppy blue cap that nearly everyone in the Border Region wears. Even toothless, aging Li Ting-ming wore his cap, sipping tea from the spout of a tiny porcelain teapot as he opened the meeting with a review of the current military situation throughout the world. He concluded: "While our allies are winning victories elsewhere, we mustn't wait for their aid but must rely upon our own efforts to fight the Japanese." He ascribed the current reverses in Central and South China to the failure of the Chungking Government troops to win the people's support. He demanded that the National Government take the half-million crack troops blockading the Border Region and send them into action against the Japanese in Central and South China. "Moreover, our troops should be allowed to join them fighting the Japanese shoulder to shoulder," he added.

Liu Pei-chi, father of Liu Tze-tan, young firebrand of early revolutionary days, rose to speak his mind about the progress of the reforestation plan. He pointed out the Government's failure to cooperate with the peasants. The latter carried out their part by planting trees, but they needed tree experts to show them how to take care of them. Then he proceeded to give some practical suggestions for tree surgery.

Ho Chu-shan, a non-Communist educator, proposed improvement of the school system, putting forward many practical ideas. He suggested the establishment of mobile schools for backwoods villagers, with teachers making a daily circuit of the villages. During busy seasons, the teachers might even go direct to the students at work in the field, thus enabling the peasants to continue their work while studying. A small blackboard with a few new characters might be placed at each end of the field so that the student-farmer could study them as he worked. Subsequent to this, by the way, I saw such blackboards erected in many villages, proving that these legislators had not been talking idly.

Brisk little Ma Yu-chang spoke on care for the dependent families of soldiers at the front. More should be done to make these families self-supporting, not only because this would lessen the public burden but also because it would enhance their self-respect. He advocated, therefore, that land, farm implements, and seed should be given to such families with members able to farm.

Pi Kwang-tao, a non-Communist doctor, advocated more intensive fostering of a program of hygiene in the more backward villages. He asked that vigorous steps be taken to win the people away from "wizards" and witch doctors. More doctors trained in Western medicine were needed to combat the high mortality among infants, over fifty per cent of whom died before they reached the age of a year.

Kao Sung-chang, a merchant and former Kuomintang public safety director, talked on current political problems. He took the Generalissimo to task in salty phrases. "You're not such a bad fellow, Chiang Kai-shek, but the trouble is you're stubborn and won't listen to others. And you listen to the wrong people. Now, Dr. Sun Yat-sen said all patriots should join to make a strong China. We will support you to the hilt if you'll tread the path to democracy and unity, and you'll then surely and truly become one of the four great leaders in the world. Meanwhile, let's stop arguing among ourselves and get busy fighting our common enemy."

During a short recess someone produced a deck of dog-eared cards and a game of "Yenan Poker" (a cross between bridge and rummy) was started on the conference table.

After the recess Chiao Sung-shan, who is listed as a member of the Kuomintang formerly employed in the Control Yuan of the National Government, took the floor for an exhaustive survey and criticism of the present system of administering justice in the Border Region. He pointed out weaknesses and offered suggestions for improvement in procedure. First, the judge should go directly to the neighbors and elders in the litigants' village or wherever the case originates. Thus, he would not only gather first-hand evidence but also save time, which testifying farmers could better spend in the fields. More encouragement should be given to mediation out of court. This method would be satisfactory in all civil and most criminal cases, with the possible exception of cases of treason and subversion. He urged further popularization of mediation as initiated by Ma Hsi-wu, the Special Commissioner for Kwangchung Sub-Region (just north of Sian). Ma Hsi-wu has made himself famous in the Border Region for the efficiency and directness with which he handles civil and criminal cases. He wastes no time but goes directly to the source of the trouble and, in seeking a settlement, invites the assistance of locally respected people. The case of Fu-Peng-erh is a good case in point. Fu Peng-erh, a comely miss, was engaged to marry Chang Po-erh. The girl's father thought Chang Po-erh was too poor for his daughter and believed he could get more "marriage money" from another prospective husband whom he had in mind. But Chang Po-erh's father, who had drawn up the original marriage contract with the girl's father, called together a group of his relatives and neighbors and, one midnight, they kidnapped the girl and married her to his son. The girl's father appealed to the local court, which ruled the marriage invalid and sentenced Chang Po-erh's father to six months in jail.

However, the case led to heated argument in the community,

and Ma Hsi-wu was asked to settle the question. In order to obtain the orthodox, legal view he talked first with the local officials. Then he consulted neighbors and relatives. Finally, he asked the girl whether she wanted to marry the wealthier man selected by her father, or Chang Po-erh, the one whose father had been sentenced for kidnapping her. She replied that not even death could stop her from marrying Chang Po-erh.

Ma Hsi-wu thereupon called an open trial, to be attended by the whole community, which was to act as judge and jury. It was then revealed that the girl's father had repeatedly "sold" her as one suitor after another raised the successive "marriage money" offers. The girl, however, was entirely innocent in all this and had insisted upon marrying the man first selected by her father, whom she said she truly loved.

The community decided unanimously that old Fu had offended the marriage laws of the state by repeatedly "selling" his daughter, and therefore should be punished. Moreover, the boy's father, old Chang, had likewise disturbed the social order by kidnapping the girl, and he, too, should be punished. The boy and the girl were to be permitted to marry in accordance with the law of Voluntary Marriage.

Chiao Sung-shan concluded: "Ma Hsi-wu's principle that the masses should rely upon the masses in matters intimately concerned with their own welfare and livelihood is even more fair and just than the law." He had in mind, perhaps, a local saying that "Three old peasants are equal to a local judge"—a basic principle that the Communists are trying to establish in their system of practical justice.

12

◇◇◇◇◇◇◇

The Japanese People's Emancipation League

THERE are no war-prisoners' camps in the areas controlled by the Chinese Communists. At the very outset of the war the Communists announced that they would "kill no captives, [but would] give them preferential treatment and release all those who wished to return to their units." Of the 2,407 Japanese deserters and prisoners taken since the beginning of the war up to November 1944, all but 322 (who voluntarily chose to remain) had been sent back to their units, or had been returned to Occupied China where they might go underground and perhaps eventually reach Japan with forged papers.

The 322 who remained enjoy complete personal freedom and are all members of the Japanese People's Emancipation League. This organization has its headquarters in a cluster of well-appointed bomb-proof caves, high up the face of a cliff in the heart of Yenan city. While depending upon the Communist Eighth Route Army for material support, the J.P.E.L. is a wholly independent organization. Its director is Susumu Okano, the assumed name of Tetsu Nosaka, famed Japanese Communist and revolutionary who only recently arrived in Yenan after years of undercover work in North China.

The objects of this body of Japanese ex-soldiers are the destruction of Japanese militarism and the establishment of democracy in their homeland. Not a few have already given their lives in carrying their propaganda of discontent and revolt into the Japanese front lines. How successful they have been is perhaps suggested by the increasing number of deserters in the past year who tell of arguments in the ranks of the Japanese over the activities of the J.P.E.L.

During the first half of 1944 over a million handbills, pamphlets, and newspapers were printed in Japanese and distributed to the very doorsteps of thousands of Japanese blockhouses and strong points among those scattered throughout North China. There is nothing abstract about these leaflets. They deal with the personal problems of the Japanese soldiers—their food, their treatment, their supply of reading material and news—as well as what may be called the characteristic irregularities of Japanese military life.

For example, in Central Hopei a company commander was notorious for his face-slapping—an insulting indignity to a Japanese. J.P.E.L. workers at the front heard of this and sent him a personal warning through handbills mysteriously distributed about his post. Thereafter he quit face-slapping. Mimeographed newspapers carrying news picked up by special short-wave receivers tuned to San Francisco and London, as well as United Press and Reuters Morse-coded newscasts, are delivered almost daily to the garrisons of Japanese blockhouses. Special attention is paid to debunking Domei reports of Japanese "victories."

Three or four times a year, on Japanese festivals, hand-painted twelve-inch-square "comfort bags" are distributed by the thousand to Japanese strong-point garrisons. These bags contain simple delicacies such as peanuts, figs, candy, and reprints of popular Japanese fiction, playing cards, and perhaps a little bottle of Chinese rice wine. In most cases the Japanese soldiers send back their thanks, often with the latest newspapers and magazines from Japan, with Japanese cigarettes, and beer or other drinks.

Japanese officers, aware of the demoralizing effect of this fraternizing, try hard to stop it, shifting their men frequently from place to place. This, fortunately, plays right into the hands of the J.P.E.L. members, who thus find fresh material to work upon without too much moving on their own part. Through letter-writing, personal connections are made with individual members in the strong points. From intelligence workers the addresses of Japanese troopers are learned, and a J.P.E.L. member from the same district will write gossipy letters to them, carefully avoiding politics or propaganda. Though the Japanese soldiers are forbidden to reply, on an average of ten per cent of such letters are answered. In south Hopei, 42 replies were received in answer to 195 letters.

Occasionally a J.P.E.L. worker finds his former unit among a garrison. This happened to Matsuda. Discovering that his company was in the Taiheng Mountains in Hopei, he wrote forty letters to various members of it—letters full of personal, intimate facts so that there would be no doubt that he was still alive; for Japanese propaganda was declaring that prisoners and wounded alike were tortured to death by Paluchun "bandits." Matsuda's letters created so much to-do in the garrison that the company commander sent word through puppets that if Matsuda would return he would be welcomed by his old comrades, and it was announced that a large quantity of ammunition and money would be paid for his ransom. Matsuda replied that he was not a prisoner to be ransomed, and invited the company commander and his men to join him in the fight against the militarism of Tokyo.

Major Matsumoto, commanding the 75th Battalion of the Independent Mixed Brigade, decided he had better do something personally about the activities of J.P.E.L. workers in his district. He wrote, promising that if they would return to the Japanese Army he would guarantee that no harm would come to them. The J.P.E.L. workers replied politely that they were being well treated by the Eighth Route Army; moreover, they were fighting for something worth while, and they urged him to join them. The major lost his temper and wrote again, calling them traitors and threatening to catch and shoot them on sight. He wrote also to the Paluchun commander in that district: "As one soldier to another, I demand that you send those men to me." The Paluchun commander, after talking it over with the J.P.E.L. workers, ordered a surprise attack on the major's headquarters. The major's staff was captured, but he himself got away by the skin of his teeth. The J.P.E.L. members chalked on the headquarters walls: "Major Matsumoto—we have returned; why have you run away?"

Three or four times a month a "shouting corps" goes into action. This is dangerous work, for the corps must move right up within megaphone-range of a Japanese blockhouse. As often as not, hard-shelled Jap troopers will fire at the voices out in the darkness, and sometimes an irate blockhouse officer will order a sally. The shouters are therefore given strong protection and usually work on comparatively isolated strong points.

The J.P.E. Leaguers have been exceptionally successful with their shouting campaigns. In the Taiheng area, shouter Kamada found a unit to which he had belonged when it had been stationed at Lucheng, Hopei. The sergeant commanding the blockhouse was his particular friend, a native of his village. This sergeant, once convinced that he was indeed talking to the friend he had long believed dead, leaned over the blockhouse ramparts to talk with Kamada, creating a sensation among the garrison.

A Shantung strong point, garrisoned by thirty Japanese and fifty puppets, was subjected to a "shouting" assault. When the puppets opened fire on shouter Suzuki and his unit, the Japanese quickly restrained them. For the next hour or more the garrison asked innumerable questions about the J.P.E.L. and its work, expressing considerable astonishment that such an organization existed, since they had been believing their officers' stories about the terrible *Paluchun dohi* (Eighth Route Army bandits).

Shouting has a distinct advantage over handbills, pamphlets, and letter-writing, because it affords an opportunity for direct conversation, in the course of which questions may be asked and answered. But an even better method is telephone-tapping. Here the danger is lessened and conversations may be carried on indefinitely; and at the same time contact may be established with a whole network of strong points linked by a common telephone system. Kobayashi-san, who had just returned from the North China fronts, told me some of his experiences with telephone-tapping:

"It was a bitter, blustery New Year's Eve. In pitch darkness we slithered along an icy mountain trail, each fearful lest an unwary step send him hurtling over an unseen cliff. I was considerably worried about the precious telephone equipment that my Chinese guards carried on their backs in addition to their rifles and light machine-guns captured from the Japanese army. The telephone set and the tools for tapping the strong points' telephone system were also booty. At last we reached our destination—a roofless, burnt-out farmhouse barely two hundred yards from a Japanese strong point. We dared not light a fire for warmth, or even a candle for light.

"On a propped-up three-legged table I set up my telephone set and leaned on my earphones waiting for the signal that would tell me that the Chinese trooper shinnying up a telephone pole out there in the dark had succeeded in his task—which was to cut my line into the system connecting a web of strong points in that area. Our guard was deployed in the snow-covered vicinity, the sergeant moving from post to post to keep his men on the alert.

"At last the signal came. I looked at the luminous dial on my watch—it was well on toward midnight. Just in time! I cranked my set four times. After a while a sleepy voice answered: 'Moshi! Moshi!' [Hello! Hello!]

"'Moshi! Moshi!' I replied. 'Is that Number Four Strong Point?'

"'It is. Who is this?'

"'May I speak with Corporal Katayama?' I asked. I had been told that Katayama was a good man; only a few days before, he had reprimanded a man in his squad for needlessly abusing a peasant. Presently Katayama came to the 'phone.

"'Is this Katayama-san?'

"'Hai—this is Katayama. Who is this?'

"'I just called to wish you a Happy New Year,' I said. 'It's nearly midnight, you know.'

"'Why, of course—so it is. I had intended to stay up for it, but I guess I must have dozed off. Thank you—and a Happy New Year to you, too; though I guess it isn't such a happy one, at that, is it? Brr-r-r-r! These North China winters are cold, aren't they? Say— by the way, who is this? Headquarters?'

"'No. This is Kobayashi, a member of the Japanese People's Emancipation League.'

"There was a long silence. Then I spoke again. 'Hello—hello! Are you there?'

"'*Hai*,' came the answer. But Katayama sounded a bit worried. I didn't want to frighten him off the line, so I spoke hurriedly: 'How did you like the comfort bags we sent you yesterday?'

"'The comfort bags? Oh, yes—I know what you mean. Did *you* send them?'

"'Yes. Were there enough for all of you?'

"'Yes, there were, thank you.' Then I heard him chuckle. 'What is it?' I asked.

"'Oh, nothing—just that our lieutenant was wild when he heard about them. He told us they would poison us!' He chuckled again. 'We made the puppets taste them first, you know.' I laughed with him. Then he sobered. 'You know,' he went on, 'I'm not supposed to talk with you.'

"I said I knew that, but that this was New Year's Eve and we were both Japanese, and homesick for our loved ones at home. I heard him sigh heavily. 'And when shall we ever see them again?' he asked, as if to himself.

"This gave me the opening I was waiting for. I told him about myself—how I had been wounded so badly that I was unable to commit suicide, which I thought was the honorable thing for a disabled Japanese to do. The Eighth Routers had picked me up on the battlefield, nursed me back to health, and even offered me my freedom. But by that time I had come to understand something of what they were fighting for. Other Japanese of the J.P.E.L. talked to me, and I decided to join them. Then I said: 'We, the Japanese People's Emancipation League, are as concerned about our families as you are. We want to stop this war that nobody wants and from which nobody will gain anything.'

"At that, he was silent. Then he asked me to tell him about the J.P.E.L., and we went on talking for the better part of half an hour, until he said that someone was coming and he would have to ring off.

"I then rang up Number Six and Number Nine and Number Seven Strong Points and talked with several more fellows. At Number Two an officer came into the room while I was talking to some of the men. He grabbed the telephone and started cursing me, ordering me to shut up and threatening to send out a party to hunt me down. I said quietly that I would take no orders from him and that it was such as he that I and my J.P.E.L. companions were fighting, and—that if he led a party out—we would not only tear up the telephone wires but also capture him alive. That made him so mad that he nearly exploded! He hung up and I went on with my telephoning."

This was but one of the incidents described by Kobayashi-san, but it is typical.

What the Japanese High Command thinks of the J.P.E.L. can be understood from the efforts made to discredit it. Counterpropaganda branding J.P.E.L. members as impostors and traitors is distributed to Japanese soldiers in North China; and special agents are trained to "desert" or to be "captured"—then doing their best to enter the J.P.E.L., for the purpose of sowing dissension, seducing the members, and assassinating the leaders.

At the time of my visit there were six of these in Yenan—self-confessed agents who were quite willing to talk. Tall, twenty-four-year-old Naoyuki Tanikawa was one of them. He said he had been expressly commissioned to kill League leader Okano, who interpreted for me. A conscript from a poor peasant family, Tanikawa had been a private in the Suzuki Fourth Independent Brigade stationed in North China. One day his regimental commander, Lt. Col. Kitagawa, called him to his quarters and smilingly offered him beer, cakes, and coffee. "I have had good reports of you," he told the bewildered Tanikawa. "It may be that you deserve promotion. You would like that, *hai?*" Tanikawa was too flabbergasted even to reply. He was dismissed, only to be called back a few days later. And this time the officer got down to business. After a sumptuous meal, Tanikawa was told that he had been selected for a special honor: he was to be trained as a spy, was to be "captured" by the Eighth Route Army, and so enter the J.P.E.L. If he succeeded in this mission, it would be equivalent to the work of an entire division. On his return he would be decorated, promoted, and given a big bonus and a long furlough back home. If he failed—well, his family would be well cared for and honored in their community.

Tanikawa said he was at first quite puzzled; he couldn't understand why he, an ordinary private, should be chosen for so important a mission. Later he realized that—just because he was an ordinary private—his superiors had no compunctions about sending him on so dangerous a mission. There was no option, of course —the request was actually an order.

So Tanikawa entered a special school at Yanghsueh in Shansi, where, together with fifteen others like him, he spent four months studying ciphering, jiu-jitsu, and the many different ways of killing a man without weapons. In the political course they were told that the Chinese Communists took orders directly from Stalin, who was using them as puppets in order to conquer Japan and the whole Far East. He was told also that he would be working in collaboration with Chinese spies, once he got into the Communist area. He was taught how to transmit messages by simple signs such as doffing his cap, mopping his brow, or picking his nose. Should his mission be discovered, he was to make only a partial confession; in any case he was to have no fear of the Paluchun, who never killed their prisoners.

"This surprised me at the time," Tanikawa said, smiling, "because we had so often been told that the Communists tortured prisoners to death."

So Tanikawa "escaped" to the Communists. When a scouting party of Eighth Routers took him to a little shack—in which he saw a portrait of Chiang Kai-shek—he thought for a moment that he had fallen into the hands of Central Government troops. "But," he told me, "as soon as I saw a picture of Mao Tze-tung on the *other* wall, I knew I was all right, though I didn't quite understand it all at the time."

The Eighth Routers sent him to Yenan, where he asked to join the J.P.E.L.

"Of course, we spotted him as an agent almost from the very beginning," said Okano. "You see, we checked his story thoroughly and found it full of discrepancies. We said nothing, however, knowing he would be so closely watched by all the J.P.E.L. that he would be unable to do anything to be concerned about."

Another of the six Jap agents in Yenan was young Arata, who had been "captured" last year after having gone through the four months' training. With him when he came, he brought a powerful bomb concealed in a pocket watch, with which he was supposed to kill either Mao Tze-tung or Chu Teh. He carried also a tiny vial of poison inside the fly of his trousers, to be used for the same purpose. He was never given the least chance to use either of these. When one day the guilt of another spy was being discussed at a meeting of J.P.E. Leaguers, Arata decided to confess voluntarily— and was considerably taken aback to learn that they knew all about him already. "But I didn't mind it, really," he said with a smile. "I never did have much enthusiasm for the job."

Kenji Koda, who had "deserted" only a few months before my visit, admitted that he, too, had been assigned to kill Okano. "I'm quite flattered by all this attention," observed Okano-san dryly.

Fifty-year-old, soft-spoken Okano, one of the founders of the Communist Party in Japan, has been a revolutionary all his life. His parents died when he was a youngster, leaving him in the care of his older brother, who sent him first to a commercial school and then to Keio University. Influenced by the Russian Revolution in 1918, he had gone to Russia and then to England. When, after he had delivered a number of speeches, Scotland Yard intimated that he was not welcome in England, he went on to France, Switzerland, Germany, and Russia. Thence he returned to Japan, where shortly after his arrival he was thrown into prison. There he languished right through the earthquake of 1923. From that year to 1931 he spent most of his time in prison until his escape from Japan to Soviet Russia. In 1935 Okano was elected a member of the Executive Committee of the Comintern. In 1937 he smuggled himself into North China and engaged in underground activities against the Japanese army. In 1943 he arrived in Yenan, expressly to transform the more or less purposeless Anti-War League—composed of zealous but inexperienced ex-prisoners—into the present antimilitarist, revolutionary League.

The program of the J.P.E. League is ambitious. Among other things, it urges on the Japanese soldiery that they demand an immediate cessation of the war, the overthrow of the militarists, and the establishment of a democratic government in Japan. It demands also that friendly relations be established with foreign powers, based upon principles of equality and true co-prosperity. It insists that the provocateurs of the "Manchuria Incident," the Sino-Japanese War, and the Pacific War be punished. Other articles of belief are that demobilization and disarmament should be carried out immediately, down to the limit required purely for self-defense. Measures should be taken to raise the standard of living, to effect complete freedom of speech, press, assembly, association, and religious faith, to grant the franchise to all over the age of twenty, and to convoke the national congress for the establishing of a democratic constitution.

On the subject of the Emperor's fate, Okano and the J.P.E.L. speak cautiously. "The Emperor is still too much of a godlike figure to a good many Japanese for us to shout 'Down with the Emperor!' at this moment. By the end of the war, however, the Japanese may have come to regard him as no more than a weak mortal, a puppet in the hands of the militarists. Already the militarists are playing into our hands by deliberately forcing the Emperor to shoulder full responsibility for the war. On the eighth of every month all newspapers must publish the declaration of war against Britain and America promulgated over the Emperor's name, with the implication that, if the war should be lost, the Emperor must perforce bear the blame. Moreover, the Emperor's frequent appearances before the people, at the militarists' insistence, have weakened public belief in his 'divinity.' In any case, our quarrel is not with the Emperor himself, but with the absolute power vested in him, which the militarists have usurped. We consider that they may well usurp that power again, in order to launch some fresh imperialist adventure."

Having thus defined the essential principles, Okano went on to disagree with ex-Ambassador Grew, who has advocated that the Emperor be retained, together with his godlike prestige. "This is wholly undemocratic," said Okano, "and fraught with danger for the future"—though he admitted reluctantly that should the constitution reduce the Emperor's status to the equivalent of the King of England's—the status of a virtual figurehead—there might be a place for the Emperor in the new democratic Japan. "It would be much better, however, without an emperor at all—as in America." If monarchy were to be abolished, he concluded, it would be wise to pension the Imperial House and treat them with the respect due to an old family.

All members of the J.P.E.L. attend the Japanese Workers and Peasants School in Yenan. After a year and a half of training they are detailed to varying terms of service at the fronts. The school —which, like almost every other institution in Yenan, occupies a series of caves—was founded in November 1940. Its principal object at the outset was to rid captives of the idea that this was a "sacred war" for Japan. The true character of the war and of Japan's part in it was patiently explained to the students in their native tongue by teachers graduated from their own numbers. The regular curriculum included an analysis of international and domestic affairs, world geography, the ABC of political economy, etc. The indirect approach was used in teaching—e.g., an analysis was made of Nazism and Hitler's dream of a "New Order" for Europe so as to suggest a parallel with the Japanese militarists' "New Order" for Greater East Asia.

Emphasis is placed today on the encouragement and development of individuality and initiative, as preparation for antimilitarist activities at the front during the war and for revolutionary work in a democratic Japan after the war. In addition to lectures on political history, economics, and social science, the students are also given courses in general knowledge to raise their intellectual level. Once a month each one individually reviews and criticizes his own work in the presence of his fellows, who bestow praise and blame where due.

Great attention is given to practical work. Students spend much time in drafting propaganda leaflets and editing newspapers. They practice "propaganda shouting" assiduously. Up to the spring of 1943 broadcasts in Japanese were made twice weekly from Yenan, in the hope of reaching not only the invaders in North China but also the people of Japan proper. For technical reasons these broadcasts were stopped, and propaganda material is now mailed or Morse-coded to the front lines for distribution by J.P.E.L. workers in the field.

Japanese students not only attend all big public meetings in Yenan, but often address them. They have been given the right to vote and the privilege of election. One of their number, Ken Mori, has been elected a Councillor in the Border Region Government, while Nakakoji serves as Municipal Councillor for the city of Yenan. In accordance with the Eighth Route Army's principle of preferential treatment for Japanese, the students get better rations than do the average Chinese soldiers. Instead of millet, for example, they receive white flour, and their allowance of meat is about six pounds a month—one pound seven ounces more than the Paluchun soldier gets. Daily necessities such as toothbrushes, toothpaste, towels, soap, and tobacco are supplied in ample amounts. They run their own kitchens and prepare their own Japanese-style dishes. While they are exempt from participation in the Production Movement, they nevertheless devote a number of hours daily to spinning, carpentry, or the raising of vegetables. They are skilled makers of toys—toys that find a ready market in Yenan.

When I first visited the League's school, the seventy-odd members present were lined up in military formation while their spokesman announced: "We are ready at any time to fight, together with our American and other allies, against Japanese militarism. For the sake of overthrowing those who have led our country into misery and degradation we are prepared to do anything asked of us."

In a reception room there was a fine exhibit of the students' activities, together with detailed statistical charts and graphs; sandtable miniatures of shouting units and telephone-tappers in action; samples of their handbills, pamphlets, and newspapers which they had already distributed to the Japanese blockhouse garrisons; "comfort bags" with their contents displayed; and a tableful of war trophies, principally such personal things as a trooper carries in his pockets—luck charms and amulets, notebooks and diaries, identification disks, and bright-colored postcard photographs of current movie and stage stars.

The statistics, into which a good deal of work had evidently been put, revealed that there had been an 88% increase in the J.P.E.L. membership during the past year; that 12% had been killed in the course of their front-line propaganda work; 34% of the members had been factory workers before entering the army, 32% farmers, and 12% tradesmen, the remaining 22% being composed of public-works employees, artisans, and fishermen—and there were even four priests; 78% were infantrymen, 66% were graduates of high primary schools, 15% of intermediate schools, and two of them had university diplomas. Especial pride was taken in the chart showing a comparison of their rations with those of civilians in Japan: with the exception of rice (the northern Chinese raise and eat wheat instead of rice), their rations were considerably higher.

Along the walls a series of large hand-painted posters illustrated the "Iniquities and Tortures Suffered by Recruits in the Japanese Army, Which Boasts Itself a 'First-Class Army'." All the posters had English captions. One of these read: "New recruits are ordered to stand underneath a shelf or table with things on top. They must keep standing in a stooped position with the head touching the under side of the table until the back begins to ache excruciatingly. Should they try to sit down they will receive a whack or kick from the older soldiers." A poster showing a gawky recruit under a bed was captioned: "Sometimes new recruits will be ordered to crawl under the bed and imitate a cuckoo. Often an older soldier will hit him over the head with a rifle-cleaning rod, much to the amusement of all others." "When quarters are found untidy," read the caption of another, "the recruits are blamed and have to line up in pairs for slapping each other. If they don't slap hard enough, an older soldier steps in and slaps the delinquent especially hard."

The students were eager to talk about themselves and their work, of which they were obviously proud. Second Lieutenant Oyama told me how he had been teaching Chinese artillerymen to use captured Japanese cannon. Nakajima taught carpentry. Yamada, an assistant surgeon in the Japanese army, was now working with the Eighth Route Army's Medical Service. Shimada was an expert with the grenade-thrower; he spoke highly of the Eighth Router's adaptability. Yoshida told stories of some of the "shouting" offensives in which he had taken part; of late, he said, the Japanese authorities were carefully spoon-feeding their troops with heavily propagandized news.

"They flatly refused," he said to me, "to believe our reports of Allied victories in Europe or the Pacific, until we pointed out that, regardless of what they were being told about Japanese and German 'victories,' the geography of the places mentioned currently in the news proved clearly that the Axis was 'victoriously losing territory.'"

Corporal Yoshida, sole survivor of a surrounded platoon, had been captured at the close of a ten-day battle. He had tried to commit suicide by slitting his throat, but he had not cut deeply enough; and he had been nursed back to health by his Paluchun captors. (He showed me the scar on his neck, while the others laughed.) On regaining consciousness he had demanded that he be killed, fearing that the Paluchun were saving him for cruel public indignities or actual torture. Instead, he had received only the best and friendliest of treatment—which had frankly puzzled him until he came to understand something of the Paluchun's policy toward captives.

Katayama, captured only some six months before, told of the shouting campaigns directed against his blockhouse, and of receiving "comfort bags." "We considered the Workers traitors," he said, "and the Paluchun an awfully queer army to send us comfort bags. We used to tell each other jokingly that if a Japanese private went over to the Paluchun they'd make him a high officer to lead their troops. This joke gained weight after a battle that we lost, when word was passed around that we had been beaten because the Paluchun forces had been led by Japanese who had gone over."

Shizuo Nakakoji told a grimly amusing story. His company, the Fourth, had fought many times against the Paluchun; but it always happened, during every sortie, that four of their number had been killed. Now, the Japanese word for "four" also means "death" —so their company commander changed the name of their detachment from the "Fourth" Company to the "Hirosi" Company, Hirosi being his own name. However, in the very next engagement, not only were the usual four men killed, but so was Captain Hirosi. The lieutenant was promoted to succeed Hirosi—but in the next battle the lieutenant was also killed, along with the usual four. By this time, the company had begun to fear that the Paluchun possessed some mysterious power, the troopers started complaining of "illness," and eventually the company was withdrawn from that sector. Nakakoji himself had been wounded and captured in the last engagement before the company's transfer to an Inner Mongolian front.

Several of the students admitted candidly that they had killed civilians, and for this they blamed their army training: they had been taught that the Chinese were little more than animals and that they themselves were superior beings. Not only did they talk freely of such matters—they also wrote detailed accounts of their own atrocities and those of other Japanese. The *Giefang Rhbao* one day published a full page of these stories. Here is a typical one:

"In 1941 the Tanaka Company of the Third Battalion, Kondo 223 Regiment, Izeki 36th Division, was stationed at Nangning and Tzechow in Shansi Province. One day a captive of about twenty-seven years of age was brought in. One could tell almost at a glance that he was merely a poor innocent peddler, but our captain insisted that he was a spy, and turned him over to our doctor for 'treatment.' The doctor ordered the fellow stripped to the waist and stretched on the ground; then he took a big syringe, which he had filled with water, and jabbed it into the man's chest—withdrawing it full of blood. Blood also began to issue from the screaming man's mouth. Even some of our own men could not stand this, and turned away. But the doctor only smiled and went on pumping water into the peddler. When the man fainted, the doctor revived him with some drug. Eventually the man died—whereupon the sadistic doctor picked up his things and walked away."

Another such account ran as follows:

"In July 1941 I was assigned to the Military Dog-Training Institute at Changsintien, southwest from Peiping. One day they brought about fifty Chinese civilians into a high-walled courtyard. Major Kato ordered us to take positions along the wall, and when we were settled he cried, 'Sergeant Oisi, begin the attack!' A little door on the far side of the courtyard opened and a pack of sharp-toothed dogs came bounding out and made straight for the throats of the screaming Chinese, who tried to beat them off with their fists. The spouting blood only made the dogs more ferocious, and they literally tore their victims into pieces. Eventually all the Chinese lay dead of their mutilations, and the glutted dogs were led away."

Still a third, written by one Tajima, read:

"In May 1940 the Third Company of the 39th Battalion, Ninth Independent Mixed Brigade, was garrisoned at Sanchiu in Chihsien, Shansi Province. One day Second Lieutenant Ono said to us: 'You have never killed anyone yet, so today we shall have some killing practice. You must not consider the Chinese as a human being, but only as something of rather less value than a dog or a cat. Be brave! Now, those who wish to volunteer for killing practice, step forward.' No one moved. The lieutenant lost his temper. 'You cowards!' he shouted. 'Not one of you is fit to call himself a Japanese soldier. So no one will volunteer? Well then, I'll order you.' And he began to call out names: 'Otani—Furukawa —Ueno—Tajima!' (My God—*me* too!) I raised my bayoneted gun with trembling hands, and—directed by the lieutenant's almost hysterical cursing—I walked slowly toward the terror-stricken Chinese standing beside the pit—the grave he had helped to dig. In my heart I begged his pardon, and—with my eyes shut and the lieutenant's curses in my ears— I plunged the bayonet into the petrified Chinese. When I opened my eyes again, he had slumped down into the pit. 'Murderer! Criminal!' I called myself."

Such episodes are terribly hard to read, I know, but because they are a part of every soldier's knowledge in invaded China I continue to quote them.

"In June 1939 I was with the Ohara Battalion of the Wataru Regiment, Houma Division, in a campaign on the Suiyuan-Ninghsia border. On one occasion I saw Sergeant Sakuma and Corporal Simazu drag an old man, a young girl, and a baby from a tiny shack. After a few moments' whispered conversation, the officers pointed a pistol at the old man and said: 'You and your daughter—*saku, saku!*' Then they stripped the man and the girl and tried to make the old man have sexual intercourse with his daughter. The man cursed and fought them, so they shot him. The girl screamed as they tore the baby from her and then forced her to the ground and stuffed pepper into her sexual organ."

The page carried a dozen more such stories. That such things have occurred not once but thousands of times, I know. But what prompted these Japanese to describe and print them is to be explained only by somebody better versed than I in Oriental psychology. I cannot explain it.

13

◇◇◇◇◇◇◇◇

Anti-Japanese Bases

WHEN the various components of
the Chinese Red Army congregated in North Shensi at the end of
the Long March, they numbered about 80,000. On the outbreak of
the war in 1937, and by agreement with Chiang Kai-shek and the
Central Government, the Red Army was absorbed into the National Army. Only 45,000 Communist troops were recognized, however, and designations for only three divisions (115th, 120th, and
129th) were given them. Collectively, these three divisions formed
the Eighth Route Army. When "Route Army" formations were
abolished something like a year later, the Eighth Route was incorporated into the Eighteenth Group Army under the direct authority of Marshal Yen Hsi-shan, commander of the Second War
Zone. Though the Communists have since fallen out with both
the Marshal and the Central Government, their troops still bear
the arm-patch military designation of 18GA. And while they still
consider themselves at least nominally members of the Central
Government forces under Marshal Yen Hsi-shan's Eighteenth
Group Army, popularly they prefer to call themselves the Eighth
Route Army—the Paluchun.

The Communist New Fourth Army was originally composed of
Red partisan detachments from the civil war period. On the outbreak of war with Japan in 1937 these partisans, by agreement with
and under orders from the High Command in Nanking, assem-

bled along both banks of the Yangtze in south Anhwei Province, and were organized as the New Fourth Army with designations for four detachments numbering a total of 12,000.

Generally speaking, during the period from the outset of the war to the fall of Canton and Hankow in October 1938, the Japanese more or less ignored the Communist forces and concentrated their attention upon the Kuomintang troops. With the fall of the two cities, the Communist Eighth Route Army—veteran guerrillas from civil war days—began intensive activities behind the Japanese lines, paying special attention to the enemy's North China communications. The Japanese thereupon turned powerful forces into their own rear in order to "mop up" these Communist guerrillas. The mopping-up campaigns reached their peak, in number and ferocity, during the years 1941 and 1942, with the result that the population under the Communists' control was reduced from a hundred million to fifty millions.

The Communists, however, continued to organize mass resistance to the Japanese. The enemy's "village purgings," "triple destruction policy," and "annihilation campaigns" were countered with cave and tunnel warfare, mine and river barricade warfare, and other forms of combat devised to meet the special conditions of this war. Moreover, over two million People's Militia were organized to harass the Japanese and to co-operate with the Paluchun regulars and guerrilla forces in their hit-and-run operations. Meanwhile, Communist Party workers helped the people to reorganize their administrative systems and to set up a form of democratic government with elections based upon the secret ballot. Reforms such as the reduction of land rent and loan interest and the guarantee of payment of rents and interest by tenants were introduced. A Production Movement was launched in which the regulars and the guerrillas participated when not fighting.

By 1943, through a long-range policy of steady, persistent pressure, the Communists had recovered their losses in North China and had actually begun to expand the territory under their control. To-day, they claim almost ninety millions of liberated Chinese under their direction. Their armies operate on a farflung front stretching on the north from Suiyuan to Manchuria, east to the Pacific, south to Hainan Island and Canton, along the Yangtze River almost to Shanghai. They stand within sight of Peiping, Tientsin, and Tsingtao.

This vast area, liberated entirely by force of arms—arms taken from the Japanese themselves—is today organized into fifteen semi-autonomous anti-Japanese bases. Five of these are in North China: Shansi-Charhar-Hopei, Shansi-Hopei-Honan, Shansi-Suiyuan, Hopei-Shantung-Honan, and Shantung. Eight are in Central China: Central Kiangsu, Eastern Chekiang, Northern Kiangsu, Hwainan (the district south of the Hwai River), Hwaipei (the district north of the Hwai River), Southern Kiangsu, Central Anhwei, and the Hupeh-Hunan-Anhwei Border Region. The South China bases are located on Hainan Island and in the vicinity of Canton.

The bases in North China lie north of the Lunghai Railway. They extend westward to the Yellow River, eastward to the Yellow Sea and Gulf of Chihli and northward to points below Paotow and Pailingmiao in Inner Mongolia, Tolun in Charhar, Chihfeng in Jehol, and Mienchou in Liaoning. They embrace the whole of Shansi, Shantung, and Hopei provinces, and parts of Suiyuan, Jehol, Charhar, Liaoning, Kiangsu, and Honan, with a total area of 370,000 square miles and a total population of over eighty millions.

The terrain is a system of broad plains intersected by mountain chains in complicated fashion, with the troops in the mountains and the people in the plains playing roles of mutual aid. In the early period of the war the enemy occupied the plains and isolated and besieged the troops in the mountains. When they found they were unable to starve out the Eighth Routers, the Japanese undertook numerous mopping-up campaigns, which also failed. Meanwhile, the enemy built new railways and over 95,000 kilometers of new motor roads. They dug deep, wide ditches flanking the railways and highways, which they fortified with thousands of strong points and blockhouses spaced within gun-range of each other. Supplementary spiderwebs of strong points and blockhouses were spread over the countryside, to cage up the troops in the mountains and to strangle the lowland guerrillas.

But in the face of all the Japanese efforts the Communists con-

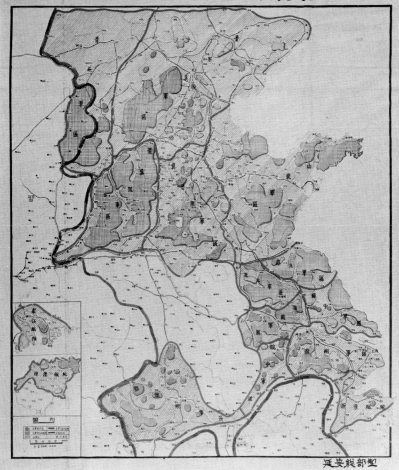

中國抗戰敵後戰塲形勢要圖 (一九四四年十月十日)

延安總部製

The Communists' Anti-Japanese Bases as of October 10, 1944. (See *inside book cover for names*.) Inserts: upper, Canton Area; lower, Hainan Island. Darker portions are base areas. Lighter portions are guerrilla areas. (*Reproduced from official map drawn by Headquarters of the Eighteenth Group Army, Yenan.*)

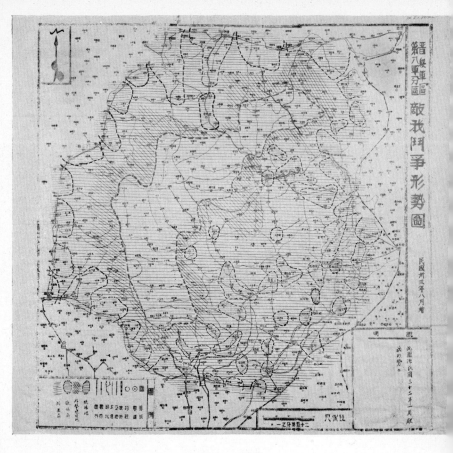

January 1943

Maps of Eighth Sub-Region of the Shansi-Suiyuan Anti-Japanese Base. Large lighter area represents actual base in hands of Communist forces at height of Japanese "draining-water" offensive. Jap strongpoints represented by smaller encircled areas. The Guerrilla operate in no-man's-land.

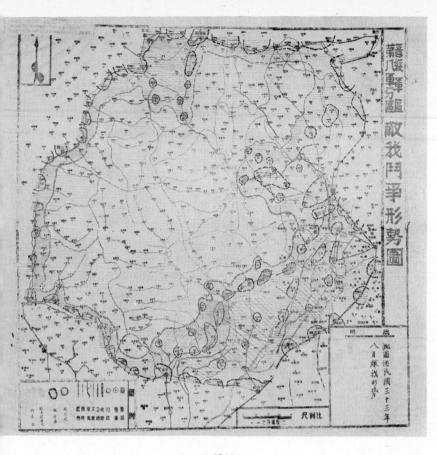

August 1944

ote how base area has been expanded in nineteen months of offensive action
unched by Communist Eighth Route Army operating from within encircled area.
Reproduced from official maps drawn by Headquarters of Eighteenth Group Army,
enan.)

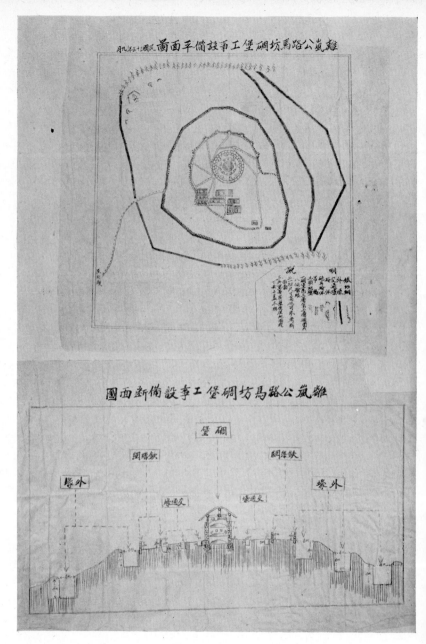

Plan and elevation of Mafang strongpoint, on the western perimeter of the Eighth Sub-Region of the Shansi-Suiyuan Anti-Japanese Base—one of 13,000 such strongpoints destroyed by the Communist forces in the year 1943-44. (*Reproduced from official map drawn by Headquarters of the Eighteenth Group Army, Yenan.*)

tinued to expand. With the co-operation of the people they were able not only to hold their own but actually to launch an offensive against the invaders. The details of this offensive will occupy a later chapter. In the twelvemonth ending with the summer of 1944 they had attacked and destroyed over 13,000 of these strong points and blockhouses. This sounds almost incredible when one considers the terrific handicaps under which they were forced to fight. I could scarcely believe it when they told me this in Yenan; but from what I saw in the two months I spent with the Eighth Route Army in action behind the enemy lines—actually participating in the capture and destruction of such strong points and blockhouses—I am convinced that there is no exaggeration in the Communists' assertion. The offensive is limited only by weapons and circumstances. Already fifty of the eighty millions in the North China anti-Japanese base regions have been freed from the Japanese yoke. Moreover, the large cities in North China such as Peiping, Tientsin, Taiyuan, Tsinan, and Tsingtao presently occupied by the enemy are under direct and constant threat by the Eighth Routers, who lack only the weapons to recover them.

The Central China bases straddle the lower Yangtze, the Hwai, the Han, and the Yellow rivers. They extend from eastern Chekiang to the northern banks of the Tungting Lake and thence north to the Lunghai Railway. They embrace the major parts of Kiangsu (up to the Lunghai), Anhwei, Hupeh, and parts of Honan and Chekiang—an area containing some of the most fertile rice-producing districts in China. They spread over an area of about 135,000 square miles with a population of over sixty millions. Surrounded by high mountains, these bases have been established in a vast plain, laced by a great network of canals and checkered with lakes and marshes. Here the New Fourth Army has fought the Japanese for the past seven years.

Communications in this area are the best developed in all China. The whole region is criss-crossed by railways, including the Shanghai-Nanking, the Tsin-Pu, the Ping-Han, the Lunghai, the Hwei-Nan, the Kiang-Nan, the Chekiang-Kiangsi, the Canton-Hankow, and the Shanghai-Hangchow-Ningpo lines. Motor roads are even better developed, with a total of something like 6,000 miles. As in the North, these communications are fortified and designed to partition and blockade the New Fourthers. The Communists counter with extensive mine-laying operations and the destruction of roads and railways. The enemy is thus forced to garrison nine and a half divisions plus 230,000 puppet troops to contain the New Fourthers. Since the outbreak of the Pacific War three major campaigns have been launched against the New Fourthers, who threaten the very heart of the enemy's key points in Central China, such as Shanghai, Nanking, and Hankow. All three campaigns failed miserably, with the New Fourthers continuing their pressure upon the Japanese, pinning down a sizable number of troops which might have been used on more active fronts elsewhere.

Since the fall of Canton in 1938, the South China guerrillas have been active behind the Japanese lines from Canton to Kowloon. By 1944 they had established themselves strongly enough to control about 7,000 square miles and about a million of the district's total population of four million. On October 2, 1943, the Tungkiang Anti-Japanese Government formally declared that it henceforth accepted full leadership from the Central Committee of the Chinese Communist Party at Yenan. The Tungkiang guerrillas concentrate their operations mostly along the Canton-Kowloon Railway, where they frequently derail traffic and assault the garrisons guarding the line. Famous for their daring, they once blew up the big steel railway bridge on the very outskirts of Kowloon.

Since the fall of Hongkong the Tungkiang guerrillas, who move in and out of the city at will, have rescued scores of Chinese, including many Chungking Government officials. Britishers and Americans, both civilians and military personnel, also have been brought out. Not a few American pilots who were shot down over Hongkong have been rescued and returned to their bases by the Tungkiang guerrillas.

Since 1939, when the Japanese occupied Hainan Island, which hangs like a teardrop from southern China, the Communists on the island have carried out numerous raids on grain depots, attacked airdromes and communications, and obliged the Japanese to keep a strong garrison on the island. It is their hope to prepare the island for an allied landing in the Pacific counteroffensive.

14

◇◇◇◇◇◇◇

The Military Record

SINCE the headquarters at Yenan for the Eighth Route and New Fourth Armies considers itself, at least nominally, still under the direction and orders from the High Command at Chungking, reports covering military activities of the Communist forces are forwarded regularly to the National Military Council.

Here is a summary of the military record claimed by the Communists for their armies from the outbreak of the war to the summer of 1944.

The Eighth Route and the New Fourth Armies together represent something less than one-fifth of the total Chinese forces facing the Japanese. These Communist troops, however, engage 49.5 per cent of all the Japanese forces in China today, as well as over 90 per cent of nearly 800,000 puppets (about which the world has heard comparatively little). In the seven years of war the Communists have fought over 92,000 battles. They have killed and wounded 1,100,000 Japanese and puppets and captured over 150,000 of the enemy. Booty includes 320,000 rifles (enough to equip 540,000 men at the ratio of five men to three rifles), 9,000 machine-guns, 600 pieces of artillery, and great heaps of miscellaneous equipment such as trench mortars, grenade-throwers, hand grenades, cartridges, radios, telephones, etc. Fifty-five high-ranking Japanese officers have been killed, including a lieutenant-general and seven major-generals, besides colonels and majors. For the same period the Communists suffered over 400,000 casualties, including 535 officers above the rank of colonel.

"All this," Chief of Staff General Yeh Chien-ying pointed out to me, "without a single bullet, a single penny or pound of food having been given to us by the National Government since 1940—with one exception: a special shipment of 120 light machine-guns and six antitank guns received through the High Command from the Soviet Union."

The above answers General Lo Tze-kai's much publicized charge that "the Communists have not fought a single battle in the past six years." Four hundred thousand casualties represent almost as many as the total number of troops today (570,000) in the combined Eighth Route and New Fourth armies.

Why are the Communists able to accomplish so much? Principally because of the extraordinary high morale in their ranks, which —according to Vice-Commander-in-Chief Peng Teh-huai—is the result of patient political training.

"The fulfillment of any military plan," he said in an interview, "depends primarily on the courage, self-confidence, fighting power, and esprit de corps of both officers and men. To heighten these qualities is the purpose of the political work in our armies. Mere slogans and posters do not help much. The most important thing is a gradual process of education—to awaken in our officers and soldiers a national consciousness, to acquaint them with the designs and substance of the enemy, and to teach them that the only way to rescue our nation from her present predicament is to resist the invader to the victorious end, and that our national independence and happiness cannot be had for nothing.

"Equally important is the cementing of good relations between officers and men. In the past, in the armies of the warlords, there was no harmony between officers and men. Officers ill-treated their men, scolded and beat them on the slightest provocation, and enforced obedience without reason. Today, it is not sufficient to do away with these evils; it is important to create a positive esprit de corps, to foster an atmosphere of friendship and respect, and to strengthen the spirit of sharing sorrows and happiness, of standing or falling together.

"In our struggle for national emancipation we must rely upon the immense potential of the people. We must organize them, educate and arm them, and lead them in guerrilla warfare. To secure their support we must observe the strictest discipline. Among other rules of conduct, our soldiers must be polite in speech and attitude, they must pay for what they buy, return what they borrow. They must pay for any breakage, clean up any mess they make, and before departing must submit themselves to a disciplinary investigation lest any wrong be unwittingly done to the people."

Once launched on the subject of political work in the Paluchun, heavy-lipped Peng Teh-huai—ordinarily a somewhat taciturn fellow—finds it difficult to stop. It is no new thing with him; this knowledge and conviction have crystallized out of an experience that goes back to the early civil war days, when together with his miserably equipped revolutionary followers he joined with those of Mao Tze-tung, Chu Teh, Ho Lung, and other leaders in a ten-year stand against the overwhelmingly superior forces and arms hurled against the Communists by Chiang Kai-shek and the Kuomintang. It was political faith, and the educational work of the Party, that sustained them on that amazing Long March, a trek rivaled in recorded history only by Napoleon's retreat from Moscow. He had talked about this when I had first met him in his South Shensi headquarters, back in 1937, on the eve of the Japanese attack on Peiping and the outbreak of the war.

"War with Japan can be expected at any moment," he had said then, "but we are ready for it. What we lack in weapons will be balanced by our men's knowledge of what they are fighting for. We are backed also by our tremendous manpower and the resources necessary for what will be a prolonged war of attrition."

Earthy, salty Ho Lung, in offering his explanation for the Communists' unusual military record, was quite unequivocal: "Our boys are not just not afraid of the Japs—that's all!" And Ho Lung ought to know. It was he and his men, whom he led personally, who inflicted the first serious defeat on the mechanized Japanese driving down from Peiping in the early months of the war. The

Japanese had boasted they would conquer China in three months. Contemptuous of the Chinese forces, proud of their own mechanized armament, the Japanese were blasting their way southward from North China, driving the Central Government forces before them like a herd of panicking cattle. Instead of joining the retreating Chinese, Ho Lung drew his civil war veterans to one side and allowed the Japs to go roaring by. In the narrow pass of Pinghsinkwan, Ho Lung, a master of guerrilla strategy, threw a cordon around the main body of the Japanese mechanized parade. Trapped tanks and artillery climbed all over each other in a frantic effort to escape. "We gave them a helluva drubbing," he mused, more to himself than to me. "We actually captured a number of those tanks and armored cars, but we could only destroy them because—well, I've got to admit it—because we didn't know how to drive the damn things. Anyway, we could have done nothing with them. They would have been a nuisance; tanks aren't much use except on level ground, and there's not much level ground in North China. What level ground there is, we can and do easily cut up to make it almost impossible for tanks to get around."

Nor did the Japanese planes have any terrors for Ho Lung and his Long Marchers. They had been bombed and strafed by Chinese planes so often in the ten years of civil war and along the eight thousand miles of their Long March, that the Jap dive-bombers did not scare them. As a matter of fact, Ho Lung boldly attacked the Japanese airdrome at Yangminpao and destroyed thirty planes. "We didn't waste a single precious bullet on the job; we went in with our bayonets and hand grenades and wrecked every plane on the field in addition to the airdrome installations."

Ho Lung's name is a legend throughout North China today. In the civil war days, they called him the "Robin Hood of the Communists." Though before the break in 1927 he was a Kuomintang general, the ruthless arrest of entire multitudes and the Kuomintang massacre of every captive who was even suspected of sympathy with the Communists thoroughly disgusted him and he took the Communists' side in their long struggle for survival. In 1935 he led his 50,000 followers out of Hunan to take part in the Long March. By the time he joined Chu Teh and the main body of the

Communist troops on the Tibetan borders, his numbers had been reduced almost half. In thousands his men had died of starvation and exposure; other thousands died in battle or of their wounds, for they had to fight at every stage of their way. They had barely arrived when I visited Ho Lung and his troops in Shensi. I was in his headquarters on the night of July 7, 1937, when word came through of the Japanese attack at Marco Polo Bridge on the outskirts of Peiping—the famous attack that touched off the powder keg of war in Asia. One might have thought that the General would have wanted nothing more than to rest himself and his men after so terrible a journey. Instead, at a mass meeting called the next morning Ho Lung and his troops declared themselves for war with the Japanese whether or not Chiang Kai-shek and the Kuomintang agreed.

In the seven years that had elapsed since that first meeting, Ho Lung had changed little. He was still the husky, exuberant warrior. He still smoked his underslung pipe, and his mischievous eyes, slit in his handsome, squared features, still mirrored his ever-youthful good humor. He was suffering from some mysterious lung ailment now, but his friends had been unable to persuade him to submit to hospitalization—he was too restless a soul for that. As we talked he paced up and down his stone-floored, mud-walled room with a fly-swatter. A man of little education, he made up for this with a depth of understanding and feeling for the sufferings of his fellow man. Among the common people throughout North China he is perhaps the most popular of all the Communist leaders. Though garrison commander for the Border Region today, his active days are by no means over, and more will be heard of him before the war is over.

When the Red Army was incorporated into the armies of the National Government, Ho Lung led the 115th and 120th divisions into Shansi to take up positions along the Tungpu Railway. He arrived just in time to disrupt the whole Japanese plan of conquest in North China by his scissoring-up of their lines of communications. As a result, the Japanese had to halt their drive southward and turn back to deal with him in their rear. This gave the retreating Nationals a breathing spell, with time enough to dig in and hold a front against the enemy. "My men then were stiffeners for these frightened Kuomintang boys," he says, perhaps a little boastfully. "We used to call them 'guides' for the Japanese, the way they ran and the Japs followed."

Although combat with the Japanese Army is a much more dangerous and difficult matter than the civil war ever was, Ho Lung still devoted considerable attention to organizing the masses wherever his troops operated. "Without the people's help we should never have been able to exist. We know that from our experience in the old days. We sent propaganda corps into the villages ahead of our troops to explain our purpose in coming: The Japs were destroying our country, and we were coming to fight them. We needed the help of the people to do this, their help in defending their own fields and homes against the enemy. If we were willing to dedicate our lives to this defense, was it too much to ask the people for their help and co-operation? Those who had money could contribute money. Those who had strength could contribute labor power, stand sentry duty, provide us with intelligence on the enemy's movements, act as guides, or carry the wounded. Our reasoning with the people before we arrived appealed to them, and our subsequent exemplary conduct caused our reputation to travel ahead of us. Our troops were welcomed wherever we went. They recognized us readily by our characteristic wide-brimmed straw hats."

"Thus were we able to live and fight behind the enemy. Thus have we been able to develop and expand, so that in the passing years we have liberated millions of Chinese from the Japanese yoke and helped them to establish free and democratic anti-Japanese bases strong enough to persist in the face of the enemy's most powerful weapons."

In Yenan at the time were a number of those who had had a personal hand in the establishment and development of these anti-Japanese bases. They were gathered for a conference, to plan for the future. There was, for example, General Nieh Yung-chen, Commander of the forces in the Shansi-Charhar-Hopei Anti-Japanese Base.

15

❖❖❖❖❖❖❖

Chin-Cha-Chi

THE Shansi-Charhar-Hopei Anti-
Japanese Base—popularly called Chin-Cha-Chi—is the largest, rich-
est, and most important of the fifteen semi-autonomous bases.

Chin-Cha-Chi embraces an area stretching from Inner Mongolia
and Manchuria on the north to the Chengtai Railway on the south,
from the Tungpu Railway on the west to the Gulf of Chihli. Of
its total population of 25,000,000, about 18,000,000 are under direct
control of the Chin-Cha-Chi Government. The 7,000,000 under
Japanese control are concentrated mainly in the larger cities such as
Peiping, Tientsin, Taiyuan, and Paoting, which are military strong
points in what the Japanese are pleased to call "Occupied North
China."

The story of Chin-Cha-Chi is the story of Nieh Yung-chen.
Snub-nosed, forty-six-year-old General Nieh, a native of Szechwan,
was sent to France in 1920 under the Worker-Student Plan to study
industrial and chemical engineering at the Université de Travail.
Later he worked at the Creusot Arms Factory and the Renault
Motor Works in Paris. In 1924 he attended a military school in
Moscow, and returned to China in 1925, where he taught at the
famous Whampoa Military Academy. He joined the Northern Military Expedition in its march on Hankow, but with the subsequent
Kuomintang purge of the Communists he joined the Red Army,
first as political advisor to Lin Piao, and later as a divisional commander under Ho Lung.

In October 1937, with the war only a few months old, General Nieh was ordered to take a picked force of 2,000 guerrilla veterans and march eastward into Hopei. Their arms consisted of a total of one thousand rifles.

The Chin-Cha-Chi area at this time was in a state of extreme chaos. The fleeing Central Government troops were joined by all the local government officials and tens of thousands of panic-stricken peasants. Those who remained were too few and too demoralized to harvest the crops standing ripe in the fields. Bandits preyed upon the unarmed villagers, and a handful of Japanese ronins with a Japanese flag could capture almost any sizable town.

In the midst of this prostration, Nieh Yung-chen and his 2,000 arrived and immediately set about bringing order to the region. Political workers calmed the people and persuaded them to comb the battlefields for abandoned weapons with which to arm themselves. With confidence thereby restored, guerrilla brigades were easily formed, besides a supplementary volunteer corps and people's militia. New officials were elected from their own numbers to replace the old appointees who had fled southward.

Three months later, by January 1938, General Nieh had so restored order that it was practicable to call a congress of people's representatives, which should elect a provisional government. The congress was representative of widely different classes. There were in attendance wealthy landlords dressed in formal silk gowns and peasants in their padded cotton suits. Several Mongols and Mohammedans came, and even a red-robed Tibetan lama, to represent their minorities. Many had had to pass through the Japanese lines. Some came from occupied cities. The discussions were conducted in a completely democratic manner upon a basis of equality. The resulting election of officials was by secret ballot. The nine members elected to the Administrative Committee of the Chin-Cha-Chi Border Region were approved in a subsequent telegram from the National Military Council and the Executive Yuan at Chungking, which also sanctioned the establishment of the Chin-Cha-Chi Anti-Japanese Base.

Meanwhile, General Nieh's original nucleus of 2,000 Long Marchers was expanding rapidly as more and more recruits enlisted.

"In the beginning we had no experience fighting an enemy armed with such powerful modern weapons as tanks, artillery, and airplanes," Nieh Yung-chen said as he paced up and down. He was a restless soul, a bundle of nerves. He couldn't sit still for a single moment. To keep his hands busy he danced a child's yo-yo on a string, or doodled with his Parker pen (Parkers are given instead of medals for outstanding achievement in the Communist armies). "On the other hand, the Japanese had never before faced an enemy so expert in guerrilla tactics as we were. To meet our growing threat to their rear they began to move against us with their traditional frontal attacks, using heavy land and air bombardment designed to capture a point we were occupying. When they captured it they thought the battle was over. We, however, had merely evacuated the point in order to swing around and attack their rear. Almost always we forced them to withdraw by cutting their lines of communication with their base."

Extreme mobility was his principal advantage against the Japanese, encumbered as they were with heavy mechanized equipment that was of little use against a foe who refused to engage in positional warfare. And since it takes two to make a fight, the Japs could engage Nieh's guerrillas only when Nieh wanted to fight, and he chose to fight only on his own terms. As an instance of this, General Nieh tells the story of the famous battle of Laiyuan. The Japanese had sent a powerfully armed column of a thousand men to seek out and annihilate Nieh's guerrillas hiding in the mountains.

"We lured them into a big pocket, then hit them unexpectedly, before dawn, and drove them into a small valley. Here we mowed them down with crossfire with such deadly effect that they didn't even have time to unload their artillery from their mules. Unless a few Japs individually escaped in the excitement, there were no enemy survivors. At least, when the battle was over there wasn't a single Jap left alive on the field itself. The artillery made fine trophies, though it took us some time to learn how to use them. When we did, we used them to good purpose against their blockhouses."

Meanwhile, Lieutenant-General Kishiu Abe, enraged at this

ignominious defeat, decided to lead personally another powerful column of a thousand men on a punitive expedition. "As before, we sat in our mountain hideouts and let them walk into our prepared trap. Then we fell upon them, and succeeded in killing General Abe and most of his staff before they knew what hit them. The surviving Japs radioed for assistance. Planes came over and parachuted ten new officers; but we killed most of these, too, in the next day's fighting." A third column of a thousand reinforcements were rushed up. They, too, were allowed to come in; and by the end of that day only 300 of the total 3,000 Japs were able to break out and run for their base.

"We collected many precious rifles, grenade-throwers, and other arms that day," Nieh added with a chuckle. His success fired the people throughout Chin-Cha-Chi and won him literally thousands of recruits. In revenge for General Abe's death the Japanese marshalled a force of 50,000 crack troops and launched an ambitious campaign, intending to encircle the Eighth Routers with an "iron ring" and so to squeeze them from their major base in the Wutai Mountains. It was from these mountains that Nieh's men had descended upon the enemy columns at Laiyuan. The main body of Paluchun troops holding Wutai at the time, incidentally, was the 359th Brigade—Wang Cheng and his men.

Using terror tactics, the Japs burned everything in sight, murdered everyone they could catch. Things were beginning to look black for the defenders. The siege attracted the attention of the world outside and caused the British Government to make enquiries concerning Nieh's chances. Hankow had already fallen, and the Japs, who had long been boasting that the Chinese could not fight positional battles, now began to claim that the Chinese were also a failure at guerrilla tactics.

In celebrating the destruction of the Wutai defenders, as they did, the Japs were too hasty. The guerrillas, who had waited for the proper moment, oozed through the tightening "iron ring" to re-form in the enemy's rear. This done, they struck hard and brought confusion upon the Japs. Disgusted, the Japs were forced to abandon the whole campaign as an expensive failure.

Now thoroughly aroused, the Japanese at last took General

Nieh's force for what it really was: a threat to their entire position in North China. They assigned one of their ablest tacticians to make an exhaustive study of Nieh's guerrilla tactics. By 1940 he had worked out what he called "widespread dispersal" and "silkworm" tactics. A network of key strongpoints, well-fortified with blockhouses, trenches, and barbed wire, was spread over the area. Then began their "silkworm" nibbling, the gradual expansion of their network, with the inclusion of more and more strong points, spaced closer and closer together. In this way the Japanese expected to reduce the areas in which the Paluchun guerrillas might move and support themselves.

The Paluchun, under the direction of Commander-in-Chief Chu Teh, thereupon challenged the Japanese with a bold general counteroffensive—the famous Hundred Regiments Campaign waged from August to mid-September 1940. First they attacked the railways and highways to disrupt and break up the enemy's communications. Then they went to work on the more isolated strong points and blockhouses. With captured Japanese artillery they began systematically to destroy them, one by one. Alarmed, the Japanese were forced to withdraw from their outposts and concentrate along the railways and highways. They built newer and more formidable strong points along these traffic lines. The new blockhouses, designed and tested for resistance to their own field pieces, were now two stories high, with a deep cellar from which to continue fighting, should the blockhouse itself be destroyed. These miniature forts were further reinforced with double lines of deep, wide trenches, several rows of barbed wire, and log-buttressed firing pits.

"We found from captured documents that the Japanese were getting ready to precipitate war in the Pacific, and were planning to prepare North China as a vast military depot for manpower and resources," Nieh continued. "We were not surprised, then, when they became impatient with 'silkworm' tactics and decided on a major campaign to rid North China of the Paluchun once and for all. They brought in a powerful force of something like 70,000 Japanese and 30,000 puppets. Having carried out a huge encirclement of the whole of the Peiyao region, they again began to contract toward the Wutai Mountains in the center. After victory they

planned to descend into the plains and destroy the last fires of resistance so that they might then give their full attention to the coming war with America and Great Britain.

"But once more they failed," General Nieh said animatedly. "In
their fury they destroyed anything and everything in sight, in an
effort to make it impossible for either people or Paluchun to exist.
This was what they called 'draining water' tactics. The fish cannot
live when the sea is empty."

Empty-handed, the Japanese retired to their strong points again.
In their press they admitted their failure, saying: "The Japanese
Army is like a ferocious lion that has not been able to catch the
cowardly mouse."

When the Pacific War had been launched, the Japs returned
once more to their "silkworm" tactics. Literally thousands of new
blockhouses and strong points were built, spaced half a mile to
two miles apart. "They made a forest of forts in the Hopei plains,"
General Nieh declared.

"But we stayed right there, operating in the spaces between the
fortresses, though seriously hampered in our movements. When
they closed in, we moved out; when they stuck out their heads, we
chopped off their tails. It was a losing game for us, however; and
steadily the enemy was able to squeeze us from more and more
territory. The Japs rounded up the people and made them build a
network of roads for their tanks and armored cars. We in turn mobilized the people to destroy these again by night. Next day the
Japs would come and make the people repair what we had destroyed. It was a hard burden for the people to bear and left them
little time for farming. It became necessary to find other measures
to meet this threat. It seemed indeed that the Japs were fast suc-
ceeding in their occupation of North China's fertile populated
plains. Well, we decided to start with the people; to organize, arm,
and help them to help themselves. This is always the point to
which a guerrilla commander must come back. We taught them
how to make land-mines and hand grenades. We taught them how
to shoot, how to destroy the enemy's communications, how to defend their homes and fields. We taught them new techniques—the
techniques of tunnel warfare, mine warfare, ditch warfare, sparrow

warfare, and a dozen other ways to fight the enemy whenever he emerged from his strong points and blockhouses. And we were successful beyond our most optimistic expectations. The people had come to realize they had nothing more to fear from the Jap—he had already done his worst—and they decided to fight back. Again the Jap retaliated with vicious punitive expeditions; but when his casualties began to mount alarmingly he recoiled, as if stung, to his strong points. And because he could not spare the necessary reinforcements for large-scale operations, with troops needed more urgently elsewhere in the Pacific, he soon found himself pinned to his blockhouses.

"Then our expanding Paluchun once again donned their uniforms, picked up their weapons, and passed from the defensive to the offensive. Today, we have already recovered from the Japanese more territory than the Chin-Cha-Chi base possessed at the outbreak of the Pacific War. And we are still on the offensive against the enemy."

It sounded like big talk. But I was to see later what he meant when I went up to the front—the front behind the enemy's lines. However, I had still some weeks to spend in Yenan and the Border Region before I could start for the front. I would see much of the People's War up there, I was promised. Meanwhile, I wanted to hear more of its origins, its problems, its development. So General Nieh introduced me to two political workers recently arrived from Hopei.

"They've had their teeth and hands in this work almost from the very beginning," he said, "and they can give you the details and inner workings to fill out what I've already outlined." They did, wonderfully.

16

◆◆◆◆◆◆◆◆

Underground Warfare

WANG TUNG-KEH and Chao Fang looked like father and son, though they were not related. There was nothing extraordinary about them, either physically or mentally. They were just plain peasants, but typical of the brave millions of North China.

Wang was a leader of the People's Armed Forces in his local hsien in Central Hopei; Chao was a member of the Youth Vanguards in the vicinity of Jap-occupied Paoting, also in Central Hopei.

Hour after hour, day after day—for almost a full fortnight—I sat and listened to Wang and Chao talk of the People's War in Chin-Cha-Chi. First one would talk, then the other. Sometimes they would get excited and talk volubly, and at the same time. And all through it I sat spellbound, fascinated by their tales. They talked and talked, and I let them race on according to their own inclinations, only rarely interrupting with a question. It is their voices I remember now, when I think of the war in North China. Its history for me will always be told by two peasant voices.

From the very beginning their job had been to develop and coordinate the peasants' individual efforts in the People's War. Trained by the Paluchun—which had picked leader-types in every community for this work—they in turn organized Self-Defense Corps units in the villages surrounding their own homes. The people, long used to handling explosives in the making of firecrackers, were making crude mines of earthenware jugs, teapots, bottles, and tin cans packed with black powder and detonated by a simple fuse. Wang and Chao and scores of others trained by the Paluchun taught them how to improve their mines by using heavy metal containers made from melted temple bells. The villagers were shown improved methods for planting and camouflaging mines as well as precautionary methods very necessary in the handling of these improved weapons. Most important, they were persuaded to defy the Japanese threat to massacre the inhabitants of every village suspected of laying mines inside the area. And when it was observed that the Japs on the march gave a wide berth to the mined villages, the word spread far and wide. Today, the approaches to thousands of villages are heavily mined. The pathways, the creeks, even the crops themselves are cunningly sown with explosives so that in many places the Japs dare no longer carelessly touch even an innocent pumpkin, for pumpkins have been known to explode when picked up.

In some districts mine warfare has been developed to a fine art. Mine fields are laid at strategic points along the highway. From each mine in the field a string runs through an underground system of brick tubes to a primitive "switchboard" in a farmhouse or other observation post near by. As an enemy column moves into the mine field the operator calmly pulls this or that string on the "switchboard." The mines explode like lights in a pinball machine as the bewildered enemy dashes back and forth in an effort to extricate himself from the field.

Innumerable booby traps litter the countryside: leaping mines, delayed mines, upside-down mines. The last is merely an ordinary mine left partly exposed, as if the mine-layer had been interrupted and had fled before he could camouflage it successfully. Jap engineers carefully pick up the mine, and as they turn it over for examination a tiny vial of sulphuric acid inside is spilled and the mine explodes in their hands. Nowadays, the Japs do not dare to touch any mines without the most elaborate precaution. And even their magnetic mine-detectors fail to detect mines made of painstakingly hollowed-out rocks, set innocently by the roadside.

With time and success the villagers have grown bolder. Today they provoke and insult the Japanese with slogans painted on flags or hung on scarecrows in the fields. When many of these exploded as the enemy tried to pull them down, he swallowed his pride and decided to ignore them. Whereupon, such slogans multiplied by the thousands—few of them actually mined, of course.

Anything within sight is likely to be mined. And in some districts almost everything is. A basket left in the middle of the road, a plowshare in the field, a paper-wrapped parcel by the wayside—all these things may be mined. A road rut is dug out, a mine is carefully buried, and an old auto tire is rolled lightly over the dusty surface. After a few Jap trucks are blown up in this way, Jap drivers will bump along the surfaces between the ruts—which are also mined. Even children make a grim sport from mine warfare by obstructing the road with small mounds that resemble ill-hidden mines. A Jap truckdriver, spying the mound, warily detours into a muddy field while the youngsters from their observation point stifle their laughter. Often, should the truck bog down, guerrilla snipers suddenly appear to pump bullets and shower grenades.

"Our most popular mine hero in Chin-Cha-Chi is young Li Yung," said Wang. "Would you like to hear something about him?"

"Yes, of course."

"Well, Li Yung is the inspiration of mine-fighters throughout North China. He's just a youngster—still in his twenties—but what he doesn't know about mine warfare isn't worth talking about. Last winter during the three months' mopping-up campaign which the Japanese launched against the Peiyao district, Li Yung with the little group under his command killed and wounded 364 Japs and puppets and blew up five trucks.

"One of Li Yung's favorite tactics was to lure the Japanese into prepared traps. Contemptuous of the big price the Japs had placed upon his head he would, in suitable conditions, reveal himself to an advancing column.

" 'Hey! This is Li Yung,' he would shout. 'Follow me if you dare!'

"In their eagerness to pursue him, the Japs would forget their caution and run into mine-traps over which Li Yung had stepped.

Sometimes he would lay a pattern of mines in the path of an advancing enemy column. When they reached a certain point he would fire a clip of shells at the leaders, forcing them to scatter to the sides of the trail into his prepared mine-traps.

Periodically, the Japs drove cattle or captive villagers through mine fields to detonate mines. The villagers prepared for such contingencies with string-pull mines. Wang told me that it was the villagers' practice to wait until the cattle or the captives had passed safely through the field, and then to explode the mines under the Japs who were following.

"When the Japs are determined to crash through the mine fields at all costs, they are often—very often—met at the village gates by blasts from our wooden cannon," Chao Fang began.

I held up a hand. I wasn't quite sure I had heard him aright.

"Now wait a minute. . . . Wooden cannon, did you say?"

"Why, yes." Young Chao paused a moment. "Oh, of course—the wooden cannon is something new to you. *We* take it for granted, you know."

So Chao described this weapon. A hardwood log, usually about ten feet long, is bored to make a barrel, which is sometimes lined with metal. The outside is tightly wound with stolen Japanese telephone wire to keep it from blowing apart. The charge, weighing anything from five pounds up, is made of broken pots and pans, glass, stones—any tough and sharp scrap material at hand. A hole is cut into the side of a house with the camouflaged muzzle opening flush with the outside wall facing the village gate. An officer watches from a peephole or the rooftop and, when the enemy reaches a given point such as the village gate, orders the crew to fire. The Japs have a superstitious fear of these wooden cannon, since the unorthodox charge, even when it does not kill, makes ugly wounds.

When the Japs carried their attack past the cannon and drove into the village, they would stumble over innumerable booby traps in the streets, in the alleyways, in the houses they tried to enter. They would be grenaded from every rooftop and shot at from every doorway or window. Then there would suddenly come a mysterious lull, and the villagers would seem to disappear completely.

"Then began a new type of warfare—tunnel warfare." And old Wang rolled up his sleeves, took a sip of hot tea, and motioned young Chao to silence. Wang was a specialist in subterranean warfare.

In the early days of the war the villagers dug cellars under their houses, in which to hide from the enemy. The Japs easily found these and rooted out the people, raping, torturing, murdering at will. The villagers then connected their cellars, until a whole village would become a veritable warren of tunnels. But when the Jap came again he would surround the village and make a careful search for every tunnel entrance, driving the people to the surface with fire, smoke, and water. Some of the villages then held council and decided to connect each village's tunnel system with that of the next. It was a staggering undertaking; but if it would save them from slaughter by the Japanese it would be well worth while.

So there exists in Central Hopei today an amazing system of tunnels linking hundreds of villages for miles and miles around, built on a scale that makes New York's subway system seem a child's toy railway by comparison. The tunnels are big enough to house the people together with their livestock and their possessions and are equipped with sufficient food and water for an extended siege.

When the Japs discovered that the tunnels ran in straight lines from one village to the next, they dug deep lateral trenches in the fields so as to cut through and expose these tunnels. Thus they were able to isolate one village from its neighbors.

At Peitan, about thirty miles south of Paoting on the Peiping-Hankow Railway, the Japanese decided to teach the tunnel-fighters a lesson they would remember. Sectioning off a half-mile of tunnel, they pumped gas into both ends, asphyxiating 800 villagers. Undaunted, the Central Hopei villagers devised new tunnel designs. Tunnels were built zigzag, and up and down; they connected, through emergency entrances, with wholly independent subsidiary tunnel systems at different levels going off in all directions. All the entrances were furnished with simple antigas devices, and provision was made to wall up and section off any portion of a tunnel system entered or exposed by the enemy.

Now, when the Japs were able to force their way into the opening shafts they ran into innumerable traps. Crawling single file through a narrow tunnel opening, a Jap might well set off a hidden mine, or be trapdoored into a spiked pit, or have his head lopped off by a village husky wielding a big sword. Sometimes a whole party would be lured into a chamber and a partition would be dropped behind them, trapping them. Then strings would be pulled and mines would go off or a grenade would be tossed into the confined space.

"Look here," I interrupted. "Perhaps I'd better not write about these things. The Japs might get hold of this information, and it might not be so good for your friends in Chin-Cha-Chi."

Old Wang snorted. "Pu yao *chin*—it doesn't matter. It wouldn't do them any good anyway. Besides, we have actually scores of different types of tunnel systems, and hundreds of different kinds of booby traps. So, go ahead and write about anything we tell you."

He paused for a moment while I slipped a fresh sheet of paper into my typewriter. I asked him if he'd ever seen a typewriter before. He shook his head. "I'm only a country bumpkin. I know nothing of such modern marvels." As an afterthought he added, "Though I do know something about fighting Japs."

He wasn't boasting. He just didn't think too much of that accomplishment. Anyone with ordinary brains could fight the Jap— this was what he was trying to say.

The tunnels were a challenge to the Japs, and they tried in countless ways to force an entrance into the tunnels, or to drive the villagers to the surface. Captive villagers would be sent down at the point of a bayonet to detonate hidden mines. But watchers below learned to provide for this with safety gadgets on the mines, to be released by remote control when the Japs followed the captives. If puppets were forced down behind captives they, too, were spared on condition of surrendering their rifles. The defenders had an understanding about this: in the less developed tunnel openings the watchers at the bottom could tell friend from foe by the footwear of the one coming down—a bare or a rope-sandaled foot meant a captive villager or a puppet, while a leather shoe could denote only a Jap.

Since every bit of food, every bit of fuel, everything of possible value was taken underground, the Japanese found little comfort in burning the houses. Moreover, they dared not remain long away from their strong points, since at any moment there might be a sudden concentration of Paluchun regulars, or the ubiquitous guerrillas might appear. (Thousands of Paluchun in the populous areas of Central Hopei live in the tunnels by day, and come out to attack the near-by Jap strong points by night.)

The Japs tried tying a canister of gas to a pig's tail, then pouring kerosene on its back; they would then set this afire, sending the screaming pig down a tunnel ramp. But the villagers merely built water traps across the tunnel floor, drowning the pig and neutralizing the gas. Of course, every such countermeasure was devised only after the Japs tried some new and devilish trick which often took its toll of lives before a countermeasure was found.

Once the Japs tried a Hollywood stunt to lay siege to the tunnels in one district. They brought with them a phonograph with a loud speaker operated by a suicide squad playing sound-effects records of trucks passing to and fro, to suggest to the villagers underground that their village was still under occupation with considerable military traffic overhead. After a few days the villagers noted a queerness in the sound of moving vehicles without the attendant vibrations which should have been felt in the tunnels. Surfacing, the villagers discovered the trick, captured the Japs, and now use the phonograph for village entertainments.

"Suppose I tell you," suggested Wang, "of the battle at Tachuti village. It was typical of scores of such battles the villagers have been fighting in the never-ending People's War."

"By all means, yes," I said eagerly.

17

◇◇◇◇◇◇◇

The Battle of Tachuti

O LD WANG lighted a cigarette, took a sip of his scalding tea, and began.

"The villagers in Kaoyang hsien, about thirty miles from the Hopei provincial capital of Paoting, had become especially defiant of the Japanese after they had perfected their tunnel and other defenses. The Japs, deciding to put an end to this, sent a strong punitive expedition under the command of a brigade commander, Shangban. [Old Wang didn't know his Japanese name; Shangban, he explained, was the Chinese pronunciation of the two Chinese characters the Japanese commander used to write his name.]

"Shangban first established his headquarters in the occupied city of Kaoyang, the county seat. Then, one day, with a force of 300 men, he started for the village of Tachuti, about six miles from Kaoyang. The villagers prepared for the attack by mobilizing their militia force—about 200 strong—while the rest of the village's 400 families were turned over to the tunnel command.

"The militia commander then inspected the village defenses. There were two wooden cannons trained on each of the four entrances to the low mud wall surrounding the village. All roads and trails leading in were mined. The streets were mined and booby traps set. When he was satisfied that all was in readiness, the militia commander took up his post on the roof of the highest building to direct the battle. He used a gong for giving commands. One beat on the gong meant 'emergency at the north gate'; two for the south; three for the east; and four for the west. He gave orders that the cannons were not to fire until the Japs were within at least fifty yards.

"Shangban approached the village warily, suspicious of the silence. He deployed his men to surround the village and then, after some hesitation, he gave the order to charge all gates simultaneously. The militia commander beat his gong. Mines detonated—cannons went off—grenades showered. It was one big explosion! When the smoke cleared, Shangban had retreated in dismay, leaving behind dozens of corpses."

Old Wang lit another cigarette. "We thought at first we'd gotten Shangban himself, but we were disappointed to find it was one of his officers we'd killed."

" 'We,' did you say? Were you in that battle?" I asked.

"Oh, I guess I forgot to mention that, didn't I?" He smiled, embarrassedly—he hadn't thought it important. "Yes, I just happened to be there—I was the political director for that district, you see."

Shangban, angered and afraid, gathered the remnants of his repulsed force and sent out a rush call for reinforcements. He was determined to annihilate this village and so wipe out his disgrace. When the reinforcements came, bringing artillery with them, he circled the village looking for a likely place to set up his guns. The village cemetery on a little height safely outside the north gate appeared to be the best spot.

"But we had mined that cemetery for just such an eventuality," Wang chuckled. "Shangban got madder still when he saw anti-Japanese slogans on the fence posts, and he ordered them torn down immediately. When a guard stepped forward, the first fence post he touched blew up in his hands, killing him and two others. But Shangban must have borne a charmed life—he was only knocked down."

If Shangban had been angry before, by now he was enraged. He set up his cannon and ordered a barrage of tear and gas shells to be laid on the village.

"But we had had some experience with this gas before, and we'd found that garlic and cold water considerably lessened its effect on us. However, when the gas got to be too much for a militiaman, we sent him down into the tunnels and a tunnel guard came up to take his place."

In the meantime, news of the battle had been signaled to all the surrounding villages. Wuniu, two miles away, sent its militiamen up through the tunnels; the militiamen from Shaowan and Nanchi also came. And when a strong unit of full-time guerrillas appeared suddenly to attack Shangban in his rear, the Japs took to their heels. "We captured more than a hundred rifles from this battle," old Wang said with satisfaction. "But the steel helmets we gathered from the field afterward were not distributed for use as cooking kettles, as in the old days—we turned them over to the guerrillas for use in their 'sparrow warfare.'"

After the battle the villagers held a meeting. It was decided that the Japs would be sure to return, if only to recover their dead, whose souls would not rest easily if the bodies were not properly buried or cremated. So the corpses were loaded into carts and sent to a point about a mile from Kaoyang, where they were piled neatly by the side of the road. A flag fluttering from the top of the pile was inscribed: "Don't come back if you want to live. We've been polite this time and sent your dead back to you. Next time we'll feed them to the dogs." Then, to soften the effect of this, another flag beside it read: "You soldiers are also farmers and workers back home. Why do you fight us? We wish you no harm. We want only to live in peace, with you and all the world."

Shangban marched his men out of Kaoyang and silently collected his dead. Soon afterward he was transferred from that district, and Tachuti was never attacked again.

For several minutes Chao Fang had been trying to interrupt—ever since Wang's mention of "sparrow warfare." Now, as Wang paused for another sip of tea, Chao Fang began eagerly to tell me about his friend Wang Ming, whose father had been killed in the Peitan tunnel gas attack. The surviving relatives of the Peitan victims had formed the "White Suit Corps" (white being used for mourning), a special group of guerrillas sworn to vengeance on the Japs, and Wang Ming was a member of the corps. One day he discovered the identity of one of the traitors who had betrayed the secret of the Peitan tunnel system to the Japanese. The traitor lived in a walled compound close to a Japanese strong point. Undaunted, Wang Ming sneaked into the traitor's house one night and took him prisoner at the point of a pistol. The traitor was brought before the hsien government for trial, condemned, and shot. Unfortunately, shortly after this, Wang Ming was apprehended by the Japs; knowing that he was in for a bad time, he slipped his bonds, by a desperate effort, jumped his jailor, and grabbed the guard's rifle and bayoneted him. The dawn was just breaking and he was discovered as he fled to a rooftop near by. Surrounded, he fought bravely until noon, killing many of the Japs and puppets below, before using his last bullet to commit suicide.

The "White Suit Corps" continued to harass the enemy like a swarm of angry hornets. A type of warfare they initiated became very popular. This was "sparrow warfare." Like sparrows they were everywhere, picking off a Jap here and a puppet there. A straggler behind a column of Japs on the march would be quietly dispatched by a knife in the hand of an innocent-looking *lao-paishing* walking down the road. A handful of shots fired from ambush would kill two and wound three, the ambushers then scattering so as to afford no target for revenge.

A refinement of sparrow warfare is segmented-worm warfare. An ambush is laid, and when the Japs recover from the first shock they start chasing the ambushers down the road. Unobserved, the ambushers drop a few men in each village they pass through. Soon the pursuing Japs discover that they are chasing the wind, though the people in each village have convincingly told them, "They've just passed through, headed *that* way." More than that, on their return they may well be ambushed again by the collected segments; and so the game keeps up until the Japs get wise and quit taking the bait.

Often the partisans disguise themselves as Japs or puppets, and boldly march down the highway. Sometimes a group of a dozen or more will do this, primarily to observe and deceive the Japs in their blockhouses. At times as many as a hundred or more may form such a disguised company, eighty in puppet uniforms, twenty in Jap—the usual proportion. They march for miles, picking up all Japs and puppets they meet on the road. The frightened puppets usually make no trouble. The Japs are quickly disarmed, stripped, gagged, and dressed in *laopaishing* dress, as if they were prisoners. Meanwhile, other partisans line the highway in hiding prepared to support this column should it suddenly meet a strong enemy force. The purpose of this trick is to intercept messengers bearing documents, to seize important puppets traveling from place to place, to capture goods in transit, and to collect weapons, ammunition, and medicines—all at a minimum cost. Such disguised partisans have secret signs which they give to identify themselves so that they may not be attacked by their own people—a rifle periodically raised three times into the air, for example.

"I was with one such company," Chao said, "when we met a string of carts coming down the road. We stopped them. They proved to be a puppet magistrate traveling with a lot of valuable cargo and protected by an escort of thirty Japs and puppets. Seeing our Jap flag, the magistrate got down from his cart and began to kowtow. He was going to Pochun, he said, on official business. We said we'd like to inspect his goods. At this, the escort got suspicious. A fight developed, but the escort soon fled down the road. Before reinforcements could come up we had looted the cargo and dispersed."

A simple, old-as-the-hills ruse that worked well for quite a while was this one. A party of disguised partisans would appear before a Jap strong point, escorting bound captives, allegedly Paluchun men. The unsuspecting Japs would let them in, and immediately be wiped out and the blockhouse destroyed. There was a time when the Japs often took this particular leaf from the villagers' book, disguising themselves as Eighth Routers in order to ferret out Paluchun sympathizers in the villages. It never worked, however, for the villagers spotted them quickly, and hugely enjoyed themselves hurling abuse or throwing stones at the "unwelcome Paluchun."

When the Japs discovered that village fighters rarely attacked the puppets, saving their mines and precious bullets for the *Jih*

Pen kwei tze—the Japanese devils—they tried exchanging uniforms with the puppets. But as these "puppets" marched through a village the people would ask them if they wanted a drink of water —and of course the "puppets" would be immediately identified as Japs, whether they replied or not. In addition, the real puppets— being dressed in the dangerous Japanese uniform—had to declare their own nationality.

"If the column was off at a distance, how were you able to spot the fact that the uniforms had been exchanged?"

"Easily—the Jap can never disguise his waddling, bowlegged gait."

To deceive the everwatchful villagers, as to their numbers, Chao said, the Japs frequently sent trucks to run the gantlet of road mines with blockhouse "reinforcements." A passing truck would seem to be loaded with men, though there might only be half a dozen living figures in it—the rest would be rubber dummies. When the truck reached the blockhouse the balloon soldiers were secretly deflated and the empty truck was sent back through the villages, having dropped its "reinforcements." The villagers, Chao told me, were highly amused by this childish trick, and frequently some sharpshooter contemptuously wasted a precious bullet on the dummy soldiers.

The Japs also used wooden cannon. These were dummies, however. Covered with tarpaulins they were hauled around to delude the Paluchun's intelligence service into overestimating the Japanese armament. These dummy cannon would often be dragged into battle and set up beside real guns. Boxes and crates, filled with pebbles and stones and prominently marked AMMUNITION were often ostentatiously moved from place to place.

Psychological or nerve warfare, both Wang and Chao said, was being waged on a grand scale by the North China villagers, and was proving tremendously successful. One of the quite unfailing devices was to spread false rumors of Paluchun movements— rumors reinforced by the imparting of "confidential information" to known spies. For example, a Japanese agent would be told that secret orders had been received to prepare stores of food in order to provision the (mythical) Paluchun concentrations; and sometimes the villagers would support the fiction with elaborate pretenses. Then the Japanese local officers would put in urgent requests for reinforcements, thus confusing their superiors into diverting troops from one point to another. When the Jap reinforcements arrived, they would rush about here and there in search of the Paluchun, with the villagers soberly leading them on: "They've just left here." "They've gone this way." "They've gone that way." A power like Japan which employs traitors and puppets is particularly vulnerable to this form of warmaking.

Meanwhile, to keep up the fictitious threat, the villagers would blow bugles, don clothes that from a distance looked like Paluchun uniforms, and march up and down with their shotguns and blunderbusses on their shoulders—convincing the worried Japs, watching them through their binoculars, that the Paluchun were really gathering in force.

At night, particularly, the war of nerves was waged with notable success, with literally thousands of Japanese strong points and blockhouses being besieged by the villagers. There might be perhaps no more than a handful of them attacking out there in the dark—but the Japs could not be sure of this, and so preferred to remain inside their fortified shelters. Sometimes the attackers would set off strings of firecrackers, accompanied by a few rifle shots to convince the Japs they were being subjected to real fire. Often the Japs would answer with a furious fusillade, firing blindly into the night. When their firing died down, a few more of the real shots would touch off a repetition of the display. Or a few dogs might be tossed into the moat surrounding the blockhouse. Their floundering about, their efforts to scale the slippery walls, would suggest an attacking party storming the blockhouse, and the worried Japs would open fire. With the dawn, the nerve-strained Japs might discover the trick and so would come to ignore it in time—whereupon the guerrilla commandos would steal up and really attack the place and inflict losses before melting away.

Often the people would co-operate actively with the Paluchun regulars in attacking larger strong points. One place, which had been besieged for twenty-eight days, was finally taken after the villagers, who had first carefully mined all the highway approaches to prevent the arrival of reinforcements, collected dogs for miles about, slaughtered them, and laid their carcasses all around the fortress. In the blistering summer sun the carcasses quickly decayed, enveloping the strong point with such an overpowering stench that the Japs were eventually forced to abandon their fortress and fight their way through the encirclement, suffering heavy casualties.

"And now how would you like to hear something about our naval warfare?" Old Wang looked perfectly serious.

"You mean *water* warfare?"

"Yes—war on the water."

"Fine. Let's have it!"

"Well, it was this way. . . ."

In September 1943 the Japanese army headquarters in Peiping issued an order forbidding the villagers in the Peiyangtien Lake area—about fifty miles south of Peiping—to shoot any more of the wild ducks which yearly flock there in great numbers. When the villagers refused to heed the order, the Japanese sent a fleet of specially constructed motorboats and steam launches to police the shallow marshlike lake.

For their duck-hunting the villagers had developed "big shoulder-fire guns"—ten-foot tubular weapons operated like a bazooka and firing a scattering charge of about a pound of scrap metal. These were now pressed into military service. Hidden in the lake-shore's tall reeds, the villagers would pot away at the passing motor-boats. After some thirty of these had been sunk or badly damaged, the Japs got mad. In the middle of the lake they built a huge fortified raft—a veritable battleship—bristling with machine-guns and deck cannon. Watchers in crow's nests atop the tall masts scanned the shores with powerful binoculars. When the slightest movement was detected in the reeds, machine-guns and cannon opened fire; or, if the range was too great, then one of a fleet of armored launches standing by was immediately dispatched to investigate.

With the Japs' adoption of these tactics, the bazooka-sniping lakemen came out only at night. The battleship's searchlights then tried in vain to find them in the reeds, while charges of old nails, of scrap from broken kettles, pots, and pans, from rusted tools, plowshares and such, continued to sweep the battleship's decks or rattle fiercely against its sides. When the crops in the fields adjacent were harvested, thousands of villagers gathered one night and quietly opened the dykes, allowing the lake water to spill into the fields. With the dawn the Japanese observed with horror that the water-level had dropped alarmingly. Hurriedly they stripped the battleship of guns and equipment and escaped by launch through the lake's outlet toward Tientsin lest they be left high and dry. Before they left they set fire to the battleship, the spectacle being viewed by thousands of gleeful villagers. They lined the shores shouting, dancing, and clapping their hands like pleased children. When the dykes were repaired, the lake filled up, the ducks returned, and the villagers were once again free to use their home-made bazookas for duck-hunting.

18

The Hopei Amazons

TANG CHENG-KUO is only twenty-five, but she is the director of 1,500 amazons in the Women's Self-Defense Corps of Nankuo hsien in Chin-Cha-Chi. She had been called to Yenan for special political training, so that I was able to have long talks with her about the activities of her Central Hopei amazons.

There was nothing hard about Tang Cheng-kuo. She was a smallish girl with a shock of bobbed hair framing a triangular face, with regular teeth and steady brown eyes. Dressed simply in tunic and trousers—faded but clean, with her sleeves rolled and a portrait of Mao Tze-tung on a tiny celluloid badge pinned over her heart, she spoke quietly, in crisp, almost military accents. She was a very self-possessed young woman.

"Only about 800 of our girls are what you might call fighters," she said. "They are recruited from the unmarried or childless women in our villages, between the ages of eighteen and twenty-five. We are armed, trained in the use of rifle, grenade, and mine, and given a knowledge of military tactics. Sometimes we engage the enemy alone as a unit, but mostly we work in co-ordination with the guerrillas and the Paluchun regulars."

The older women were trained in intelligence activities, taught how to take care of the wounded, and given courses in what might be called the household duties of an army. During battle

154

they were stretcher-bearers and food and ammunition porters, and upon occasion they fought.

Nor were Tang Cheng-kuo's amazons the only ones in Chin-Cha-Chi—there were thousands more like them organized in local units having little connection with one another. These groups were not, of course, regarded as mobile units, their work being principally to defend their villages and their homes. During quiet periods they stood sentry at village entrances or guarded road crossings, checking the credentials of all passers-by. On the arrival of Japs, the girls joined with the guerrillas, the militiamen, and the regulars in giving battle. They ambushed Jap transport, sniped at Jap columns, grenaded them from walls and rooftops when the enemy entered the villages.

She continued briskly, with gestures of her very expressive hands. "Every year, usually around March 8th—International Women's Day—we hold general maneuvers. The girls gather from all the hsien villages, bringing their weapons and enough food for ten days. The meeting place is secret, of course, and is changed from year to year. The last meeting over which I presided before coming to Yenan was held within four miles of the nearest enemy strong point and only ten miles from the Peiping-Hankow Railway.

"We try usually to work out some practical problem. On this occasion our problem was to destroy communications between the Jap strong points at Peilu and Ankuo, about two miles apart. And, if need be, we were to be prepared to fight, too. First I sent out scouts to find out how many Japs there were in each of the strong points. This information they got from the villagers near by. The scouts went out in pairs, one staying on watch while the other returned with a report."

I offered her a cigarette. She refused it. "I never smoke," she said smilingly—and I suspected that what she really meant was, "I have no time or thought for such things." Then she went on with her story.

"Before giving them their orders, I drew them up at attention and told them that the operation was to be entirely voluntary. All but five of the 432 present immediately raised their hands. The five who didn't had mild temporary ailments and offered to do the cooking for the battalion. I drew up a plan. First I detailed twenty-five girls to watch each of the twin strong points." She went on with a long and exact description of the strong points. Located just outside the village, each consisted of several block-houses with a high wall surrounding the compound. The top of the wall was covered with broken glass and barbed wire. Outside the wall was a broad moat, wider at the bottom than the top, so that it was easy to leap into but very hard to climb out of be-cause of the overhanging sides. These two strong points were each manned by sixty Japanese and an equal number of puppets, the two groups living in separate quarters within the compound.

The highway between these strong points was bordered by deep, wide ditches, and no paths or roads were allowed to cross it, ex-cept within range of the defenders' guns. The road itself was raised three feet above the fields, in which it was forbidden to grow high crops such as kaoliang or corn, since these might afford cover for lurking guerrillas. The garrisons obtained their food, fuel, and labor from neighboring villages without payment; sometimes girls were demanded. The villagers were under orders to report daily, particularly on the appearance or presence of any Eighth Routers, and were constantly threatened with the massacre of all inhabitants should they fail to report truthfully. These conditions, of course, obtained only for villages directly under the Japanese guns.

Having described the two miniature fortresses, Tang Cheng-kuo continued her story: "With my sentries posted to warn us should the enemy come out from his strong points, I then divided my girls into squads of about a dozen each and gave them their as-signments. Some squads were to fell the telephone poles; others were to roll up the wire and carry it off—the army pays us well for telephone wire, you know. Others were set to digging ditches across the highway, while still others planted mines to trap re-inforcements, which could be expected as soon as it should be dis-covered that communications had been cut.

"When we had finished our night's work, we crept up to the two strong points and set off firecrackers and threw grenades over the wall. The Japs raised quite a racket with their machine-gun fire, but they were firing mostly because they were scared."

The girls spent the next morning celebrating their success; and, as they were preparing to scatter to their villages, word came of the arrival of a battalion of Paluchun. When the battalion commander heard what the girls had done, he at once decided to ambush the Japanese, who would be sure to emerge from shelter in order to repair the damage of the night before.

"I asked the commander if we might join him. He said there were too many of us—we would only be in the way; but that he could let fifty go along. So we drew lots, and the fifty lucky ones stripped of all papers or other identifying articles that might give information if we were killed or captured—information that might be used punitively against our native villages. Then we were assigned a position behind some grave mounds not far from the highway. With the commander, I had devised a scheme that proved to work wonderfully. A column of Japs at last came down the road. We waited until they were quite near—then we threw our grenades, screamed, and dashed into the fields. The Japs let out exultant whoops and started chasing us, hoping to catch us alive—and ran right into the machine-guns of our waiting Paluchun. Twenty-one Japs were killed before the detachment could recover and run for all they were worth to the protection of the Peilu strong point."

At a meeting held after the battle, the commander praised the girls for their bravery under fire and awarded each participant four hand grenades. The people in the vicinity assembled and heaped presents on them—fruit, peanuts, and rural delicacies. The Japs pulled up their drawbridges and stayed inside their strong points for three days afterward.

But, Miss Tang told me, such tasks and operations as these were not the only ones the girls undertook. They helped in other ways that were perhaps less militant but certainly just as necessary. In the neighborhood of a blockhouse system the Japs often combined in a day or a night raid upon a village, with the intention of capturing Paluchun or political "transients." It was not always possible, in the vicinity of strong points, to construct a tunnel defense, so that other means must be found of dealing with such emergencies. Nowadays, whenever such a visitor arrived in a village he immediately reported to the local leaders, who assigned him to a family, of which he was thenceforth considered a member, with "relatives" in the village. Enough rehearsals were held—and here the defense girls had duties—until even the children could say without hesitation, "That is my uncle" or "my cousin." The unwritten records of the war are full of incidents arising out of this practice and the dangers and oppressions it was designed to meet.

For example, the village of Chiaotienchuan was being occupied by the Japs on one of their searches. Suddenly an unsuspecting guerrilla messenger came into the village—and was promptly arrested. But he shouted, "Why arrest me? I have come merely to visit my aunt here." And an old woman who heard him picked up the cue instantly. "My nephew! My nephew!" she cried as she came running toward him. Then, turning to his captors, she explained: "It's my sister's Number Three son—San Erh. Let him go!" The Japs hesitated. Another woman ran up, asking: "Oh, what are they doing to your nephew? Has he done anything wrong?" This cinched it—the Japs turned him loose with a kick and a warning not to be so careless in his movements.

Such demonstrations of collective security are often dramatized and performed in towns and villages throughout North China. I recall seeing one such play, which impressed me deeply, harsh and violently dramatic though it was. It consisted of one scene only, swiftly told in metric language. In it, the Japs had reason to suspect that a Paluchun officer was being sheltered in a village that they had surrounded. But every one present had a convincing story and an indisputable identity. Exasperated, the Japanese officer seized a young boy and began twisting his arm.

"Who is the Paluchun officer who is in this village? Answer me—answer me, or I'll twist your arm off!"

The boy howled with pain, but refused to talk. His father was brought forward. "Make him talk!" screamed the Jap officer angrily, setting the point of his sword against the father's side. "Make him talk or we'll kill both of you."

At this the boy began to weaken—whereupon the father snatched the officer's sword and killed his son. As he turned then on the officer, the soldiery ran him through with their bayonets.

At the close of this brief play there was no applause—it was, for that audience, too real to be watched as mere entertainment. Admittedly, such incidents as it dramatized are found described in the balladry of every nation under the sun; but here, in the bleak hills of North China, the conflict between a ruthless invader and a resisting people is actually going on every day—now, as this book is being read. One curious feature in the play I have described, I confess I cannot explain satisfactorily to myself: the sadistic Jap officer was played by a real Japanese—a member of the Japanese People's Emancipation League—and played with vigor and histrionic integrity. I find here a strange problem in psychology.

19

◇◇◇◇◇◇◇◇◇

The New Fourth Army

IT IS IMPOSSIBLE to get a clear idea of the political and military situation in China without a minimum of knowledge of the nature and extent of the anti-Japanese bases organized by the Communist Party. First, however, it is essential to grasp the fact that the Japanese occupation of Chinese territory is not in any degree comparable, in its thoroughness of security, with the Nazi occupation of parts of Europe. Wherever the Chinese people have been organized they resist, actively or passively. It was this will to organize that struck me most in Yenan. When once resistance has been organized, the vast areas of China represent an intolerable problem for the Japanese.

Thus, what the Japs call "Occupied North China" may be generally analyzed into zones as follows: 1. The areas that actually are occupied—those within gunshot of Japanese strong points, which in the thickly populated parts of North China are built one to every two or three villages. 2. The anti-Japanese bases—areas completely under the control of the people, with their own elected governments. These areas, in which Paluchun regulars have their mobile centers, are entered by the Japs only in force, on their periodic mopping-up campaigns or when they are engaged in battle by the Paluchun and its auxiliary organizations. 3. A no-man's-land between Zones 1 and 2—this is the true guerrilla area.

The anti-Japanese bases in Central China resemble those of North China, of which Chin-Cha-Chi is typical. We may therefore consider the Central China bases collectively in relation to the story of the New Fourth Army.

Since its inception in May 1938 with a force of 12,000 ex-partisans, the NFA has grown to over 180,000 trained and uniformed regulars, extending their protection to something like 30,000,000 of the 60,000,000 people in the Central China areas where they operate. In the six years of its life this army has fought over 17,500 battles, has had to resist 120 big mopping-up campaigns launched by the enemy, and has killed and wounded more than 240,000 Japanese and puppets, and captured more than 34,000. Its booty includes 124,000 rifles and small arms, 2,600 machine-guns, and 100 pieces of artillery. Losses have amounted to 45,000 officers and men killed and 65,000 wounded.

According to Chungking, however, the New Fourth Army has not been in existence since the Anhwei Incident of January 1941. Just what happened then is not entirely clear. The Communists say the NFA had received an order from the Central Government High Command to move north from the Yangtze River. They were dutifully complying with this order, they insisted, when they were suddenly set upon by Kuomintang troops. Ten thousand New Fourthers were either killed or captured. The commander-in-chief of the NFA, Yeh Ting, was taken prisoner and is still being held. When the NFA was officially disbanded, its surviving elements turned to Yenan for guidance. From its ranks a deputy commander-in-chief was selected who reorganized the New Fourthers on the Paluchun pattern, and they continued their resistance against both the Japanese and the Central Forces in their rear.

Here is what Generalissimo Chiang Kai-shek had to say about the Anhwei Incident: *

"The behavior of the New Fourth Army, its disregard for orders, attacks on comrades-in-arms, and even acts of mutiny and sabotage had necessarily to be put an end to; it was purely a matter of the assertion of military law. There was not the minutest admixture of issues belonging to the sphere of politics and party relationships. . . .

"In November [1940] the New Fourth Army was ordered by the High Command to move northward to engage the enemy in a certain

* In a speech reviewing home and foreign affairs delivered on January 27, 1941.

appointed area. It elected not to respond, but waited until after the expiry of the period of time allotted, then to make an arbitrary move southward, executing a premeditated maneuver leading to an attack in broad daylight upon the headquarters of the 40th Division. This plainly mutinous proceeding caused its disbandment as a disciplinary necessity. . . . The Government had limited itself last year to adjurations, calling upon the New Fourth Army to have done with its constant failure to comply with orders. It obstinately persisted, however, in its evil courses and at last went beyond all bounds. The situation developed in a way imperatively demanding the most rigorous action.

"My own feelings were of acute pain and shame, for the errors and failings of subordinates are to be laid at the door of their commanding officer. I felt personally responsible for this unhappy affair, wherein you must none of you find any cause for gratification. . . .

"All of you will recall the New Testament teaching of forgiveness unto seventy times seven. The misdeeds of the New Fourth Army even exceeded that number; there was no further room for pardon if I myself were not to become criminally negligent of my country's welfare."

To all this—"Rubbish!" said Chen Yi, acting commander-in-chief of the NFA, when I talked with him. "Why, the simple, bald facts prove just the opposite. Who attacked whom? Who killed whom? With our much inferior numbers, how should we have dared to attack—'in broad daylight,' mind you—a force that proved strong enough to annihilate 10,000 of our best fighters, commanded by our commander-in-chief himself? Bosh!"

General Chen Yi had just come up to Yenan, having been months on the road. He had traveled via Shantung and the Tai-heng Mountains, and had crossed scores of Japanese blockade lines. He is a chunky, puggish sort of fellow, in his early forties. Born near Chengtu of a wealthy landlord family, he studied chemistry in an industrial high school in his native Szechwan. After the First World War he went to France and spent three years in Paris and Lyons preparatory to entering the electro-technical college at Grenoble. When he learned that the usurpist administration in Peking * was negotiating with the French Government for a large

* The name was changed from Peking to Peiping with the entry of Kuomintang forces in 1928.

loan, in return for a monopoly in railway construction in south-west China, he joined a group of Chinese students to stage a protest. In a fiery speech he charged that the money obtained through this secret treaty was to be used by Peking in the suppression of Sun Yat-sen's revolutionary movement in Kwang-tung. As a result of the speech he was asked to leave France.

"This incident had a decisive influence on my life," he told me. "I realized that there was no use working for technical progress so long as government was corrupt."

In 1921 he returned to Szechwan and founded the *Hsin Hsu Pao,* a leftist newspaper in Chungking. For two years he tried, through his paper, to bring about some social reforms, but failed entirely to influence local warlords. So he went to Peking and joined the Kuomintang (and the Communist Party, too, secretly). Shortly afterward he went to Canton to participate in the Northern Expedition. When the successful revolutionaries reached Hankow he became a professor in the newly established military academy. In an effort to enlist the support of the Szechwan warlords, the Generalissimo sent him to Chungking and Chengtu as a special emissary; and from this mission he returned to find the Kuomintang's 1927 purge in full swing. With some of his leftist students, Chen Yi fled to Nanchang and joined the Red Army in its fight for existence. But when the Red Army began its Long March from Kiangsi in 1934, Chen Yi was ordered to remain with a nucleus of volunteers in order to keep some contact with the region and to organize partisans.

It was, of course, impossible to maintain the agrarian and social reforms instituted by the Communist Party except in the inaccessible mountain regions to which the Kuomintang "purge" forces could not penetrate in sufficient strength to destroy the partisans. Chen Yi paused to emphasize that the Communist Party and the Red Army were not driven out of their bases in Kiangsi, nor did they deliberately desert the people there: "The Communist Party and Red Army voluntarily gave up its bases in Kiangsi in the interests of internal peace, in the face of the growing threat of Japanese aggression."

With the beginning of the Japanese invasion in 1937, the pressure upon Chen Yi and his partisans in the mountains was relieved by the departure of "punitive" Kuomintang troops for action in the north. Chen Yi and his associate commanders asked to join the Kuomintang in the fight against the Japanese. After lengthy negotiations an agreement was effected whereby only 12,000 of the many thousands of partisans scattered over eight provinces in Central China were to be selected to form the New Fourth Army. These were to be concentrated in Kiangsu, in the Shanghai-Nanking area along the Yangtze River. The Government, in turn—according to Chen Yi—promised to solve the land question in the regions of the Central China Red Bases, to allow Communist Party members to participate in the local governments, and to supply the New Fourth Army fighting the Japanese.

"The Kuomintang broke all these promises," asserted Chen Yi. "Our offer to fight the Japanese was purely voluntary; we could easily have remained in our bases and have held them indefinitely against all comers."

On their march to the Yangtze the selectees for the New Fourth Army were not permitted to enter any of the cities. Nevertheless, thousands came out and begged to join the New Fourth Army—which, according to Chen Yi, could easily have recruited 100,000 men; but they had been strictly forbidden to add to their numbers. There seemed not to be any desire to rush them to the Yangtze front for, though they reached Nanchang and established headquarters there in January 1938, it was not till July or August of that year that they finally arrived at the Yangtze in the Shanghai-Wuhu-Nanking area. There were 8,000 men in the force that arrived from the south; the other allotted 4,000 had reached the north bank of the Yangtze, opposite Wuhu, in June.

"By this time, however, the Kuomintang troops had practically abandoned this area," continued Chen Yi, "and the districts were overrun with banditry and puppets, the latter being in control of the local governments and the people. Our uniforms were khaki—much like those of the Japanese—and the people, mistaking us for the enemy, dutifully came out with Japanese flags in their hands and knelt before us. They were so happy to learn that we were *not* Japanese.

"We began immediately to fight the Japanese, the puppets, and the local bandits. By the end of the year our forces had increased to 30,000—an expansion due wholly to our successful guerrilla warfare. After the fall of Hankow the Japanese felt only contempt for all Chinese forces, and they paid little attention to us. So we found it easy to take them by surprise, often wiping out whole companies of Japs in well-planned ambushes.

"The people, seeing our successes, readily joined with us. They were especially pleased to find our men so well disciplined. Our troops were strictly forbidden to take anything from the people without their permission. On the march we always made a point of first discussing the matter with the local village elders before quartering our men on the people for the night. And the quarters were scrupulously cleaned and everything set back in order before we left.

"Is it any wonder, then, that many asked to join our ranks? We welcomed all who wanted to fight the Japanese. We armed the people with weapons taken from the enemy and trained them as People's Militia.

"As our forces grew in numbers, we found it more and more difficult to confine ourselves to the small area in the vicinity of Nanking to which our activities were restricted by order from the High Command. Moreover, the Japs were beginning to take serious notice of us and were directing powerful forces against our too heavy concentrations. We therefore found it imperative to spread our forces and infiltrate behind the Japanese lines. This, then, is perhaps the first and one of the main points of friction between us and the Kuomintang High Command, which insisted that we remain concentrated in this assigned area—an obviously vulnerable target for the enemy."

At about this time, Chen Yi said, increasing numbers of Kuomintang troops were going over to the Japanese. Among these were the Loyal and Faithful National Salvation Corps under Tai Li's direction, who were operating in the Shanghai-Nanking sector under the immediate command of Yu Tso-pei. Part of these immediately joined the puppets in the cities; the rest stayed in the villages outside.

"By thus dividing their forces they were able to play both sides and get along without fighting," Chen Yi charged. "Meanwhile, our New Fourthers were ordered to fight a battle at least once every ten days. But, whenever we attacked the puppets in the cities, Tai Li complained, 'You are fighting my troops.'

"After March 1939, following the establishment of traitor Wang Ching-wei's puppet government, 50,000 of Tai Li's men under Ho Shing-chin went over to the Japs. In 1941 another 50,000 under Li Chang-chang joined the enemy. So our New Fourthers had to fight these, too. And because these new puppets knew the local terrain well, we experienced increasing difficulties in fighting them."

In spite of all this, the NFA continued to grow and expand its influence and operations. Following the Anhwei Incident, the Military Affairs Committee of the Central Executive Committee meeting in Yenan appointed Chen Yi to replace Yeh Ting as NFA commander. The NFA was, the Party decided, to be placed under the supreme command of Chu Teh's headquarters in Yenan.

In battling the New Fourthers, the Japanese have employed the various types of campaign employed against the Paluchun. Their mopping-up campaigns are usually undertaken after harvest time, when the crops have been cut and there is little or no cover for the New Fourthers in the plains. The "village purging" campaigns are designed to uproot the New Fourthers and keep them on the move. The Japs say that their mopping-up campaigns are like combing hair, while "village purging" is like shaving hair.

"We, in turn, feel like wrestlers in a never-ending contest," Chen Yi said. "Because we have no rear base to supply us with the wherewithal to fight, we must always be on the initiative to search out the enemy's weak spots so as to attack these for weapons and supplies. Moreover, offense is the best defense. But when the enemy concentrates and we find ourselves hard-pressed, we merely melt away. In battle we fight mostly at night, using bayonets and grenades, since our weapons are inferior and ammunition extremely scarce. We fight the enemy, too, with propaganda, handbills, shouting campaigns, and good treatment for prisoners."

While the guerrillas with the NFA operate just outside the city limits of such big Yangtze cities as Shanghai, Nanking, and Hankow, the regulars are based within an average day's march away. They hold areas up to about sixty miles north of Shanghai along the coast, twenty miles from Nanking, and thirty from Hankow.

"When the counteroffensive comes," said Chen Yi, "we'll be in the vanguard for the recovery of these three most important cities in Central China." He did not, of course, mean that this could or would be done by New Fourthers alone. "The most we can do—considering our lack of arms and equipment—is to keep wrestling with the enemy. To drive him out altogether we'll need full co-operation and co-ordination with the Kuomintang Central Government troops and the military, aerial, and naval forces of our allies."

20

◇◇◇◇◇◇◇◇

Civil War?

IN MY EFFORT to assess the Communist contribution to the war, I had numerous talks with Chu Teh. In the first place, he says, as far as the Communists are concerned this war is merely a continuation of the long struggle for national independence and a democratic way of life—a struggle that began with the Revolution and the overthrow of Imperial rule in 1911.

"In this respect, our struggle today has much in common with your own Revolutionary War. You won that because your people knew what they were fighting for. And we shall win our war because we, too, know what we are fighting for. Unfortunately, the bulk of the Kuomintang conscript troops, for the present at least, are only vaguely aware of what it's all about—which undoubtedly accounts for their continued reverses. Our Eighth Route and New Fourth Army volunteers, however, are in striking contrast to this: they are soldiers of the people and they are supported by the people; in this they resemble Washington's volunteers. And they have initiative and fighting power, which enable them to fight not only as regulars but also as guerrilla partisans."

Chu Teh revealed that he had made a thorough study of Washington's guerrilla tactics, which had proved so successful against the better-armed British mercenaries. And with his men, as with Washington's, the combination of extreme mobility and intimate co-operation with the people has baffled a formidable invader. Occupied territory does not stay "conquered" when these principles are applied. Enormous numbers of Japanese troops are used up, immobilized, by the necessity of constant military action in the rear of their own "front lines."

"Our Eighth Route and New Fourth armies are definitely inferior to the enemy in arms and in strength. Yet many Japanese commanders complain that whenever they strike a blow at us they meet air; but, when attacked by our forces, they are hit a powerful wallop. The reason is simple: through the help of the people we are provided with invaluable intelligence. We know every move of the enemy. We meet him only when we choose to, and on our own terms. When he sends a big force against us, we refuse to stand against it; but—and this is most significant—instead of retreating before such a force, we advance to its rear, confident that the people there will support, protect, and feed us. When we are confronted by small numbers, however, we don't hesitate to attack immediately.

"Employing these tactics, we are continually on the offensive. We keep harassing the enemy, giving him no peace or rest in which to consolidate and exploit his gains. Many Japanese officers have actually complained to us of what they call our 'unorthodox warfare.' In 1938, at Tamochiao, about 70 miles southwest of Taiyuan, the Japanese garrison had suffered a number of defeats in brushes with a regiment of our elusive Paluchun. The exasperated Japanese commander finally sent a letter to our regimental commander, Yang Yung, challenging him to a stand-up battle on such-and-such a date at such-and-such a place. 'Personally,' wrote the Japanese, 'I should praise your tactics; but they are not soldierly—they are sneaking and underhand. Do you dare come out for a showdown battle?' Of course, this wasn't the first or the only instance of such letters received by us from Japanese commanders; and naturally the challenges are not accepted."

Chu Teh told me of one such challenge sent to Chen Yi by a Japanese commander of a garrison near Nanking. "I and my New Fourth Army troopers accept your challenge," Chen Yi replied; "but we propose that, for an honest decision as to the better fighters, we should fight equally armed. Moreover, we should ask representatives of neutral states to referee. If we are defeated, I will take my men to some other front, publicly acknowledging you to be superior fighters. *But*—if you are defeated you will take your forces back to Japan." No answer came from the Japanese commander.

Technically, Chu Teh continued, General Washington began the revolution against the British with whatever guns there were at hand. As the war progressed, his troops supplied themselves, in part, with weapons taken from the British. So, too, with the Eighth Route and New Fourth armies: they have taken their weapons from the enemy during the course of the war. "In the last stages of America's Revolutionary War, Washington received help from the French, help that came through the British blockade. If China is likewise to get support and supplies from her allies—especially if weapons are given to those who will use them against the enemy —victory over Japan will not be long delayed."

Suppose, I suggested, that such aid were, for one reason or another, not forthcoming?

"Then we should not be able to drive the Jap from China—at least, not by military action. Lacking modern offensive weapons we can carry on a war of attrition only, and must depend on other factors for final victory."

"Specifically," I asked him, "what weapons do you need?"

Here, instead of talking unrealistically about heavy artillery, tanks, and warplanes, Chu Teh went straight to the point. "Our most urgent need at present is for infantry arms, such as good rifles, light and heavy machine-guns, some antitank guns and field guns for mobile warfare, and high explosives for blowing up blockhouses, bridges, and trains. With these, we can meet the enemy anywhere in mobile operations and defeat him."

Chu Teh admitted, nevertheless, that for the recovery of the big cities now occupied by the Japanese, the striking force of tanks, artillery, and airplanes would be necessary. "We ourselves, however, are not prepared to use these—though we warmly invite Allied personnel to bring and operate them in co-ordination with our forces." He was well aware of the problems involved, both political and physical. Officially, the United States and Britain can deal directly only with the National Government of China. War supplies given to China must be handed directly to the National Government, with no strings attached. The two Western powers could not, for example, earmark certain portions of these supplies for the Communist forces; and Anglo-American hands would therefore be officially tied if the Kuomintang were to refuse to give any of them to the Communists.

The exigencies of war, of course, may necessitate some change in procedure. We may, for example, decide that if many thousands of Chinese in North and Central China—quite apart from any consideration of their political principles—are willing to kill Japanese, we should give them weapons. For this there is some measure of precedent in our attitude toward the Soviet Union when it was attacked by the Germans. With this thought in my mind I asked Chu Teh whether the Communists were prepared to enter into negotiations directly with the American and the British military High Commands, if it should prove impossible to send aid through the Kuomintang Government.

"For the quicker defeat of our enemy we need the help of our Allies," he replied. "If, therefore, they should prove willing to negotiate with us directly, we should gladly welcome the opportunity."

But there would remain the physical problem of *how* we could supply the Communists directly. To truck or fly them in across Kuomintang-controlled areas would be, to say the least, embarrassing. But the Communists control considerable lengths of coastline. The Japanese hold only the important ports, such as Shanghai, Tsingtao, Tientsin, and so on. Even so, Communist guerrillas are operating in the very suburbs of these cities. At the present moment, indeed, blockade-runners (submarines perhaps, at first) could land supplies at hundreds of points whence they could be carried inland by the Paluchun itself. Later, with the crippling of the Japanese navy and air force, we could send in armed convoys, perhaps protected by our own planes operating from a beachhead established on the Communist-controlled coastline.

Such direct contact with the Communists would be necessary only if the Kuomintang and the Kungchantang find it impossible to get together. While negotiations for the settlement of these differences have been in progress since the early spring of 1944, few observers in China hope for anything more than an armed truce between the two parties—a truce for the duration of the war. They are too far apart in fundamentals to expect anything more unless some miracle should occur. Many observers in Chungking are convinced that no permanent solution is to be hoped for save after recourse to civil war *or* without the definite separation of the country into two Chinas—a Kuomintang and a Kungchantang China.

With all this in mind I raised the problem frankly, thus: America and the other Allies who will be operating in China will unquestionably, after victory, leave most of their implements of war there, since it would be too costly to carry back any considerable part of them when we withdraw. If the Kuomintang are then still in power, and still recognized as the directors of the Government of China, they will get all these weapons—except for those we might possibly have left in the Communist-controlled battle areas. What I was asking was this: Were the Communists apprehensive lest our arms be used against them after the war? The Communists, I knew, have often charged that the Kuomintang is deliberately avoiding fighting the Jap so as to preserve sufficient strength to annihilate the Communists after the war.

Chu Teh took a few moments to consider seriously. Then he replied: "We do not want to think of civil war in China, and we shall certainly never initiate such a war. But we, and other democratic forces in China, are ready to defend the democratic gains of years of struggle, and to fight any reactionaries who may wish to destroy these. Such a war would not be merely against the Communist Party—it would be against the people of China. For the people are with us, and should the Kuomintang wish to fight us they must fight the entire Chinese people. Such a war would be continuation of the present one—it would mean that the Second World War would not have ended with the defeat of Germany, Italy, and Japan."

He then asked me whether I believed that the United States would help the Chinese Communists in such a civil war. "I'm sure I don't know," I replied. "It would depend on the state of the world at the end of the war, and on the extent of our war-weariness. Of course, something like a new League of Nations may be set up—one with teeth in it; though I doubt whether it would be empowered to meddle in the internal affairs of a nation. As for us Americans—well, we have always been notoriously isolationist. . . ." I had very little encouragement to offer him, beyond mentioning the Americans' traditional sympathy for the underdog.

Chu Teh shook his head thoughtfully. "Nevertheless, we have faith in President Roosevelt and we are confident that he will help the democratic forces in China. *He's* no isolationist. We are familiar with his humane principles as expressed, for example, in the Atlantic Charter. The purpose of all of us in this war is to fight for democracy and against dictatorship. If, after the defeat of the dictators in Italy, Germany, and Japan, a war against democratic forces in China is allowed to start, then there can be no peace or prosperity anywhere in the world as long as it goes on. To uphold the democratic principle in the postwar world, the United States must help the democratic forces in China—not the dictatorship. May I remind you that you Americans in your war for independence and democracy were also helped by foreigners? We shall ask that you do the same for us."

I asked whether, as a contribution to peace and solidarity in a democratic China, the Communists could accept Chiang Kai-shek as the nation's leader.

"All things, we believe, are subject to change," he replied. "For Chiang Kai-shek there are two directions: If he were to work hard to promote democracy throughout China and to help seriously in the struggle against the Japanese, he would be supported by the people, and we should help to elect him as the first President of a truly democratic China. He might then become the Washington of China. But if he were to try to imitate Hitler, or to follow the example of our Chinese emperors, if he were to pursue indefinitely his present dual policy of fighting anti-Japanese forces while himself abstaining from combat with the Japanese, if he were to continue to suppress the Communist Party and other democratic elements in China, even to the point of risking civil war—then he would soon find himself without the support of the people. It is the *first* course that we Communists expect and hope that the Generalissimo will choose and follow."

Thereupon, since he and other Communist leaders talk of it so much, I asked for his ideas on the form and content of a postwar democratic China.

"Its government should be elected by the people," said Chu Teh, "with the co-operation and support of all classes and all parties."

"Including the Kuomintang?"

"Yes—including the Kuomintang. Basically, the Kuomintang is sound; and even now there are democratic forces within it—such as Madame Sun Yat-sen and Sun Fo—who, if given a chance, will bring the party back to the right track. For such anti-Communist elements as General Ho Ying-chin, H. H. Kung, and Chen Li-fu, there can be no place in the new democratic government. The people don't trust them and won't elect them."

There was still the question of the Communist-sponsored anti-Japanese bases, which now cut across provincial borders and reshape the map for North and Central China. "What," I asked, "will be the status of these in postwar democratic China?"

"They will remain constituted as they are today," he replied firmly. "They will have a semi-autonomous status, local autonomy being necessary because China is a big country and its various regions are in different stages of development. And we have yet to achieve social and political unity on a national scale such as you have in the United States."

The democratic nation that he envisaged for the China of the future did not resemble either the USSR, the United States, or Britain. His proposed New China would consist of a weak central government with strong semi-autonomous states—in contrast with the American model: a strong central government with states autonomous only with respect to local affairs. What Chu Teh had in mind was something on the pattern of the British Commonwealth of Nations—on a smaller scale, of course: a federation of states autonomous even with respect to finance, economy, and foreign affairs.

"Again," he emphasized, "may I point out that the reason for this is the unequal political, social, and economic development of the various regions of our country. Unification *can* be attained eventually, but only through a gradual process—and by starting it from below, not forcing it from above."

21

✧✧✧✧✧✧✧

Are They Communists?

For Americans, Communism has always been a big bogy. The average American will grudgingly admit that the Russians have done a pretty good job at fighting the Nazis, but he still wants no truck with their Communism. Two questions arise, then, in considering the Chinese Communists: First, what is their connection with Soviet Russia? Second, how Communist *are* these Chinese Communists?

Answering the first question, I can say this: In the five months I spent with the Chinese Communists I saw not the slightest tangible connection with Russia. There were no Russian supplies—no guns, planes, or equipment. There were no Russian military or political advisers. The sole Russians in the Border Region were a surgeon who seemed to stay at the operating table about sixteen hours a day, and two representatives of Tass News Agency who had come in under passports duly visaed by the Chinese Government. These two Tass men were not, so far as I could see, sending news despatches to Moscow—they were merely receiving and issuing a regular news service like that put out by the American OWI in strategic political centers all over the world today.

Occasionally I saw portraits of Marx and Lenin; but these seemed like relics of a revolutionary past. For every portrait of Marx or Lenin I found a hundred of Roosevelt, Churchill, Stalin, and Chiang Kai-shek. The portraits of these four hung everywhere—in government offices, in shops, in army barracks, in peasants' huts. Stalin's was there not as the leader of Communism but as the head of one of the United Nations—allies in the struggle against fascist aggression.

Here is that answer: the Chinese Communists are not Communists—not according to the Russian definition of the term. They do not, at the present time, either advocate or practice Communism. It is true that in the early days, when the Chinese Communist Party was founded, Marxian Leninism constituted the philosophy and the practical guide of that party. But, as the years moved on, the CCP found it increasingly hard to persuade the individualistic Chinese peasant to exchange his ambition to be master of his own little patch of land for faith in the new-fangled collectivism. Repeated compromises were required, until today the Chinese Communists are no more Communistic than we Americans are. I discussed this point with Mao Tze-tung, principal leader of the CCP.

In Yenan, incidentally, Mao is no unapproachable oracle, not the sole fount of all wisdom and guidance, his words unquestioned law. To be sure, Mao's ideas and suggestions have great influence in shaping policy, but they are taken only as a basis for discussion and final approval by a committee of Party leaders who are certainly no rubber-stampers. What Mao says for publication, therefore, is first carefully thought out and worked over by his Party associates, the final form being thus the composite expression of the Party committee rather than merely Mao's own ideas.

He sent his private car to fetch me—a half-ton Chevrolet delivery truck with a big red cross painted on the side above the word "Ambulance." Under this was printed: "Donated by the Chinese Hand Laundry Alliance, Inc., of New York."

Mao Tze-tung met me at the entrance of the little compound fronting a series of half a dozen ordinary caves where he lives with his family and immediate aides. His comely, youngish wife was with him—the former Lan Ping, well-known Shanghai movie actress, an extremely intelligent woman, a member of the Communist Party since 1933. In 1937 she gave up her movie career and went to Yenan to work in the Lu Hsun Art Academy. Here

Mao's interest in the drama brought them together, and they were married quietly in the spring of 1939.

Both were plainly dressed, she in a practical pajamalike outfit belted at her slim waist, he in a rough, homespun suit with baggy, high-water pants. I was taken to the "parlor"—one of the caves with a simple brick floor, whitewashed walls, and solid, rather lumpy furniture. It was evening, and the only light was furnished by a single candle fixed on an upturned cup. For refreshments I was served with weak tea, cakes and candy made locally, and cigarettes. Mao chain-smoked his abominable Yenan cigarettes, while youngsters ran in and out during the whole conversation. They would stand and stare at me for a few moments, and then, seizing a piece of candy, race out again. Mao paid no attention to them.

He is tall for a Chinese, broad-shouldered and loose-boned. About fifty years of age, he seemed less than forty. His full face, with an unusually high brow topped by a shock of bushy black hair, is enlivened by wonderfully expressive eyes. He smiles easily, speaks softly, and is almost boyish in his enthusiasms. His one annoying mannerism is to suck his breath in noisily between puffs on his cigarette, which he smokes with puckered lips.

"To begin with," he said to me, "we are not striving for the social and political Communism of Soviet Russia. Rather, we prefer to think of what we are doing as something that Lincoln fought for in your Civil War: the liberation of slaves. In China today we have many millions of slaves, shackled by feudalism. Over 80% of our population are peasants living on small plots of land, most of which belong to big, unscrupulous landlords. And since about 80% of the tenant-farmers must pay from 50% to 80% of the produce of the land for rent, it amounts to virtual slavery."

He cited the example of Wu Man-yu, who had to pay such an extortionate rent for his land that he had not enough left from what he raised to feed his family. "There are many millions oppressed like Wu Man-yu in China today—many whose wives die from starvation and who have to sell their sons and daughters or drown them, and themselves become beggars or bandits. Because of such poverty, many peasant women are forced into prostitution. For lack of enough food our peasantry falls easy prey to disease.

Even in the Border Region today, infant mortality is still as high as 50%.

"In trying to liberate these millions and improve their livelihood by means of agrarian reforms, however, we do not intend to go so far as the Russian Soviets—to take the land from the landlords and redistribute it to the people. We did do that in the past, I admit; but, by agreement with the Kuomintang and the Government on September 22, 1937, we gave up this policy for a modified one—a policy of persuading landlords to reduce their rents to a reasonable figure, while assuring them that these lowered rents would be paid regularly by the tenants. In this we differ from the Soviets, in an economic sense.

"Politically, too, we differ from them in that we neither call for nor plan a dictatorship of the proletariat. We do not advocate a collectivism that discourages personal initiative—in fact, we encourage competition and private enterprise. And under a reciprocal arrangement we will permit and welcome foreign investments in trade and industry within the areas we control. What we ourselves can do, we shall, of course, want to do. But there are many things that we cannot do, and we shall welcome foreigners and foreign capital that come in and do those things. We are a backward country and so have great need of foreign investments.

"As for government—as you know—we believe in and practice democracy, with the one-to-three system to limit any possibility of one-party dictatorship as practiced by the Kuomintang today. In this respect, too, we differ widely from the Russian Soviet system, in that our form of democratic government includes landlords, merchants, capitalists, and petit bourgeois as well as peasants and workers. In Soviet Russia today there are no landlords, no merchants, no petit bourgeois."

"But then," I demanded, "if you don't practice Communism, why do you call yourselves Communists?"

His reply was that the name was a carry-over from the old days. "You've seen enough here to confirm what I've been saying," he added; "enough to know that we are no longer Communists in the Soviet Russian sense of the word."

"Then why," I persisted, "don't you change the name—change

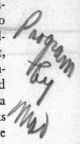

Program by Mao

it to 'Neo-Democracy,' of 'Democratism,' or some such—anything but 'Communism'?"

He shook his head. "It doesn't matter to us or to our consciences what we or others call our system. And if we were to change suddenly to some other name, there are those in China today—and abroad, too—who would make capital of it, would accuse us of trying to cover up something. No—we cannot, we must not, change the name. Nor do we need to. It is the content and the practice that are important—not the label!"

To be sure, there are those in the Kungchantang who still hope for a form of Communism in the future China. One of them is Chou En-lai, Secretary-General for the Kungchantang, who stands next to Mao Tze-tung himself in prestige and influence.

"Our ultimate ideal," Chou told me, "is the socialist collectivism of Communism—which, however, I don't believe can be achieved in China for a long, long time to come. China's development will not proceed along the same lines as Soviet Russia's. There will be stages. For example, on the basis of individual production we have adopted the mutual help or labor-exchange method, rather than an immediate and drastic establishing of collectivism. Second, from the principle of private ownership we hope to move to the nationalization of big enterprises—communication systems, banks, war industries. Third, we shall progress from the reduction of rents and interest to the stage of land owned by the tillers, and eventually to state ownership or nationalization of the land. Fourth, on the basis of equal suffrage for all social classes, we shall enable the majority—the laboring classes—to obtain the privilege of suffrage. The intention is to make rule by a minority less likely. This is the spirit incorporated in the one-to-three-ratio system. Fifth, under conditions of equality we shall strive for international peace and co-operation. These five points summarize what we call our New Democracy. They are also incorporated in the program of the revolutionary San Min Chu I as interpreted by Dr. Sun Yat-sen in the Manifesto of the First Congress of the Kuomintang in 1924."

22

Kuomintang versus Kungchantang

O<small>N</small> O<small>CTOBER</small> 10, 1944, the 33d anniversary of the founding of the Republic of China, Chou En-lai issued a significant statement on behalf of his Party. It is especially worthy of examination because it sums up the Kungchantang's whole attitude toward the Kuomintang and the deep-seated differences between them. It also suggests how difficult it will be for the two ever to get together. The following pages, containing its most significant passages, should therefore help toward a clearer understanding of the issues between the two parties.

"Today, throughout the world at war [it begins], great victories are being won; our allies are advancing steadily. But in our country, the regular battlefront and the battlefront behind the enemy's lines stand in contrast to each other: on the regular front there is defeat after defeat, while behind the enemy lines there is victory after victory.

"In the Honan campaign, China has lost forty-five cities within forty-four days. In the Hunan and Kwangsi campaigns, many big towns like Changsha and Hengyang have already fallen, and others are falling one by one. Why has this continuous series of defeats occurred this year? Why did they happen at a time when Japan's situation with respect to other fronts than China has become increasingly unfavorable? This is certainly not mere coincidence. No —it is due to the Kuomintang's defeatist policy of waging a half-

181

hearted and superficial war of resistance, of depending on foreign aid alone while preparing for civil war. It is due to the Kuomintang's policy of one-party dictatorship in the areas it controls, to its practice of excluding all other parties, while oppressing and exploiting the people through fascist procedures.

"Militarily, the Kuomintang authorities have always allowed only the Government to carry on the war of resistance—have not wanted the people to join the struggle. Because of this, our rousing of the people to resist the enemy behind his lines has been slanderously called 'partitioning by armed force and disobeying military orders' —and this, while in the areas controlled by Chungking the Government has absolutely refused to mobilize or organize the people. Instead, it gathers conscripts by force and drives them along roped together like prisoners. At the same time, the system of conscription is itself used as a source of 'squeeze' and corruption. Recruits for the army have therefore grown fewer and fewer, and the more the army fights the weaker it becomes. Meanwhile, the Kuomintang Government persists in its abnormal policy of combining halfhearted effort in the war with active opposition to the Communist Party. And so, when we fight vigorously behind the enemy lines, we are abused as a 'traitor party' and a 'traitor army,' and encounter sabotage and continued attacks from the Kuomintang. They, on the other hand, look on passively at the war from their positions on the regular front, without any thought of launching an offensive. If the enemy does not come, they work with him to run contraband and prey upon the people. When the enemy attacks in small numbers, they make a show of fighting to delude the people; when he attacks in force, they retreat without stopping for hundreds of miles.

"And worse: On the one hand they pretend to carry on the war in order to deceive the people and to get aid from our allies, hoping to enjoy the fruits of victory gained by the sacrifices of our allies. On the other hand they contact the enemy and his puppets, hoping to slow down the attack on themselves and to direct it against our forces behind the enemy lines.

"The British prime minister, Mr. Churchill, therefore has to regard the serious setbacks and defeats of the Kuomintang Govern-

ment as 'very regrettable,' 'most disappointing and vexatious'—and
this despite the fact that the American President, Mr. Roosevelt,
announces the increase of Allied aid to China from 3,000 tons to
20,000 tons monthly as a great achievement. Thus is refuted the pre-
tense of the Kuomintang Government that the military defeats in
China are due to the insufficiency of Allied supplies.

"Moreover, it is untrue that without foreign supplies Chinese
troops cannot win victories. On the front behind the enemy lines,
our Eighth Route and New Fourth armies are winning battles
daily, though they receive nothing either from our allies or from
the Kuomintang Government.

"Politically, the Kuomintang authorities cling like death to one-
party despotism and personal dictatorship. They forbid existence
alike to other parties and to a people's democracy. The 837,000
square kilometers of Chinese territory that we have recovered behind the Japanese lines, the ninety millions of people we have liberated, and the various local governments composed of all classes
elected by the people—these are termed 'traitor regions' and 'puppet
governments' and are refused recognition. Yet in the areas controlled by Chungking there is only party rule and no popular election. The various ranks of the People's Political Council, from
county to province and the entire country, are all appointed by
the Government. All officials, from the head of the smallest village
up to the chairman of the National Government, are appointed
by the Kuomintang. And these appointments are made exclusively
by a small ruling clique in the Kuomintang, the rest of the Kuomintang members and the democratic leaders having no share in
them. It is therefore less appropriate to call this 'party rule' than
to call it an oligarchy.

"Moreover, the Kuomintang authorities have set their minds on
establishing fascism and so refuse to put into practice the Three
People's Principles. When, therefore, we keep our promises sin-
cerely, when we realize energetically the Three People's Principles,
when we persist in fighting the Japanese and their puppets, when
we carry out the one-to-three-ratio system, when we develop production and reduce rents and interest in places behind the enemy's line as well as in the Border Region—when we do all these

things, the Kuomintang authorities decry them as 'bolshevization' and 'disobedience to the Government and its orders.' In areas controlled by Chungking, they rob the people of their freedom, bureaucratically dominate the so-called self-government, control public opinion, trample on culture, practice monopoly in industry and commerce, levy extortionate taxes and duties, let loose the Kuomintang Gestapo to tread down rights, and allow bureaucratic capitalists to undermine the people's industrial enterprises. Through all these measures they have brought about an extremely serious political and economic crisis. They ban the propagation of the revolutionary Three People's Principles, and prohibit advocacy of unity and friendly relations with the Communist Party. What *is* this but fascism? If so mistaken a policy of fascism and defeatism is allowed to continue, there are indeed even greater crises looming ahead for the Chinese nation!

"In order to save China in this crisis, to co-operate with our allies in the war, and to prepare effectively for the counteroffensive, we Communists advocate that the National Government convene an emergency National Council by calling together representatives of the entire country. We propose that the Government abolish one-party dictatorship and set up a coalition government. And we suggest that the following concrete steps be taken toward carrying this out:

"*First*—These representatives should be elected by the various anti-Japanese parties (Kuomintang, Kungchantang, and others); the various anti-Japanese armies (Central Army of the Kuomintang, local troops, and Communist-led armies fighting behind the Japanese lines); the various local governments (the provincial governments in areas controlled by Chungking, and the democratically elected governments in the liberated areas behind the Japanese lines); and the various people's organizations (those in the Chungking-controlled areas and those in liberated areas behind the Japanese lines which are national in character and are representative of every class and stratum of the people). The number of representatives should be based on the ratio of real strength in the various places. In order to meet the pressing needs of the situation and to facilitate their being called, the number of representatives should be large.

"*Second*—The National Government should call this national emergency meeting in the near future, so that further delay may not plunge the Chungking areas into irredeemable disaster.

"*Third*—This meeting should take Dr. Sun Yat-sen's revolutionary Three People's Principles as its basis and should pass a program that will meet the requirements of the situation and save China from her crisis. This program must thoroughly change the erroneous military, political, economic, and cultural policies at present pursued by the Kuomintang Government.

"*Fourth*—On the basis of a program organized in common, the Emergency Council should establish a coalition government of all parties and groups to replace the present one-party dictatorship. This new aggregation should absorb all leading persons in the entire country who are determinedly supporting the war of resistance and the pursuit of democracy and unity. Defeatists and fascists should be eliminated in order to guarantee the realization of a democratic government.

"*Fifth*—This coalition government should have the right to reorganize the High Command, to invite representatives of all the principal armies into the High Command, and to establish a united High Command to guarantee victory in the war of resistance.

"*Sixth*—After the establishment of this coalition government, steps should immediately be taken to prepare for a National Congress, elected by all the people. This congress should be convened as quickly as possible in order that constitutional government may be initiated.

"Only such a national emergency meeting and coalition government can provide a real starting point for democracy the whole country over. Only such a united High Command as we propose can obey the Government's orders, work smoothly with our allies, repel the enemy's attacks, and co-ordinate our own national effort with that of our allies in the counteroffensive."

Chou En-lai then turned to the question of the negotiations for solving the differences between the KMT and the KCT, which since April 1944 had been carried on with but little progress. The

Kungchantang had put forward twelve written and eight oral suggestions which their representative, Lin Chu-han, took to Chungking. After considerable wrangling and delay, they had on June 5, 1944, received the Government's counterproposals. The first, the third, and the seventh of the latter (under the heading Military Problems) had raised a whirlwind of protest from the Kungchantang. The National Government proposed to recognize only four armies with ten divisions—a total of approximately 100,-000 men—out of the 570,000 regulars that the KCT claimed to have under arms. The Kuomintang demanded, moreover, that all armed forces, with the exception of these ten divisions, be immediately disbanded, including the 2,200,000 People's Militia in the Anti-Japanese Bases. The remaining 100,000 men were then to be withdrawn from their present theaters of operation and be "concentrated for use."

Politically, the National Government made some concession toward recognition of a special status for the Shan-Kan-Ning Border Region—with its "administrative office directly affiliated with the Executive Yuan"—but demanded that the governments set up by the Communist Party in the anti-Japanese bases "be handed over to persons sent by the respective provincial governments."

To these proposals of the National Government, Chou En-lai replied caustically: "To disband several hundred thousand anti-Japanese troops, as the National Government demands, is beyond reason. If we accepted these demands, it would be equivalent to aiding the enemy—we should really be 'destroying the war of resistance and endangering the country.'" Even so, how *could* the anti-Japanese troops and the people's governments behind the enemy's lines be ordered to liquidate themselves? Everyone knows that this cannot be done. During the seven years of war, the people behind the enemy lines have established 591 local county governments, representing 82% of the 721 counties lost by the Kuomintang Government. This meritorious achievement has already become the guide to action for the whole of the Chinese people. Even to consider 'abolishing' it is to threaten the will to resistance of the Chinese people—a threat that would indicate a readiness to sacrifice all China!

"To recapitulate: We consider that the only correct proposals for rescuing China from her present crisis which will meet the needs of the situation are the reorganization of the Government and the High Command, the establishing of a coalition government and a United High Command that shall include all parties and groups, and the cessation of defeatist 'military orders' and fascist 'government orders.'

"We continue to demand that the Kuomintang Government recognize all anti-Japanese troops and all elected governments in places behind the Japanese lines, and we resolutely oppose the disbandment of several hundred thousand of anti-Japanese troops and of elected governments behind the enemy lines.

"The twelve written proposals put forward by the Central Committee of the Chinese Communist Party, and the eight points forwarded orally by our representative Comrade Lin Chu-han, should still be the basis of negotiations between the Kuomintang and the Kungchantang."

PART II

The Front

23

Off to the Front

I<small>T WAS</small> threatening rain as we mounted our ponies for a thousand-mile horseback trip to see something of the Eighth Route Army in action. There were just three of us left now, and an interpreter had been assigned to each because we planned to go off in different directions on reaching the fronts.

The youngest interpreter was Li Shao-tang, a husky thirty-two-year-old who had majored in Shakespeare at Nankai University. His English, though good, was heavy and bookish, loaded with long words and complicated phrases. Always helpful, full of enthusiasm, he was eager to learn conversational English, and he was especially quick in picking up American slang, which he mixed oddly with his Shakespearean English.

The quaintest was Lin Chung, a curious, heavy-spectacled little fellow with a turned-up nose and pouting lips. He was a Fukienese, and Mandarin—the dialect of North China—was therefore as foreign to him as Welsh is to a Londoner. In his thirty-five years he had traveled widely—had lived in Russia and the Philippines and had wandered all over Malaysia. He spoke fair English, understandable Russian, and passable Spanish; and when he got excited he mixed them all up.

Ko Pe-nien was an old-time Party man who had grown up with the Communist movement in China. He was always impressing on us how much better things were with the KCT than with the KMT in the "Big Rear." He had a burning hatred for the Kuomintang. They had killed his brother in the 1927 purge.

The trail led out past Yenan's airport, flanked by cave-pocked loess cliffs surmounted by a thousand-year-old pagoda. The cotton fields were spotted with bright red and white blossoms—and here is perhaps the origin of the charge that the Communists were growing opium, for cotton plantations in bloom look from a distance much like poppy fields.

The heavy traffic was composed of donkeys, mules, horses, and occasional iron-wheeled or auto-tired carts—but none of the human carriers seen in other parts of China. Much good anthracite coal from the newly opened mines was being transported in big chunks, two to an animal. Incoming traffic chiefly carried cotton cloth, while outgoing carried salt. The animals plodded along in strings, and one noted the efficiency of the transport co-operatives, with one muleteer tending two or three animals in a string instead of one man for each animal.

Everyone along the road was munching ripe red apples or the luscious watermelons that, by the way, were unknown in the Border Region before the coming of the Communists, who introduced a great variety of fruits and vegetables. The rains had been heavy in the past few days. In crossing one river my pony stepped into a patch of quicksand, and in a moment had sunk up to his neck; and, as I slipped from my saddle, I went in up to my hips. Fortunately I had enough presence of mind to throw myself forward, so that I was able to claw my way a few yards to within reach of helping hands. It was a close shave, and I was scared—really scared.

Our quarters for the night were in an old temple that had been turned into a primary school. The Catholic cathedral next door had been built in 1931 and evacuated in 1935 with the coming of the Communists. The pews, the altar, and other furniture had been removed, and weaving machines had been installed. These were operated by retired soldiers. Next morning we followed a trail that ran through a broad, fertile valley parallel to the course of a muddy torrent which boiled through twisting narrows cut into the shale rock. In the fields, labor brigades worked co-operatively, chanting as they swung their hoes. As we rode by they paused to stare at us. This, we knew, was the ancient invasion route traveled by barbarian hordes as long ago as the days before Christ. Sweeping down from the Gobi and beyond, these barbarians left their indelible stamp on the people of North Shensi. We saw many Chinese with blue eyes, brown hair, and long noses—heritage from the Mohammedans who had swept across North Shensi in the course of the Great Rebellion of the 1870's.

We passed through a number of ghost cities, some of which must once have been of considerable importance. Ravaged by successive waves of invaders, these were now but crumbling ruins, with battered walls and heaps of rubble where once must have stood imposing buildings. A few families still lived in crude homes built from the rubble of the stone heaps. These houses were shaped peculiarly—they looked like huge cubes of piled stones, with tunnels drilled through them. The tunnels were closed in front and rear by a wooden framework or lattice which formed windows and a door. Although primitive, they were quite substantial and serviceable—though it did seem that the inhabitants must have used a lot of effort in piling stone just to secure a little tunnel space.

At Chingchien—the first important city north of Yenan—the peasant women were in the final day of a convention, and we were invited to attend. The first speaker said she had just had word from her husband at the front. She was proud that he was fighting for a new, democratic China in which she and her children would be able to enjoy a freedom never before known in their country. As her contribution toward this goal, she promised to organize at least five groups of illiterates to study reading and writing so that they might be worthy of the new freedom. Another woman contrasted the new emancipation with the old days when women had to obey their fathers, their husbands, their sons, and their mothers-in-law. In the midst of her talk she saw Li Shao-tang coming up the aisle to translate for us, and she got panicky and fled from the platform. The heritage of thousands of years of subservience to Man the Master had suddenly risen up to banish all thought of this new-fangled emancipation. It will require at least a full generation for these women to take in fully what emancipation means for them.

Chingchien's magistrate took us to an old temple on a hill to visit his problem child—a Buddhist nun. For a long time he had been trying to get her to participate in the Production Movement, urging that it was not only a personal but a civic duty for everyone to engage in some form of production. Though he had tried every argument he could think of to induce her to change her ways, she refused to listen. "You are setting a bad example here," he told her now, as we stood by. She smiled but said nothing. "You're little better than the laziest loafer," he went on, trying to find a weak spot in her resistance.

Then she spoke. "What would you have me do?" she asked.

"Well—you could get married, for one thing, and help some man in production."

"But who would marry me?" she chuckled. "I'm already over thirty."

The magistrate quickly seized this opening. "I'll help you to find a husband."

"No." She shook her head. "Marriage is not for me. I became a nun because I would not marry the man my parents had chosen for me when I was still no more than a little girl."

He frowned. "But suppose we *make* you reform?"

"Ah, but you must not threaten me like that," she returned. "We are told that under the Communists' new democracy we all have our freedom!"

The magistrate threw up his hands at this, and quit. "You see . . . ?" he began, as we took our leave.

That evening a Yang Ko was given in the town's open-air theater. The play was *The Reformation of a Loafer*—a dramatization of the story of the ex-*erh liu tze* Labor Hero, Liu Shen-hai. I have already told this story. Did they like it? Well, you should have seen that audience. They loved every word of it. It was real, honest-to-goodness, down-to-earth stuff for them. Stuff they could easily understand; and told in their own dialect, too. They seemed actually to live the story with the actors—who, incidentally, were not professionals but members of the local amateur dramatic group.

Suiteh was the next important city to the north. Built more than two thousand years ago, Suiteh, where the Hun invaders were turned back, is today only a ghost of its former self. Its massive, picturesque city walls, which had resisted barbarian invasions for centuries, had been unable to protect its inhabitants from treachery within; and during the Great Mohammedan Rebellion "fifth columnists" delivered the city to the fanatical Moslems, who slaughtered over 80% of the population of 50,000. Today, barely 4,000 live within the walls in the rebuilt northern section of the city. The houses were well constructed and neatly painted, the shops well stocked, and the people apparently prosperous. There was a fine library in an old temple atop a hill within the city, as well as a big, modern auditorium for meetings and dramas.

Suiteh is known in the Border Region as the home of big landlords and wealthy gentry. We met many of these at a dinner given in our honor, and I talked at length with some of them. Most respected of these was seventy-year-old An Wen-shing, who is vice-chairman of the Border Region's People's Political Council. He is one of the biggest landlords in the Suiteh district, with family roots there that go back to the Sung Dynasty—a thousand years or more. Raised in the old traditions—he is a *Shu Tsai,* a scholar who had passed the first of the Imperial Examinations under the Manchus— he had nothing but high praise for the agrarian and democratic reforms instituted by the Communists. "Even the lowliest peasant today," he observed, "has the time and the opportunity to learn to read and write, to broaden his vision and free himself from the old slavery."

Eighty-year-old Wang Wen-ching vaguely remembered the Mohammedan massacre, having at the time been a lad of six. He was the only one of the company who wore a long gown with a jade bracelet on his wrist, and had the long fingernails which were once the mark of the aristocracy.

Near Suiteh is the site of Kangta, the Communists' Military Academy. There were 10,000 students enrolled at Kangta, divided into four battalions—all front-line veterans, who were getting two years' intensive military and political training. The first battalion, which we visited, was composed only of majors and colonels, who drilled like privates to enable them to understand better the problems of the men under their command when on active duty. Like everyone else in the Border Region, they were obliged to put in at least two hours daily on production. They hated this—hated puttering around vegetable gardens or spinning thread like women. But Political Commissar Li Tsing-chuan—himself an old battle-scarred veteran—only smiled at their grumbling. "Of course, it's women's work, as they call it. But we keep them at it purposely, because working in a garden, for example, makes them appreciate what it means to the farmer to have troops march over his fields trampling crops. And the spinning of thread teaches them patience—which they've got to have in the type of guerrilla warfare we are waging."

Mitze, about thirty miles north of Suiteh and a full week's horseback travel from Yenan, is one of the most prosperous little towns I have seen in fourteen years of travel in China. Incidentally, Mitze is only a mile and a half from the northern limits of the Border Region. From a height near by could be seen the line of blockhouses forming the Kuomintang blockade line on the northern hills. A little beyond is the Great Wall of China, with the vast deserts of the Gobi stretching to the north.

It was the late afternoon of a market day when we entered the south gate of Mitze. The city's single long street was thronged with the *laopaishing* from the countryside. In contrast to the monotonous blue worn elsewhere, here all wore homespun white, since dyes were unobtainable. Despite the dust whirled up by the brisk North Shensi wind, all were surprisingly clean. I saw no patched garments, no underfed bodies, no beggars; even the children who swarmed after us wore shoes of good quality.

Mitze was a comparatively new city, its walls in a perfect state of preservation, and its massive city gates with towering observation posts overhead making an impressive picture. The shops were well stocked, the shop fronts freshly painted, the flagstoned street swept clean. Before our evening meal I took a stroll down the street and talked with shopkeepers, merchants, and *laopaishing* in the markets. All spoke with real enthusiasm of the improvement in conditions brought about by the Communists. The rug-making House of Chow, composed of six brothers, was typical. Two years ago they started with a capital of 60,000 *pienpi*. Today they are worth several millions. The Border Region Government is a substantial stockholder, having one-third of the company's shares though it exercises no control whatsoever over the business. All the employees are stockholders and draw their share of the substantial profits.

Mitze, which we left an hour after dawn, is the last sizable town in the Communists' hands on the long, tenuous line of communications from Yenan to the war fronts in North and Central China. This line sweeps northward from Yenan through Suiteh and Mitze, and then turns northeastward to cross the Yellow River, whence it branches off to the various anti-Japanese bases. The trail now became rougher and passed through barren mountains. Occasional mountain villages were well fortified, though banditry had been almost completely suppressed by the Communists in recent years. We began now to see the People's Militia standing sentry day and night to guard all strategic points and village approaches. They were armed mostly with quaint, red-tasseled spears, broadswords, and home-made blunderbusses. Their duties were to halt all travelers and examine the required *lu-tiao*—road passes. These northerners were at least half a head taller than the average for those in Central and South China—some of them strapping six-footers.

Long after dark one night we reached Chiahsien, a Yellow River defense point. Like a medieval fortress, Chiahsien is perched atop a sugarloaf mountain, so that reaching it necessitates a breath-taking climb up a steep and slippery trail. At certain points long flights of steps had been cut into the solid stone face of the mountain, and up these our stout little ponies scampered like goats. At length a huge city gate loomed up in the darkness, and we were guided through the narrow, winding streets by spooky lantern light to the garrison headquarters, where we put up for the night.

Though Chiahsien was a picturesque city, as a fortress it made little sense. It had no water supply of its own, and every drop had to be carried up by coolie-back from the Yellow River, 2,000 feet below the city walls. Probably the city had been built by some corrupt or incompetent official centuries ago, though I could find no one able to tell me anything of its history or to give me a sensible reason for its existence at all. At one time the Japanese had driven through to the opposite bank of the Yellow River and had shelled the city for several days; but the prospect of crossing the treacherous river and storming up the steep, exposed trail to the mountain-top fortress must have daunted them, for they had withdrawn.

From Chiahsien we followed the northward course of the river for several days. Where it narrowed, confining itself to steep-sided stone cliffs, we were forced to travel over undulating ranges, zig-zagging up and down endless 2,000-foot mountains; but where the river's shifting currents had left beaches, we made good time galloping over the hard-packed yellow sands. *Laopaishing* in little groups were sifting the river sands for bits of coal washed down from the coal deposits far up north somewhere. Others were skimming the muddy river waters with nets for driftweeds, which they spread on the banks to dry for firewood.

Tucked away in these mountains was a string of army hospitals, each established in a series of caves. General Lo Tze-kai had told us at Sian that one proof that the Communists were not fighting the Japanese was that we should see no wounded Eighth Route Army troopers. Well, we saw many wounded troopers—yes, scores of them; some with wounds received in engagements only a few days before our passage.

Hospital conditions were primitive, of course. It was the old story: no medicines, no apparatus, no trained medical personnel—though these patients were issued with special hospital clothes as well as white sheets for bedding. The doctor in charge of a string of seven hospitals was an intelligent, serious-minded young man who, though he had had only a year and a half of training at Yenan's Medical College, was performing major operations. Doctors with long training are scarce, and needs are pressing.

In a quartermaster's depot we inspected decentralized units for making uniforms, repairing weapons, and manufacturing ammunition. The lathes and other machines were powered by a blindfolded donkey. In warehouses we saw piled cases of Japanese tear-gas and choking-gas canisters captured from a Japanese mule-train. The Japanese must be running short of silk, to judge from some captured parachutes we saw; they were made, not of silk, but of poor-quality cotton fabric. These had been picked up from beside some dead pilots, and had apparently torn when they cracked open on the jump. In the courtyard stood a pile of steel rails brought in by the Paluchun; from these, gunsmiths were making rifle barrels. A pile of Jap shell cases, iron piping, and caterpillar treads from wrecked tanks were being melted down for recasting into spare parts for captured machine-guns.

The crossing of the Yellow River into the Shansi-Suiyuan Anti-Japanese Base was even more exciting than our original entry into the Border Region. Our heavy, open, flat-bottomed boat tossed about crazily as we were swept into the rushing current. The oarsmen pulled mightily at their huge four-man oars until we were freed from the current's grip. When at last we set foot on the other bank, we were in an active war area. A half-day's ride, and we reached the military headquarters of the Shansi-Suiyuan Base—Chin-Sui, it is called.

24

◇◇◇◇◇◇◇

North China's Minutemen

THE SHANSI-SUIYUAN Anti-Japanese Base is the pivot for all the bases in North and Central China. Through it runs the main line of communication between the various fronts and the Communists' High Command at Yenan. From the Yellow River on the west it extends eastward to the Tung-Pu Railway and borders with Chin-Cha-Chi. To the northwest it reaches up to the Peiping-Suiyuan railhead at Paotow, while to the north it extends to the Taching Mountains and the grassy plains of Inner Mongolia. On the south it leans on the Fenyang-Lishih highway. It occupies an area of something like 40,000 square miles and contains about 3,000,000 people, under an administration headed by their own elected government.

Except for the stretch along the Yellow River, the base is bordered by a powerful Japanese blockade line. Additional blockade lines crisscross the base, for the Japs are trying to cut it up in readiness for eventual absorption through "silkworm" tactics. Its military commander is General Lu Cheng-tsao, a tall, scholarly native of Manchuria. When the war began he was a regimental commander of Central Government troops stationed in the Peiping area. On the retreat of the main body of the Central Government forces southward before the Japanese advance, he remained behind the enemy's lines and eventually joined with General Nieh Yung-chen and his incoming Paluchun. In October 1943 he was appointed commander of the Shansi-Suiyuan base.

Chen Man-yuan, General Lu's chief of staff, gave us a military survey of the base. We sat in a little room of a house which the Japanese, sweeping through on their periodic mopping-up campaigns, had twice set on fire. The furniture was simple and completely portable. It was interesting to observe that almost everything else in the room was Japanese: the teacups, the fruit bowl, the flower vases, the pencils and ink and paper, even the cigarettes—all of them captured from the enemy. The nearest Jap garrison was barely a day's march away.

General Chen began by dividing his military survey into three periods:

1—The period from the outbreak of the war to the end of 1940. During this time the Paluchun fought not only Japanese but Yen Hsi-shan's men, with whom they fell out over a dispute for the control of the New Army. The New Army had been raised in Taiyuan from a nucleus of leftist students and other volunteers. With the defeat and withdrawal of Yen's troops, the Paluchun had set up the new Shansi-Suiyuan Anti-Japanese Base.

2—The period from 1941 to 1942. During this, the most crucial stage, the Japanese were extremely active. They launched numerous mopping-up campaigns and doubled their strong points and blockhouses in an effort to liquidate all resistance. They varied their "silk-worm" tactics with occasional expeditions to "kill-all, loot-all, burn-all"—the "triple-sweep policy."

3—The period from 1943 to the present. The Paluchun, having met and defeated the worst that the Japanese could contrive, now passed from the defensive to the offensive. This was the record up to July 1944. Of the 297 strong points which the Japanese had built around the base in 1941 and 1942, the Paluchun had already destroyed or caused the evacuation of 128 by the summer of 1944. The offensive was still gathering momentum. In the month prior to our coming, an additional 25 strong points had been reduced. Even as General Chen told us this, a messenger came in with word that two more strong points had been destroyed the day before. The general offensive had already liberated 2,685 villages in an area with a population of 364,500 people. The General declined to make predictions for the future. "We talk about deeds only when we've accomplished them," he said.

After dinner one evening we walked about a mile to a big, raw auditorium to attend a dramatic performance. The auditorium was built in a little cul-de-sac almost surrounded by high hills which served as protection from air raids. The play was a dramatization of an incident in the mopping-up campaign of the year before. A force of 700 Japs had been trapped and besieged on a mountain top some ten miles from the auditorium, and only about a hundred of them finally succeeded in making their escape. It was wonderfully acted and beautifully staged. With a minimum of props an intense atmosphere was created.

The play opened with a scene before a farmer's home. A mother and a little girl—the family of a militia leader—were packing a few things before escaping to the hills. The Japs were coming. It was a crop-looting expedition, and the Paluchun were helping the farmers to harvest and carry off their crops while another force was harassing the enemy's advance until the expected Paluchun reinforcements should arrive.

There were the usual propaganda touches—or perhaps they should be called educational touches, since they were intended as lessons to the troops who composed the audience. Soldiers entered with a bowl, an ax, a chair—things they had borrowed and were returning. One of them helped the woman to pack and hide what things had perforce to be left behind. She offered him some bread. He refused—the Paluchun would accept nothing for their help. Another soldier set to work sweeping the house. A private, engaged in conversation with his officer, who was filling his pipe, casually asked for a pipe-load and the officer just as casually handed over his tobacco-pouch. All these were skilfully worked into the action. They bore out the Paluchun's claim that they strive to encourage a close relationship between the army and the people.

The battle began. With the arrival of the Paluchun reinforcements, the Japs were herded on to a mountain top, where they were besieged. Jap planes bombed the Paluchun; but they only moved closer, so that the planes no longer dared to bomb and strafe for fear of hitting their own men. The sound effects were primitive but effective. Firecrackers exploding behind the scenes sounded like real rifle and machine-gun fire.

There was an excellent scene of the Japs behind their mountain-top defenses. They were not caricatured, not depicted as frightened cowards. (The Paluchun is honestly respectful of the enemy as a fanatic who will, with occasional exceptions, fight to the end.) The actors who played the parts of the Japs gave an excellent representation of the hopelessness of the Japs' position in China. It was epitomized in a single pidgin-Chinese expression, commonly used by the Japanese: *"Paluchun, ta ta ti yu!"*—"The Paluchun, they are everywhere!"

All through the play ran the theme of co-operation between the army and the people. The militiamen joined the regulars as guides, as advisers, as fighters. An old man brought boiled drinking water for the troops crouching behind cover. Four *laopaishing* with a stretcher entered to carry off a wounded trooper.

The best propaganda touch of the play came at the very last moment, a few moments before the curtain dropped. The Japs had made their last attempt to break through. There was hand-to-hand fighting, as they vainly attempted to charge through the Paluchun lines. Two survivors of the charge surrendered. There was a tense moment as the Paluchun officer approached them with his hand on his pistol holster. You expected him to whip out his gun and execute the prisoners. Instead, he reached out to shake their hands.

After the show the soldiers in the audience marched back to their quarters. I had not noticed it before, but now I saw that they had brought along their beloved weapons—their Jap rifles, Jap machine-guns, Jap grenade-throwers. In single file they skipped silently from rock to rock in the boulder-strewn valley, silhouetted against the shimmering reflection of the moon on the river close by. These are the Paluchun. These are the fighters the Japanese admit they fear. They are feared because they are fighters with principles, because they are volunteers, not conscripts. They are feared because they are proud, because they have achieved a miracle in China— the respect and co-operation of the people. The Chinese, it must always be remembered, for centuries looked upon the profession of arms as the lowest in the social scale.

There were several thousand troops in camp near the headquarters. These had been brought up from their various operating sectors for special training. While the Paluchun seems to be able to supply itself amply with weapons taken from the Japanese, it suffers seriously from lack of ammunition. The troops were therefore undergoing intensive training in the use of the bayonet and the grenade. They were also learning new methods of ambush and the sudden surprise attack. Models of Japanese strong points were closely studied, and the many problems of attack and destruction worked out to the smallest detail.

In camp with the regulars were about a thousand Min Ping—People's Militia, whose training placed special emphasis upon the problems of co-operation with the regulars. They made an unforgettable sight, with their very mixed assortment of weapons, including red-tasseled spears and broadswords, shotguns, blunderbusses, flintlocks, land-mines, battered old rifles, and Chinese-made Tommy-guns. The Tommy-guns were made in Yen Hsi-shan's Taiyuan arsenal before the war and were captured by the Paluchun from puppets who had gone over to the Japanese from Yen Hsi-shan's army. Since there were no more than a handful of bullets for each of the captured Tommy-guns, the Paluchun gave them to the Min Ping.

The quaintest of their weapons was the wooden artillery. I saw a whole company of Min Ping heaving their home-made cannons on their shoulders. The cannon of three-inch bore were made of elm logs about three feet long and twelve inches in diameter. In action they were loaded with scrap iron, stones, or anything at hand, and fired by a matchlock mechanism tripped by a long string.

The 2,200,000 Min Ping—the "Minutemen" of China—are the backbone of resistance to the enemy in the anti-Japanese bases in North and Central China. They are the armed people, and they have been armed by the Communists. To me they represent the most conclusive answer to the question what the people truly think of the Communists, for it is axiomatic that no armed people would for long tolerate an unpopular government or an unwanted army in their midst.

The Min Ping are part-time fighters, going into action only when their own homes and villages are threatened or attacked. Ordinarily, their duties are to provide the regulars with intelligence and to supply transport and stretcher-bearing services during action in the vicinity of their own villages. They also act as guides or messengers when necessary, though their principal duty during times of inaction is the protection of the roads and trails. They mount a sentry service twenty-four hours a day. It is to them the traveler must present his *lu-tiao,* or official safe-conduct, without which movement is impossible.

The Min Ping may not be ordered into action by either the army or the Government; they are a purely voluntary organization. When they do participate in battle, however, their wounded are given the same treatment as the regulars and the dependents of casualties are given the same benefits. Special labor exchanges—sometimes with whole villages as units—are organized to care for the crops and the fields of the Min Ping during large-scale operations when the Minutemen are absent for long periods. When a village is attacked, the Min Ping organize and direct its defense, if no regulars are available. When evacuation is unavoidable, they superintend it and provide what protection they can.

The guerrillas stem from the Min Ping, but operate independently. These are full-time civilian fighters whose spheres of activity are limited more or less to their own districts. Their tasks are threefold: First, to protect the local government personnel and assist the civil government in the execution of its duties; second, to protect the people's interests and fight with them when the enemy enters the district; third, to co-operate with the regulars in local operations.

The guerrillas differ from the regulars in that, though they may be full-time fighters, they are purely a local force. Their forms of organization vary, depending upon local conditions and the tasks to be performed. The units may be large or small, and there is no uniformity in their weapons—they carry modern rifles, old blunderbusses, mines, or any weapon at hand. Because they are local folk they are more mobile and more flexible than the regulars. When pressed too hard it is easy for them to disperse to their homes and merge with the people.

As units, the guerrillas are directly under the control of the regional army headquarters which, for practical purposes, delegates authority to the commanders of regular units operating in the sub-districts. Unity in command is thus secured. Guerrilla units may, of course, operate independently of the regulars; but for any sizable operation—such as a frontal attack upon a strong point—they must first obtain the consent of the local army commander. However, should an opportunity for surprise action against a strong point present itself, they are authorized to attack without orders.

Where possible, the guerrillas are given full military training with a view to eventual incorporation into the ranks of the regulars. They are fed and paid by the army and receive the same benefits. Their military organization, while based on that of the army, is not quite so rigid. Their leaders are elected from their own ranks, subject to the approval of the army. Except in moments of emergency, these leaders discuss all plans with the others before orders are issued.

Noticing some Chinese-made Stokes mortars with the regulars' stacked guns on the training field, I asked about them. They had been captured in a scrap with the puppets under General Pang Ping-hsun. (In Chungking it had been denied that this Kuomintang General had gone over to the Japanese some months previously, the official story being that he had been captured after a heroic battle with the Japanese.)

"Perhaps we're not entirely justified in saying that we get no weapons from the Kuomintang," observed a Paluchun officer sarcastically. "We do get weapons from them—through ex-Kuomintang puppets such as Pang Ping-hsun."

The battle with Pang's men had been quite brief. After a mild exchange of shots, the puppets jumped at the chance to surrender, bringing their guns with them. A former gun crew of Pang's, composed of four men, were in camp and I had a long talk with them.

"The first we knew that our General Pang had gone over to the enemy," said one grizzled old soldier, "was when a party of Japs suddenly appeared and began passing out Japanese flags to us. This took us completely by surprise. We didn't like it, I can tell you. We'd been fighting Japs and traitors for years; and now suddenly we found ourselves traitors fighting our own people. That's why, when we were ordered to fight the Paluchun shortly thereafter, we took the first opportunity to desert and join the Eighth Route Army." He was one of a whole battalion which came over together with their officers and full equipment. Some of these were later sent back to their homes, but many like himself were old soldiers and preferred to join the Paluchun to fight Japanese.

One batch of troopers had finished their course and were gathered for a talk from General Lu Cheng-tsao. He told them that while their achievements might not be compared to the big battles in Europe and the Pacific, nevertheless their efforts were every bit as essential to the grand strategy of the war. They were a tiny cog in a huge wheel which for its full efficiency depended upon the firmness of each cog.

"You've done good work already at the fronts, but we expect even more of you after this training. You must teach the people, too, what you have learned here. And, since it will soon be time for the autumn harvest, you must help to bring in the crops while protecting them from the enemy should he attempt to loot the people's grain. Meanwhile, those of you who haven't already done so should learn to spin, to weave, and to sew. In the winter you will come here again for more training. And in the spring you will help the people with their planting. All this while you are still actively fighting the enemy, performing your individual parts in the general offensive we have launched against the enemy surrounding our Shansi-Suiyuan base. Is this asking too much of you?"

With a single voice they yelled, "No!"

Then the local Labor Hero, Wen Hsiang-shuan, got up to address them. He was a member of the Min Ping and wore his cartridge bandoliers crossed on his chest. He spoke in the broad local dialect. He was grateful, he said, for the better conditions in this district since the coming of the Paluchun.

"Under the Kuomintang's rule we people had little to eat. Today, even though our fields are in the very front lines of the war, we have more to eat than in the old days. More than that, under the Kuomintang we had no freedom. Today, we are proud of our own government which we elect ourselves. We are allowed to discuss our own problems and to take active measures to meet and solve them with the help, guidance, and protection of the Paluchun. Is it any wonder, then, that we willingly—yes, gladly—co-operate with the Paluchun, who are giving their lives to protect our homes, our families, and our fields? We are grateful also for this training we have received to help us work together with you to protect our harvests from the enemy."

The meeting was then addressed by Ken Mori, one of the most trusted members of the Japanese People's Emancipation League. He spoke in Japanese which was translated by a Chinese political worker.

"Soldiers of the Paluchun," he began, "I represent not just the Japanese People's Emancipation League, but the Japanese people, too." He spoke in clipped, short phrases. An intelligent fellow of a superior type, he inspired confidence with his simple directness. "It is only right for the people and the army here to work together to defend themselves," he continued. "In Japan, too, our soldiers are trained to fight; but the training is not willingly accepted because the soldiers know it is for aggression abroad. They fight well because they have good weapons. If you had such weapons you could fight as well as they—better, in fact, because you are fighting for your homes. In their hearts the Japanese soldiers know this; and when the time comes, the people in Japan will rise to meet the liberating Allies as did the oppressed French with the coming of the American and British forces of freedom."

In honored seats in the front row of that meeting sat three Japanese prisoners captured only a few days before. Their faces were expressionless masks as they listened to Mori-san. I wondered what they thought of him and what he had said. I wondered, too, what they thought of that impressive display of captured Japanese equipment, and of the determination of these Min Ping who were ready to fight the Japanese with such primitive weapons as spears and swords. They were, perhaps, quite contemptuous of it all, since they were freshly taken prisoners. Yet the seeds of doubt must already have been planted, for, instead of being tortured and killed, they were being treated as guests.

This privileged treatment of Japanese prisoners was certainly not a show put on for our benefit. In the following weeks I saw dozens more of them, some captured only a matter of hours before, some of them weeks before, our coming. Without exception they were being treated almost like special guests: comfortably housed, and given good-quality clothes and rations superior to those of the Paluchun trooper. A significant detail about the three Japanese attending that meeting was that each had a fountain pen in his tunic breast pocket. One of the regulations concerning prisoners is that their personal belongings must not be taken from them. Paluchun captured by the enemy hardly received such treatment.

On the fourth and last day of our stay at headquarters two Koreans and a Japanese military gendarme arrived. They had just come over voluntarily—at least, that was their story, and it was one of the fishiest stories I ever heard. I have no doubt they were trained spies. Ken Mori, who was present at my interview with them, must have agreed with me, for—though he said nothing—his expression as he took down their story told volumes.

The two Koreans spoke Chinese. Pak Tsen-chi said he was a merchant, who had been a civilian employee in the Japanese Army —a copyist in their intelligence division. Li Kon-ho was a photographer who had set up a little shop in Fenyang. The two Koreans had met Takao Sato, the Japanese gendarme, in Fenyang while dining together one rainy night, and they had all three discovered that they wanted to join the Paluchun. No sooner said than done —they had got up from their dinner and walked out of the city until they met the Paluchun.

"Why did you come over?" Ken Mori asked. Sato replied: "There are many poor people in this world. I come from the poor, oppressed masses in Japan. I hope to learn something of Communism here so that I can take it back to my people. But first I want to go to Russia to shake hands with Stalin."

Once started, he talked and talked; I could hardly stop him. I got the feeling that he was repeating a long-rehearsed story—the story of his miserable oppressed life, and of how he hoped to get an education so that he might do big things for his oppressed people. What did he know about Communism? Communism was good for the poor people, he replied glibly. Where did he learn about it? While in the gendarmerie he was given elementary instruction in the principles of Communism with special emphasis on how to fight it; but his conscience had told him that its principles were really good. So he had decided to desert. Because he had been in the gendarmerie, I asked whether he could tell me anything about what happened to Japanese soldiers who returned after having been taken prisoner and freed by the Paluchun. He was a bit wary in his answers, now—not quite sure what I was driving at. He denied having ever seen any such. Then, after some urging, he admitted that returned prisoners were first worked over by the gendarmerie, then court-martialed. Those who had returned unwounded were given death sentences. Executions were not publicly announced, but word got around. Sometimes, he said, a returned prisoner may be secretly executed by his own colleagues to save the unit from disgrace.

Chin Yano, one of Ken Mori's companions in the J.P.E.L., then spoke up. He had been listening to the interview, and at this point he revealed that he had once been captured by the Paluchun and freed; and when, on his return to his own troops, he learned that he was to be executed, he had escaped to the Paluchun again. He had been one of a squad of five who had been captured by the Chinese in an ambush. The other four had been wounded. When the four asked and were granted permission to return to their units, they tried to persuade Yano to go back with them. They stood a good chance of being let off easily because they could show their wounds to prove they had been captured in battle. But Yano-san most certainly would be accused of cowardice and desertion; so he refused to go back. After three weeks as a Paluchun prisoner, he grew lonesome and decided to ask for a release. He would take his chances of bluffing his way out of a death sentence. Perhaps, by offering to tell his superiors all he had seen and heard in the three weeks he had been with the Paluchun he would earn forgiveness.

Upon his return he was turned over to the gendarmerie who

third-degreed him for three days and nights, whipping him until he lost consciousness. Then they revived him and whipped him again. They accused him not only of disgracing the Japanese Army, but of being a traitorous spy for the Paluchun, and tried to make him confess to this. On the fourth day he was told he was to be sent to headquarters for court-martial. As they were taking him away, his company commander, who had always been friendly to him, handed him an envelope. The envelope contained no letter— only 34 sen in coins. He was at first puzzled; then he understood: the number 34 in Japanese suggests death. "You will die," was what the company commander was trying to convey to him. He made a quick decision, broke away from his guards, and dashed for the fields. Though they shot at him, he was quickly swallowed up in the tall kaoliang and eventually made his way to the Paluchun.

Through all this, Sato and the two Koreans said not a word; indeed, they seemed little interested. I was particuarly curious about Sato's reaction. He had been a member of the gendarmerie—he would surely know about these things. But then, perhaps he knew I was watching him.

As for Yano-san, had he some ulterior purpose in telling this story before these "escapees"? Was there something passing between them —something unspoken but meaningful? I felt sure Yano could be trusted. Was he, then, warning Sato and the Koreans that their story was too suspicious to be acceptable?

Some time later I saw Okano in Yenan. He had talked with Sato and the Koreans, who had been sent on to the Workers and Peasants School here. When I asked him what he thought of their story, Okano chuckled. "I didn't believe a word of it," he said. "Still, we let them think we were being taken in—we still do, because we are thus able to study the mentality of the militarists who sent them. Besides, there's no harm they could do anyway—we watch them too closely."

I am not yet sure that I understand it. This much is plain, however: the matter is left entirely in the hands of the Japanese, and the Communists keep scrupulously clear of it. They are letting the J.P.E.L. work it out for themselves. In so doing, they are perhaps taking the wisest course.

25

Behind the Japanese Lines

Where did we want to go? What fronts did we wish to visit? What did we want to see? They were reasonable, direct questions. I said that for my part I didn't know. I wanted merely to see enough to be convinced of three things: 1. That the army was fighting. 2. That the people were fighting. 3. That the army and the people co-operated and supported each other.

Maps were brought out at once, and we studied them. What about going down to the Eighth Sub-Region, at the southeast corner of the Shansi-Suiyuan base? This was an area about a hundred miles in diameter, completely ringed by Japanese strong points which stood almost within gunfire of one another. There, I was assured, I would see enough to convince me on all three points. There would be action, too, I was promised.

"We're on the offensive now, you know," said the General; "an offensive from *within* this area. Its intention is to destroy the enemy's blockading ring and so to liberate the half-million people living there."

That was bold talk, I thought. And a fascinating story, too—if true. An opportunity to live and fight with the people and the army behind the enemy's lines—surrounded by the enemy, in fact—sounded almost too good to be true. The others agreed. So it was decided.

We were accompanied by Li Shu-sen, an English-speaking political secretary attached to General Lu's headquarters. Secretary Li

Shu-sen was a character. Still in his early thirties, he looked like a college professor with his intelligent face and patched spectacles. His speech was subdued, almost feminine, his body soft and on the fattish side. Yet the way he rode that ornery black riding mule of his was a marvel to behold. The mule kicked and bucked and bit savagely. Secretary Li merely took him in his stride. A dozen times an hour he should have been thrown, riding as he did perched atop a huge pile of bedding. But he had ridden that mule for seven years, he explained, and knew all his tricks.

Our route from headquarters led down through the battlefield where the 700 Japs of some months before had been ambushed. We saw where they had made their last stand, and where they had burned their dead, before their last attempt at breaking through the Eighth Routers' ranks. The commander of the Paluchun who had participated in this battle was with us, and he relived vividly the whole battle for us. His story was full of colorful incident— how, for example, knowing that the Japs disliked leaving their dead behind, he had planted a mine under a Jap corpse. A Jap platoon headed by an officer returned after nightfall to recover the body; the mine blew up, killing the officer and five others.

The Paluchun had warned the people in advance, the commander told us. The Min Ping rendered invaluable help by leading the regulars along short-cut trails over the mountains to head off the Jap column. We stopped in one of the villages to talk with some of these Min Ping. There were eight of them working in a labor exchange brigade. Of the eight, only one had a serviceable rifle, and another had a pistol. These they had picked up on the battlefield the year before. The fellow with the rifle said he had had only twelve cartridges when the Japs came the last time.

"I fired four of them at the enemy," he said. "I just couldn't resist the temptation." No, he did not think he had hit any Japs with those four precious bullets; but, he grinned, they had paid dividends indirectly, for he had taken a whole cartridge-case full of bullets from a dead Jap.

The Min Ping were guarding every inch of the trail. One stood within sight of the other, and they let no one pass without a *lu-tiao*. Even the troops with whom we were traveling had to produce a *lu-tiao*. At one point a ten-year-old boy with a sword as long as he was tall stood in the middle of the road and demanded to see our road-pass. The commander at the head of our forces gravely showed it to the youngster, who examined it closely and waved us on with great dignity. No one dared laugh until we were well out of hearing, for the youngster did, after all, represent the silent might of the peasantry without whom the army could not exist.

Two companies of regulars—about 200 men—were attached to us as bodyguards. They had just completed the special course of training at headquarters and were returning to the Eighth Sub-Region. After some days of uneventful travel we approached the blockade line—the highway from Lishih to Lanfeng. It was planned for us to cross the line by night somewhere between two of the Japanese strong points. I had pictured the crossing of this blockade line as a secret, stealthy dash across the highway with a handful of men—a guide and a bodyguard or two. We would sneak up to the road at midnight, a scout would go ahead and signal back to us—a hoot like an owl's, perhaps—if the coast was clear. Then I should get a nudge from behind with a whispered "Go ahead, and good luck," and I would crawl on my belly in expectation of a hail of machine-gun bullets from a strong point.

Instead, the crossing seemed to develop into a major operation. In our cave quarters we held a council of war by the flickering light of a single candle. Our commander spread his maps. "Now, the Japs are over here. . . ." He told us there would be two more companies of Paluchun scattered over the area to form a protective corridor for our crossing. They were in command of all vantage points. Scouts were posted almost at the very doorsteps of the Japanese strong points, ready to signal us at the slightest indication of danger.

"Well, that's that," said our commander when all was clear. "Now let's get a couple of hours of sleep, because we've got a long ride ahead of us tonight. And oh, yes," he added, "perhaps you'd better wear your new uniforms."

My Paluchun uniform fitted me like a tent. It looked like a super-zoot-suit with a tunic that reached almost to my knees. I did not like it, but they insisted that I wear it, "in order to be less conspicuous"—as if a six-foot two-hundred-pounder could be "less conspicuous," especially among troopers barely half my weight and size. They laughed at me. *"Ta pi-tze Palu,"* they called me—"Big-nosed Eighth Router." (All Westerners are called Big Nose by the Chinese.)

But we did not start at midnight, as we had planned. Word came in that there was fighting ahead. No one knew what was happening. Had the Japs emerged from their strong points and run into the Paluchun? Had the enemy received word of our coming and were they now trying to intercept us?

With the dawn came a full report. The officer commanding the troops assigned to protect our crossing had taken his orders literally: to protect us from the enemy in those two strong points. The best protection, he had apparently considered, was to destroy the two strong points. He had done that. He attacked the first one, and after a couple of hours of fighting the garrison of fifty puppets in the first blockhouse had surrendered. Then he had taken the puppet captain over to the other strong point and had forced him to persuade that garrison also to yield.

So we got a good night's sleep and proceeded to cross the blockade line in broad daylight. Mafang, the nearer of the two captured strong points, was still burning. Perched high atop a promontory, it had commanded two important valleys and the Lishih-Lanfeng highway. The highway, incidentally, was lined with telephone poles, but there were no telephone wires. The guerrillas and the Paluchun had so often stolen the wire in the night that the Japs had given up trying to maintain a telephone service. Even traffic on the highway was rare, since every truck had to run a gantlet of mines laid by the Min Ping.

Japanese troops had garrisoned Mafang from the time it was built in late 1941 to the spring of 1944. Finding it necessary to withdraw many troops from North China for more urgent needs elsewhere, they had turned over to their puppets many such places as Mafang. They do not trust these puppets, however, for the fifty men holding Mafang had been equipped with old, discarded weapons and given practically no ammunition.

The Paluchun had inside information concerning the true state of affairs, and the commander decided the time was ripe to take advantage of it. His men surrounded the strong points, and during lulls in the firing he shouted to the puppets, telling them he knew just what their strength was, what equipment and how much ammunition they had. He named them one by one and advised them to surrender. If they did not, they would be stormed and killed to a man. The puppets thought it over and surrendered. The Paluchun then set fire to the place.

Mafang was typical of the many thousands of strong points in North China. Its hard core or center was a circular blockhouse about twenty feet in diameter and twenty-five feet high, built of stone, mud, and bricks. It bristled with loopholes for machineguns. Adjacent were the garrison's quarters, built half underground. Three rings of rifle trenches spaced about ten feet apart encircled the blockhouse. Just beyond these was a double line of barbed-wire fencing. Cut into the slope of the hill were three deep ditches, about fifteen feet deep and fifteen feet wide, encircling the promontory; and across these, drawbridges were flung. Eighth Routers had scrambled down and up each of the ditches and cut the ropes holding the drawbridges, whereupon the others had raced across under cover of their own machine-gun fire.

The puppets, a sorry-looking lot, were bewildered and frightened, since this particular batch had a bad reputation for mistreating the people in the vicinity. Obsequiously, they answered all our questions as they thought we would like them answered. The Japs beat them often and treated them badly, they said. Then why did they stay? Why did they not revolt and go over to the Paluchun? Well, they were only poor fellows, and they were not able to earn a living any other way than by being puppets for the Japs. Yes, they *had* thought of revolting—often; but they had never had the nerve to do it. They were not very convincing.

The puppet captain was afraid that, when the Japs learned of this incident, his wife and family living in the village near Mafang would be killed. Could he bring them along? The commander agreed. A cart was obtained, and the puppet captain piled it high with all his household effects. His wife and three children sat on top. He must have known he would not be held prisoner long. The Paluchun have no permanent prison camps. He, and the rest of the puppets, would be lectured and then given the choice of joining the Paluchun or being sent back to their native homes.

It was dusk as we left the smoking ruins of Mafang. The *laopaishing* were gathering from the entire countryside with picks and shovels to complete the destruction of the strong point during the night. The Japs were expected to return, of course. They would round up these same *laopaishing* to rebuild the strong point. The *laopaishing* knew this—but they knew also that it would take time, for which the Japs were somewhat pressed these days. Actually, the Japs arrived the next morning with a force of several hundred men. They inspected the ruins of the strong point, gathered the people from the village nearby, lectured them on the undying glory of Dai Nippon and the "New Order for Greater East Asia," and departed—with no attempt to rebuild the strong point.

We were now inside the blockaded Eighth Sub-Region. Powerful forces of Japanese, bent upon obliterating any possible sources of support, had swept through on numerous "kill-all, burn-all, loot-all" campaigns. For miles and miles as we moved from one end to the other of the Eighth Sub-Region we saw nothing but burnt-out villages. At first the villagers rebuilt their homes; but when the ravaging Japs returned time after time to burn them again, the people took to the hills and dug cave homes. The Japs followed them even there, burning the wooden doors and windows of their miserable dwellings, which was about all the destruction they were able to wreak. Now, the doors and windows were made collapsible and portable, and could be carted off and hidden in caves up in the hills.

Meanwhile, though this was technically "occupied territory," the people maintained their own elective government while supporting thousands of Paluchun regulars.

The village of Mifu was an example of what the Japs meant with their talk of a "New Order for Great East Asia." Once a prosperous trading village with substantial, ornately decorated shops and homes, Mifu was now only a heap of rubble. So thorough had the Japs been in their destruction of this village that they spent three days there methodically leveling every building. The people had tried bravely to rebuild their homes; but, when the Japs came back and destroyed these for the second time, the villagers resigned themselves to living in caves back of the village ruins.

But the Japs had not cowed these villagers, who were allotted more and more arms by the Paluchun. The peasants now challenged passage to all but large forces of the enemy. We saw them in the fields with rifles slung over their backs and grenades swinging at their hips, ready for instant action.

The people of a fertile valley near by had for a long time tried co-operating with the Japs, hoping thereby to save their homes. But some months previous to our coming, the Japs had descended upon this valley without warning and burned every village, slaughtering 300 of its 1000 inhabitants. Grim-faced survivors told incredible stories of the Japs' bestiality. Women stripped and raped, then tied to trees and used for bayonet practice. Babies were tossed into the air and spitted on bayonets. Boys were drowned slowly by having their heads ducked in and out of ice-holes in the river. I heard these reports not at second hand, but from the husbands, mothers, brothers, and sisters themselves, who showed me the places where these crimes had been committed. It was no wonder, then, that these people were now so wholeheartedly supporting the Paluchun.

Cave dwellings like these at Kenanpo house millions of people in Northwest China. They are carved out of the fine, hard-packed loess soil of the region, are cool in summer and warm in winter. And they are bombproof.

▲ The headquarters of the Japanese People's Emancipation League is in this cluster of caves above the ruins of Yenan.

▼ Intensive Japanese bombing pulverized the former city of Yenan, capital of "Communist" China. Today its inhabitants live in caves pockmarking the thousand-foot cliffsides of Yenan Valley.

⋀ The massive city walls are all that is left of pre-war Yenan. Outside the south gate of the deserted city is a mushroom growth of temporary shacks. Gauze masks on people at extreme left are protection against wind-driven dust.

Timber cutters bring ➤ mule-loads of wood into Yenan from the mountains and barter it in this market. The white building in the background is the Border Region Bank.

▲ Five top-ranking military figures in the Chinese Communist Armies. Left to right: Peng Teh-huai, Vice-Commander-in-Chief; Chu Teh, Commander-in-Chief; Yeh Chien-ying, Chief of Staff; Nieh Yung-chen, Commander of the forces in Chin-Cha-Chi (largest of the anti-Japanese bases in North China); Chen Yi, Deputy Commander of the New Fourth Army (operating in the Yangtze Valley).

▼ Mao Tze-tung, Chairman of the Chinese Communist Party, with his wife, the former Lan Ping, a well-known Shanghai motion picture actress. She has been a member of the Chinese Communist Party since 1933.

▲ On the left, Wu Man-yu, Labor Hero Number One of the Border Regions, with General Wang Cheng, youthful commander of the famous 359th Brigade.

▼ General Wang Cheng's men, veteran Jap-fighters 10,000 strong, have become self-sufficient farmers tilling fields reclaimed from wasteland in the Nanniwan district.

▲ Tsuo Chi (on the left), Chen Wai-ou, and Liu Chuan-lien, three heroes of the 717th Regiment. Tsuo Chi lost his right arm in the engagement in which these Japanese heavy machine-guns were captured.

◄ Members of the Min Ping, or People's Militia, armed with a typical assortment of weapons ranging from home-made flash-pan bird guns to fairly modern Tommy guns made in the Taiyuan arsenal before the war and subsequently captured from puppet troops. Taiyuan arsenal is now in Jap hands.

Border Region democracy in action—a joint session of the Standing Committee of the People's Political Council and the Border Region's elective government. This picture was taken in Yenan in 1944.

▲ A *Living Newspaper* dramatization of the opening of the second front in Normandy, produced just three days after D-Day, depicts a Hitler weeping over the news of Eisenhower's success.

▼ "Hitler" begs "Tojo" to help him by attacking Russia in Siberia, but Tojo tells him the island-hopping Americans are keeping his hands full. In the background, portraits of Churchill, Stalin, and Chiang Kai-shek.

⋏ Posters like these are displayed at mass-meetings in the Communist-controlled areas.

⋎ The *Living Newspaper* dramatization of Eisenhower's landing in France. He stands on the deck of a human "battleship." In the foreground, two men with raised arms represent the prow of the ship.

⋀ Prisoners of war in the Chinese Communist areas either are released immediately or join the Japanese People's Emancipation League and train themselves for anti-war work.

⋁ Members of the J. P. E. L., writing propaganda leaflets and preparing news broadcasts in the cave quarters of the Japanese Workers' and Peasants' School in Yenan.

⋏ Rehearsal of an anti-Japanese war play. The two coatless men in the center are Japanese members of the J. P. E. L. playing Japanese officers.

⋎ A chart prepared by members of the J. P. E. L. comparing rations issued to them with those received by civilians in Japan.

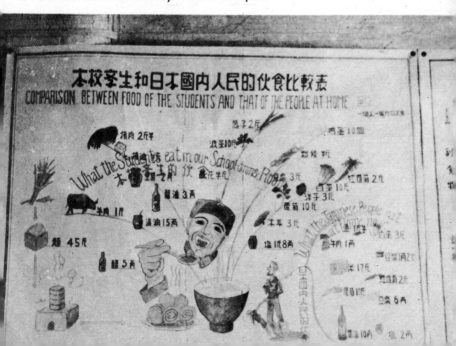

▲ The oil wells at Yenchang. The Communists trade kerosene, gasoline, and other by-products from these wells at the blockade border for cotton cloth and other much-needed materials.

▼ Makeshift machinery has to suffice at Yenchang.

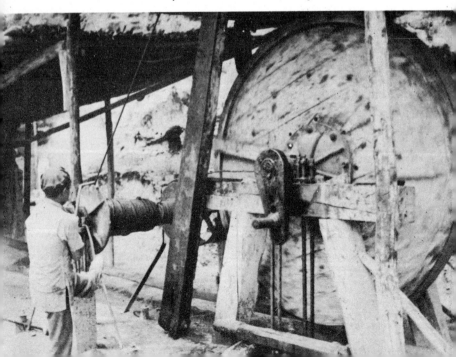

A wall map of the Eighth Sub-Region in the Shansi-Suiyuan anti-Japanese base. The slogans at the left read: "Oppose the Enemy! Fight to Win the Final Victory! Continue to Do Your Best to Resist the Enemy!" Wall maps and wall newspapers are widely used Chinese methods of popular education.

Thousands of villages in north and central China have been periodically looted and burned by the Japanese in an attempt to make it impossible for the people to feed and support the Communist Armies.

⋏ To defend their homes and their fields the people post sentries to watch for the Japanese.

⋎ Sentries of the Min Ping guard all roads and trails. Every traveler must carry a road-pass.

◄ A member of the Min Ping teaching his son how to use a home-made potato-masher hand grenade.

▼ The children's toys are dummy hand grenades, mines, and guns.

A company of the Min Ping with their home-made wooden cannon. The guns are made of elm logs, have a 3-inch bore, and are loaded with stones and scrap metal. They are fired by a match-lock mechanism tripped by a long string.

▲ A Min Ping hero holding oversized home-made mines and with a hand grenade stuck into his shirt.

▼ The author watching the manufacture of the home-made firecracker powder which the Min Ping use for their mines.

⋏ Where metal is scarce, stones are laboriously hollowed out to make mines.

⋎ Porcelain crocks, bottles, teapots, and tin cans are sometimes used for mines.

These three men are characteristic of the Border Region citizenry. In spite of primitive weapons, their fighting spirit and the fact that they are always ready to take up such arms as they possess have made life miserable for Jap garrisons and effective military occupation of their fields and villages impossible.

Mines are planted everywhere. The villager below is ready to detonate a string-pull mine.

(Top, left) Typical soldier of the Eighth Route Army carrying a Japanese rifle.

(Top, right) General Ho Lung, a master of guerrilla strategy, is perhaps the most popular of the Communist leaders in north China.

(Bottom, left) General Wang Chang-chiang, commander of the forces in the Eighth Sub-Region of the Shansi-Suiyuan anti-Japanese base.

⋏ The Min Ping setting a booby trap for the Japanese before they evacuate a village.

⋎ Japanese booty for the Communist armies. The lengths of rails will be used for manufacturing small arms. The telephone wire will extend the Communists' communications and intelligence system.

⋀ The populace and the army work hand in hand; each trusts and supports the other. Here a soldier gets a drink of water from a village woman.

⋁ Villager volunteers help to carry the wounded after an engagement with the Japanese.

▲ The people have planted tens of thousands of mines in their roads and trails. The mine, in this pattern, is planted in the center pit, while the four others are for step-trips. Ready for action, all five holes are skilfully covered with dirt and twigs.

▼ Where rifles and gunpowder for mines are not available the people arm themselves with the traditional "Long Knife" of the ancient Chinese warrior.

∧ The Lishih-Lanfeng highway, eastern boundary of the Eighth Sub-Region of the Shansi-Suiyuan anti-Japanese base. Japanese strong points are spaced along it almost within gunshot of each other.

∨ These soldiers of the Eighth Route Army marched all day with their rifles at parade slope on their shoulders. An officer blew his whistle at intervals and the rifles were switched in unison from one shoulder to the other.

⋏ Men of the Eighth Route Army are cheerful and possessed of great energy and stamina. On the march, they sing endlessly, whoop, and shout.

⋎ Even during rest periods, military order and discipline are closely maintained.

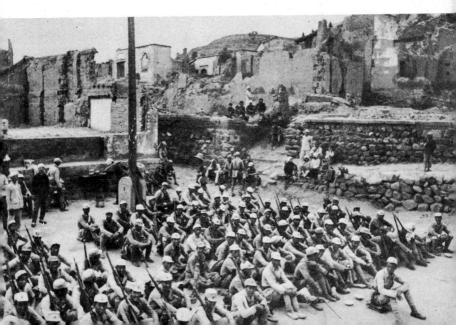

⩘ Attacks on Japanese strong points are carefully briefed.

◄ The attack on Lo Fan strong point. Lacking artillery, frontal attacks are rarely possible. Here, local villagers are carrying up a thousand pounds of gunpowder to go into a tunnel already dug under the strong point.

Mafang strong point, ➤ typical of the thousands of fortresses erected by the Japs to try to hold their North China conquests. This one, like thirteen thousand others, was destroyed by the Eighth Route Army. In the foreground, one of three concentric defensive ditches and the remains of the drawbridge which spanned it.

▼ The blockhouse of the Mafang strong point, still burning. A strong force of Japanese arrived a few hours after this picture was taken. The Japs inspected the damage but did not rebuild.

Scouts of the Eighth Route Army. These men wear no uniforms and are often armed, as here, with captured Japanese rifles.

Three of the Eighth Route Army's front-line nurses. They, too, go armed with rifles, grenades, and mines.

▲ Gifts for the troops being distributed by local women.

▼ This group of puppet soldiers was captured in an attack upon a Japanese strong point a few hours before.

◄ A jubilant soldier of the Eighth Route Army with booty secured in an attack on a Japanese strong point. The telephone is a specially valuable prize.

▼ The commander of the attack discusses the battle with the local populace: He is sorry the troops were not able to do more because the Japanese refused to come out from behind their protective walls and accept battle on more or less even terms with his men. Even so, his men succeeded in storming and destroying one strong point, capturing fifty prisoners and enough booty to equip a full company of new recruits.

26

The Fireworks Village

THE EIGHTH SUB-REGION is in the heart of one of the most mountainous areas in North China, its average elevation being from 7,000 to 8,000 feet above sea-level, and some of its ranges reaching 12,000 feet.

When the Sub-Region Base was established in 1940, the Paluchun occupied almost the whole of its 10,000 square miles, with the exception of the large cities such as Taiyuan and Fenyang. In 1941 the Japs began intensive mopping-up campaigns, combined with their "silkworm" tactics, and by 1942 they had reduced the area held by the Paluchun to almost a negligible fraction. But when they had spent their fury and retired to the network of strong points they had built to hold what they had gained, the Paluchun quietly came out of hiding and, together with the people, started their counter-offensive. In little more than a year's time, this counteroffensive had grown to such proportions that the Paluchun had already recovered all they controlled in 1940. The network of Jap strong points within the area was destroyed—point by point—leaving only the fortresses on the perimeter. Now the Paluchun were systematically at work destroying these last strong points also. A fourth of them had already been reduced during the past year by Paluchun troops operating from within the encircled area.

Periodically the Japs send in strong forces in a determined effort to liquidate the elusive Paluchun. The Eighth Routers merely melt

away, refusing battle except on their own terms. There really is
nothing the Japs can do about it. Little is left to destroy; the villages
are already in ruins, and green crops cannot be burned. At harvest
times the Paluchun and the people take measures to contain the
Japanese in their strong points until the harvest has been gathered
and hidden away.

One much-used method of containing the Japs is to plant thousands of mines in the vicinity of all strong points. I remember one
village which had found these mining operations so successful that
they decided to rid themselves altogether of the menace of the
near-by strong point. A solid mine field was laid around the strong
point, with Min Ping detailed for day and night sentry duty to prevent any attempt on the part of the Japanese to break out. They
were unable to come out even for water, and their emergency water
supplies must already have been running low when we arrived on
the twentieth day of the siege. We asked the villagers whether they
wished our troops to stay and help them storm the place. "No, no—
we'll handle this ourselves," was the reply. Ten days later we heard
that they _had_ handled it themselves: they had stormed the besieged
strong point, and the weakened garrison had put up little resistance.
Half of them had been killed, and the other half surrendered.

That village was one of the most belligerent I have ever seen.
Every approach, every trail, was heavily mined; and mines were set
not only on the trails but also out in the fields, where the wary
Japs might be expected to move. This was a precaution against possible Jap reinforcements. Warning notices, easy to remove should the
enemy approach, were stuck into the ground over every mine. It
gave you a goose-pimply sensation to zigzag your horse carefully
in and out between those marked mines—you hoped they hadn't
missed marking any!

Even the village street was mined. The villagers moved about nonchalantly, as though oblivious of death underfoot. Everyone carried a weapon of some sort—a rifle over his back, a potato-masher
grenade at his hip. This weapon-carrying had grown so natural
that even the little boys and girls wore dummy grenades dangling
from their waists.

In prewar days this village was locally famed for the manufacture of firecrackers, and the inhabitants had now turned their firecracker-making skill to the making of mines. In one courtyard I saw men, women, and children at work making black powder, casting mine-molds, and piling up loaded mines in neat heaps. Because of a shortage of metal for the mine-casings, some of the villagers were hollowing out big rocks to make stone mines; others were filling bottles, jugs, and even teapots; and one man was fashioning a wooden cannon of his own invention.

The significance of all this lay not in the effectiveness of such primitive weapons; it lay in their clear reflection of the fighting spirit of the people. A people must needs be brave who would match such puny contrivances against the deadly weapons of the enemy.

And what the Japs thought about it all, we learned from five of them who had been captured when their strong point was attacked and destroyed some days before. They were still scared, still expecting to be put to the torture. Four of them were over thirty and had been in the army less than three months. They were the equivalent of our 4F-ers and had been called up from their civilian jobs. The fifth was a smart youngster of twenty-four who had already seen four years of service in the army.

Did they know what they were fighting for? Did their people back home know what they were fighting for? What did they think the Allies would do to the Japanese if the Allies won the war?

Now the four oldsters, at least, being just fresh out of Japan, would, if they answered honestly, express the opinions and sentiments of not only the Jap soldier in China but also of the average civilian at home. Here were their answers.

Slow-speaking Matsushita spoke first: "Should we lose this war, all Japanese men will be taken abroad for slave labor, while our women will be distributed among the Allies as concubines."

Matsubara, whose wife and young son lived with his family on the family farm near Nagoya, said: "All our men will be slaughtered by the Allies, leaving the women and children to starve to death."

Tanimura, who has a family of four children now dependent upon relatives, answered: "I believe that only the soldiers will be executed, leaving the old men, the children, and the women in Japan."

Harada agreed with Tanimura; but Tanaka, youngest of the five, said he thought that the old and the very young would be massacred, while the soldier class would be enslaved. All five of them—if they believed what they were telling us—had good reason to be fanatical soldiers. Their answers suggested that what keeps the Jap going today is rather the fear of defeat than the desire for victory. He has the tiger by the tail and he can't let go. This is particularly true of the Jap in China. Here he has won many battles, yet he has failed to conquer the people. They hate him—and he knows it. He can only sit in his fortress and brood and wait for inevitable death. *"S'la s'la ti yu!"* he cries despairingly in his pidgin-Chinese—"Everywhere is death!"

The commander of the Eighth Sub-Region forces is chunky, Hopei-born General Wang Chang-chiang, a professional soldier from way back. Graduate of the Paoting Military Academy in 1921, he has fought under almost every important military figure since, including Wu Pei-fu, Feng Yu-hsiang, and Yen Hsi-shan. When the Japs marched into Manchuria in 1931 he fought them until he was ordered to withdraw—it then being the policy of Chiang Kai-shek and the Government to appease the Japanese, while hoping for support from abroad. When peace was signed with the Japs in 1932, he was sent to Nanking to receive special military training from the German and Italian mission. At Nanking there were a few tanks and some artillery for the students' practical education, but they did not really learn much. All of them were specially selected officers, to whom there was too much pandering on the part of the instructors, who had a keen eye on future orders for German and Italian supplies. "To give you some idea of the slackness of this school," said General Wang with a laugh, "the students always rode out to the training field in rickshas!"

With the outbreak of war with Japan in 1937, Wang was the commander of two regiments of Central Government troops in North China. Ordered by his superior officers to attack the recently arrived Paluchun forces, Wang balked, and eventually led his men in a revolt, as a consequence of which they all joined the Eighth Routers under Lu Cheng-tsao. When General Lu left Hopei to take up his new post as commander of the forces in the Shansi-Suiyuan base, General Wang accompanied him. Some six months before our coming, Wang had been given command of the forces in the Eighth Sub-Region. "My orders were simple and clear," he said. "These were to fight, to carry on production, and to encourage education."

Wang arrived in the midst of a large-scale mopping-up campaign which the Japs had launched at the beginning of the year. They were trying out some new tactics—"hair-combing," they called it. They would set out in force, then quickly divide into small units of about twenty men each, who marched forward like the teeth of a comb; if any Paluchun forces were encountered, these teeth would instantly converge in an encircling movement.

"At first we were taken completely by surprise by these new tactics," said Wang. "But we recovered quickly and dispersed our forces into even smaller units—of five or six men—which adopted 'sparrow warfare' as a countermeasure. These units, knowing the terrain well, first harassed the enemy with a handful of shots here, a mine laid there, a shower of grenades from a hilltop vantage point—and then scooted away along little-known bypaths before the enemy could catch his breath. Eventually the Japs were forced to return to their strong points, their new 'hair-combing' tactics having proved a complete failure."

General Wang is one of the Paluchun's best tacticians, and he has given special attention to the reduction of strong points. In the absence of the necessary weapons—artillery and high explosives—to drive the Japanese from their strong points by direct attack, other means had to be found. First, an attempt is made to lure the enemy from his fortress to a place in which he may be met on more equal terms; though, even so, an attack is not made unless the Paluchun commander is quite sure it will be successful. The Paluchun works so close to the bone that it cannot afford failure.

Should this attempt at luring not work, the strong point is subjected to intensive harassment. It may be attacked every night, in order to rob the enemy of peace and rest. It may be sniped at daily, to keep the garrison jittery. It may be surrounded by mines, to make them virtual prisoners—and relieving forces will need to be very strong to discount the possibility of ambush.

Meanwhile, every angle is probed for weakness, and, when the time is deemed ripe, a blow is struck—a blow that rarely fails to achieve its objective. The strong point of Tsaochuan is an example. The men from this strong point often came to the village below and raped its women. In the strong point there was a puppet whose wife had been one of those raped by the Japanese. The ever-watchful Paluchun learned of this and got into contact with the puppet. One night, when he was on sentry duty, he let down the drawbridge. The Paluchun sneaked in, tossed grenades into the Japs' quarters, and killed twenty-five Japs and captured fifteen. The booty: one trench mortar, one heavy machine-gun, three light machine-guns, one grenade-thrower, a radio transmitter, thirty-five rifles, and 20,000 rounds of ammunition. The cost: two Eighth Routers killed, one wounded; only fifty rounds of rifle ammunition and forty grenades expended.

Tsaochuan was one of the key strong points, dominating forty-seven villages. These were liberated, together with a population of about 10,000.

Another typical example was the strong point of Lijun. The five Jap prisoners with whom I had talked (as described above) came from Lijun. The coolie who brought in their water every morning was frightened one day when Harada-san playfully accused him of being a Paluchun spy. He wasn't—but the Paluchun heard about it and went to work on him. He was persuaded to co-operate. During the night a Paluchun unit crawled up and hid themselves near the drawbridge. With the early morning, the coolie began making his usual trips for water to the river below. On the fourth trip he signaled to the hidden Paluchun that the Japs were at breakfast. The Paluchun dashed across the lowered drawbridge and, as they rushed in on the Japs with fixed bayonets, one of the Eighth Routers shouted in Japanese, "Don't be afraid—the Paluchun doesn't kill prisoners!" Those who resisted were shot; the five who surrendered were spared; the strong point was demolished.

27

Over High Hills

"**A**CTION? Well, let me see." The General studied his wall map. "We're about due to blow up Lofan. That should be interesting, but I don't think we're quite ready for it—not enough powder manufactured. Suppose you take a trip down to the southern border first, down around Fenyang. There's always something going on down there. I dare say you'll find plenty of action with our Sixth Detachment operating in that area."

So, one morning on which rain-clouds hung threateningly, we started south, to traverse at least four nine-to-ten-thousand-foot passes before we came to the last notch. Here we looked down on a great, fertile plain with the Jap-occupied city of Fenyang nestling in the foothills close by. The two companies of regulars, still with us, were now no longer mere bodyguards—they were troops on operation. We might expect a fight at any moment, for we were never more than a day's march from the nearest Jap strong point.

Leading our detachment was an army scout in civilian clothes. I dubbed him "Kit Carson" Wong because of his picturesque appearance as he rode his pinto pony with his long-barreled Jap rifle slung carelessly over his shoulder and his bandoleers crossed over his chest. It was Kit Carson Wong's job to dash ahead and talk with the *laopaishing* to learn whether the Japs had begun to concentrate at any point.

These Paluchun regulars may not have been the best-equipped

troops I had seen in China, but they certainly were about the best-trained and best-disciplined ones. Soldiers in almost any other army on a route march carry their rifles as they please; these carried them parade-fashion, angled on the shoulder, and marched all day that way. An officer would blow a whistle every few minutes, and the rifles would be switched from one shoulder to the other, in unison. When a rest was called, the troops did not simply drop where they were—they formed orderly ranks and at a signal from their officers squatted in neat rows. And then, utterly unlike the average Chinese soldier, they brought out rags and carefully cleaned the tiniest speck from their beloved rifles. I picked up rifle after rifle and looked down the barrels; they were all spotlessly clean—which alone told me volumes about these men.

They were the most cheerful lads you ever saw. And they were possessed of the most tremendous energy and stamina. They sang endlessly, punctuating their songs with whoops and shouts even while scrambling up and down stony, slippery mountain trails, some so steep that my big red riding mule panted and puffed like a steam-engine. Whenever we started up a steep grade they began to yell: *"Chia yu! Chia yu!"* "Pour on the oil! Pour on the oil!"

Presently the rain began to fall, but we kept on marching since it was inadvisable to stay more than a single night in one place. On that first day we marched for nine straight hours in a blinding, driving rain, slithering up and down the roughest of mountain trails without a moment's stop for either rest or food. That night we dried out over fires, and the next day marched again in the rain for six more hours without a stop. The men did this with full packs, including rifles, machine-guns, grenade-throwers, ammunition, and other equipment.

In a small hidden valley we stopped for a visit at what, to all intents and purposes, was a front-line hospital. Everything was so arranged that the hospital with its patients could be evacuated within an hour. A labor exchange had been arranged with the villagers, who provided stretcher service in exchange for help in the fields from the hospital staff. The three uniformed nurses kept their bedding and few belongings packed when they were not in use. A brace of grenades and a rifle for each stood beside their knapsacks.

In case of emergency, it was their duty to protect the wounded as the stretcher was being carried up to some hidden cave near by.

The doctor in charge of the hospital had had only six months' medical schooling, though he had been an army nurse for something like a dozen years. He was performing major surgical operations, admitting that he was not too good at it—but *mei yu ban fa*, there was no other way.

For lack of medicines they used much hot water and sunshine for treatment. Surgical instruments, such as knives and saws for amputations, were made in the near-by arsenal. Sheepgut was used for lack of catgut, and salt-solution served as disinfectant. Calcium was obtained from ground-up eggshells, willow-twigs boiled in vinegar substituted for aspirin. Toasted wheat husks wrapped in cloth took the place of hot-water bottles. They were even raising a few silkworms from which they hoped to get silk thread for sutures.

The arsenal near by was really not much more than a repair shop. Even with the limited materials at its disposal, however, it was turning out about a thousand mines and about two thousand grenades per month. It could double this production if sufficient materials were available.

It was getting dark as we came down over the last mountain crossing for the day and entered the tiny, burnt-out village where we had planned to spend the night. The village head met us and reported in a curiously calm, matter-of-fact way that two hours previously he had received an interrupted telephone message from the village six miles to the west to the effect that a force of 200 Japs and 100 puppets had suddenly appeared there. (The telephone instruments and miles of wire had all been captured from the Japs. The lines, laid mostly underground or skilfully hidden in the underbrush, provide an amazingly efficient intelligence network for prowling units of Paluchun such as ours.)

The enemy had come out the day before and were apparently seeking revenge for two strong points which had been destroyed in that sector within the past week. Or perhaps they had heard of our coming and were planning to kill or capture us. They knew we were in the Eighth Sub-Region, for they had spread handbills in the villages near their strong points slandering us and offering rewards for information.

The village head told us that his informant had been in the midst of describing the enemy's equipment—two mountain guns, five heavy machine-guns, several trench mortars—when the line had gone dead. Apparently the intelligence man had continued to report up to the last possible moment before disconnecting his telephone instrument and running for safety.

Our commander listened thoughtfully. We had marched ten hours that day, up and down ankle-twisting mountain trails. And he had the responsibility of protecting his foreign guests. I would not for a moment have blamed him had he decided to withdraw. However, he elected to remain and fight. Quietly he ordered a squad to this hill, another to that house, a third to that point. The head of the village Min Ping came in for orders, and the Min Ping were dispatched to mine all the trails leading into this valley. Scouts were ordered out to ascertain the enemy's location. This done, the commander folded his maps and we sat down to our meager evening meal, feeling sorry for the tired, hungry troopers out there on watch with only a single thin Jap blanket to keep out the mountain chill.

Our commander, incidentally, was the political commissar for the Eighth Sub-Region, Lo Kwei-po. Commissar Lo, still in his early thirties, has been a revolutionary since boyhood. He joined the Kuomintang when he was only fifteen and had become the head of the propaganda department in his district. After the split with the Communists in 1927, he joined the Reds in exile; he was then only sixteen. He organized guerrilla detachments and fought numerous battles with the Kuomintang regulars, making such a good record for himself that by the time he was twenty-one he was appointed vice-commander of an army unit of 5,000. While still in his early twenties he had become the vice-director of the Red Army Military Academy in Kiangsi. When the Long March began in 1934, he was given the command of the High Cadres Detachment. At first this unit was made up purely of political workers; but as the Long March stretched on and on, these workers needed military training, since everyone had to fight the pursuing Kuomintang forces. The war with Japan began shortly after their arrival in North Shensi, and Lo joined Ho Lung as political commissar of the famed 120th Division. Later he was assigned to the Eighth Sub-Region, where he had been both political commissar and commander of the small forces there until the coming of General Wang with his troops at the beginning of 1944. Lo then gave his full time to political work in the growing counteroffensive against the encircling enemy.

We slept in our clothes that night. But the Japs failed to put in an appearance. We had word later in the day that another Paluchun unit some miles away had ambushed the enemy column on the move, but apparently they had not done so well. Or, at least, we gathered as much from the report of their casualties—the unit's political commissar and two squad leaders had been killed and several more wounded; there were no details of casualties inflicted upon the enemy. The strike had not been enough to stop his march, but had merely deflected it to the south. Commissar Lo regretted he was unable to contact the other unit during the night, for together they might have given the Japs a sound drubbing. "But don't worry," he said. "We're moving east today, and tomorrow we'll join with other units to attack Fenyang. That ought to be a better show, don't you think?" He smiled wryly.

The walled city of Fenyang, with a population of over 20,000, was a sizable objective. It was the most important Japanese base in this area outside of the provincial capital of Taiyuan itself, and a principal concentration point for the start of large-scale mopping-up operations.

28

Action at Fenyang

WE LEFT our mounts and our bedrolls behind and joined the troops for the night march over the hills to a little village barely five miles from Fenyang. By the dim light from a vegetable-oil lamp, Commissar Lo unfolded the plan of action. The attack was set for 3:00 A.M. The installations at the Fenyang airdrome were to be burned. The city's power plant near by was to be blown up. The match factory and the bus station outside the east gate were to be destroyed. If the Japs came out of the city they were to be engaged and the city itself stormed. Apart from these general orders, the officer in command of the operation was to seize whatever opportunity presented itself.

A battalion of Japs—400 or so—were garrisoned inside the city, with three hundred more in strong points near by. In addition there were about 700 puppets. This, then, was to be no mere hit-and-run show. The attacks on the airdrome, the power plant, the match factory, and the bus station were designed to goad the Japs into coming out of the city, where the Paluchun was ready to meet them on something like equal terms.

It was a hellish climb for us up a slippery, stony path in pitch darkness to a mountain-top observation post. They *said* it was less than a mile, but we thought they must have meant one vertical mile and a horizontal league. It was bitterly cold on the summit, with a biting night wind blowing off the high ranges at our backs.

When we arrived, a platoon of bodyguards were already there, sitting shivering in their flimsy Jap blankets. Yet this was only early fall, and much snow would fall in these parts during the severe North China winter.

About 3:30 we heard firing and then saw flames shoot up at three separate points. The operation was apparently going well. With the dawn we saw great clouds of smoke billowing over the city's rectangular walls. But there was no more shooting and no sign of activity in the vicinity of the city.

A report came in shortly after noon. The men had accomplished only part of what had been planned: they had burned the airport's installations and planted mines on the runways in case the Japs sent in a call for planes; and they had blown up the power plant and had destroyed the bus station. At the match factory, however, they had met stronger resistance than they had anticipated and, since dawn was approaching, they had had to break off. With daylight they would have been at the mercy of Jap machine-gun and artillery fire from the city, with little or no cover available.

But this was not to be the end of it. The troops were hiding in a little village a mile or two from the city, waiting for the Japs to emerge. If the Japs refused to come out and fight, their orders were to attack again that night. Later in the afternoon we inspected the village's anti-Jap tunnel. It was perhaps a mile long and big enough for all the women and children in the vicinity. The men would take to the surrounding hills to snipe at the Japs if they made a sortie. The tunnel, incidentally, had been used only the week before. This attack on Fenyang was in part retaliation for a minor mopping-up campaign which the Japs had carried out in this area during the past two weeks. This campaign had ended only some three or four days before our coming.

We climbed a winding path to a hillside farmyard. The tunnel entrance was in an abandoned cave, of which there were many thousands in this country. It consisted of a series of upright and inverted U's connected by manholes, and could be easily defended from the inside with a baseball bat. Our guide gave us full details of its construction, its history, and all its secret defense features. I noticed a badge he wore over his heart. "Oh, that? That's a Good

Citizen Certificate from the Japanese garrison commander in Fen-yang!" He grinned.

No wonder the Paluchun were prepared for every move the Japs planned. I understood a little better then how the Eighth Routers were able to live and operate within a surrounded area such as the Eighth Sub-Region.

We slept for a few hours; then, some time before midnight, we started for another village closer to Fenyang whence we might better observe the night's action. The Min Ping were out in force. The eyes and ears of the Paluchun, they were scattered along the hilltops flanking the trail, and again and again they challenged us from the dark. Before we were allowed to move forward we had to give the password for the night—tonight it was *"lien chang,"* company commander. It was well after midnight when we arrived at our destination. This was a Japanese strong point whose garrison had been squeezed out only a few weeks ago. The people, in co-operation with the guerrillas and the regulars, had laid siege to the strong point, starving the garrison until it had withdrawn.

We sat up on its wall, huddled in our blankets, looking like a row of vultures waiting for the kill. The sheer audacity of the whole business appealed to me. We could hear the shooting plainly and see the gun flashes coming from the city. Then, suddenly, a big flame began to blossom—the match factory. The flame was shot with blue and green and orange from the combustion of the chemicals.

The battle continued until just before dawn, and ceased almost as abruptly as it began. The Paluchun had broken off and withdrawn according to order. With the dawn we, too, picked up and moved back about three miles to a mountain-top village. There we set up headquarters in an ancient temple filled with fierce-visaged, gold-leafed warrior gods. The walls of the temple and the village houses were bravely plastered with big bold white characters—slogans reading, "Down with the Japanese Fascists!" "Hail to the Victory of the Allies!" Encouraging, too, was the welcome that the villagers gave us. There was no need to requisition quarters for our men—the people voluntarily took them into their homes.

We were waiting now to see what the Japs would do. Would

they come out and fight? Perhaps, suspecting a trap, they had called for reinforcements from Taiyuan, and these were already on the way. Commissar Lo decided we could not afford to stay there much longer. We had already won a terrific moral victory—had made the Japs lose a lot of face and had done considerable damage. We would wait for our fighters to come up from the city and then move off.

About noon we walked to a promontory overlooking a string of Jap strong points leading up over the hills only a couple of miles away. We sat there, thumbing our noses at the enemy. Soon a platoon of our men came up from behind and quietly deployed around us. They set up machine-guns in the cornfield on the right and mortars in the kaoliang on the left.

Presently one of them let out a yell. A string of villagers were moving up the trail from below. He called to them to halt, to send up one of their number to state their business. An old *laopaishing* came up, grinning. He was carrying a basket of eggs—a present for the Paluchun heroes. They all had presents, having heard of the fighting of the past few days. Though they lived in villages directly under the domination of the Japs, they wanted to prove how much they welcomed the fighting Paluchun.

The rest of them came up. They were all dressed in their best clothes and carried baskets of fruit, bunches of vegetables, pumpkins, nuts, and chickens. One was dragging a protesting goat. Some of the older women who had bound feet hobbled along painfully. All were laughing and joking as though out on a picnic. It was a touching scene, and an eloquent expression of what the people who lived directly under the Japanese guns thought of the Paluchun.

Someone shouted, "There they come!" The warriors were returning. A long single file of men snaked up the twisting trail. What a sight! They were loaded with the dog-gonedest assortment of booty—rifles, machine-guns, swords, helmets, telephones, battle flags, blankets, overcoats, sacks of salt, bags of rice, cases of cigarettes and matches, even a few bicycles. Some carried bottles of soda water and Japanese saki. One wore a dead Jap's glasses. It seemed that they had gone beyond their orders. Before leaving they had decided to storm a strong point about a mile and a half from the east gate of the city. It was well protected, with deep wide ditches surrounding the inner defenses. But the Paluchun knew its weak points; some days before, a Paluchun officer disguised as a coolie had entered and cased it from within.

They had killed all but two of the Japs. These were wounded, and they had brought them back, together with about fifty puppet captives. Among these latter were thirty-eight members of a nearby puppet government which had taken refuge in the strong point during the attack on the city. The Paluchun's own casualties were three killed and nine wounded. The wounded were presently carried in on stretchers borne by the local Min Ping.

Dead tired though they must have been, they were still in the highest of spirits. As they formed ranks and squatted, the women began to move among them distributing their gifts. Then they joined the rest of the *laopaishing* sitting off to one side with pride and admiration shining in their eyes.

After a while Commissar Lo addressed them. He was proud of their achievements. They had delivered a blow at the enemy which he would not soon forget. They had brought increased hope and courage to the people. But there was still much more to be done, and a careful analysis must therefore be made of the whole operation so that defects and mistakes might be avoided in future ones. Then he called for a few moments' silence in memory of those who had fallen. All rose and stood with their heads bowed; many had tears in their eyes.

They were a most generous bunch of men—they heaped us with souvenirs of the battle: war flags, insignia, helmets, and a photograph album. They themselves were anticipating a great feast on the bags of rice and flour they had captured. They had hundreds of cartons of bad Japanese cigarettes, which they shared with the two companies of men who had come down with us from headquarters and who were bitterly disappointed at not having been allowed to share in the battle.

So we took our leave of them, for we had to march clear up to the northern perimeter for the Lofan show, which was just about due.

29

The Assault on Lofan

THEY HAD been at it three nights now, these two. Kaida and Otani were members of the Japanese People's Emancipation League. Every night they had crept up to within thirty yards of Lofan strong point and shouted to their countrymen inside to come over to the Paluchun.

"Did they listen to you?" I asked.

"Oh, they listened, all right," said Otani. "But that's about all. They didn't fire at us, which was some encouragement. They even hushed up the dogs they kept there. We could hear them plainly."

"Private Sato did answer us on the third night," Kaida cut in. "He said: 'Come in. Come in. We won't hurt you.' We thanked him, but replied that we'd rather stay outside and talk. We shouted that we were former Japanese soldiers ourselves. We'd been told we'd be cruelly tortured if we were captured by the Paluchun. Instead, we had been given excellent treatment, and had subsequently joined the J.P.E.L. Then we told them about the J.P.E.L., and also gave them a summary of the latest military developments in Europe and the Pacific."

If Private Sato and his companions in Lofan had been influenced by the shouting of these two, they waited too long to make up their minds, for they were killed when we blew up Lofan two nights later. Kaida and Otani knew we were going to blow up the place, and they were sad about it; but they felt they had done all

235

they could to save the lives of a few more of their misguided countrymen.

It was drizzling lightly as we set out in the gathering darkness for Lofan, which lay in the Fen River valley about five miles across the hills. The General had wanted us to watch from a mountain-top a couple of miles back from the strong point, but we insisted on going right in with the troops. Reluctantly he consented to take us to an old temple about 300 yards from the strong point's outer defenses.

As we were leaving, two reports came in. One said that 300 Japs were moving in our direction from the east; they were only about ten miles away. The second reported that 1,000 Japs had arrived at a point about 25 miles to the northeast. These latter were believed to be the vanguard of a concentration to begin a general mopping-up campaign in the Eighth Sub-Region. It was harvest time, and the Japs were probably after the grain.

The General considered these reports for a bit, and then decided to continue as planned. "The Jap devils won't dare move in the night," he said.

We knew what he meant as soon as we started our march. The trails in that area wound along the narrow ledges of thousand-foot cliffs with certain death as the consequence of a misstep. And, as if that was not enough to discourage night travel, every trail was heavily mined. The Min Ping had been out earlier in the evening to clear the mines from the trail along which we were to march, and the mine-holes remained as ominous reminders of how thorough the protection had been. At some places the holes were bunched together in a narrowing defile; elsewhere they were spaced about ten or fifteen yards apart. But always they were laid in the only available line of advance, and it would have been suicidal to move over this mined trail by night.

In the pitch darkness we moved in Indian file, stepping carefully, relaying back: "Mine-hole"—"Step down"—"Keep to the left." We spoke only in whispers, which enhanced the suspense; though really there was hardly any need for much caution until we got up really close.

As we neared the strong point, ghostlike shapes loomed up in the drizzle. These were the troops resting before they marched the last mile and began the battle. With them were the guerrillas, the local Min Ping, and a file of *laopaishing* carrying boxes and sacks of gunpowder. Others carried picks and shovels for the tunneling, and scaling ladders for the crossing of ditches. The stretcher-bearers squatted and smoked their pipes nonchalantly.

The general was disturbed to find them there; they should have been at their tunneling two hours ago. But they, too, had heard the reports of the Japs on the loose, and on his decision would depend whether they were or were not to proceed with the night's plans. This two-hour delay was now become a serious matter. It was estimated that it would take at least eight hours to dig that tunnel. They had planned to start just after dark—about 8:00 P.M.—and had hoped to finish the job and be ready for the blow-up by 4:00 A.M., which would be about an hour and a half before dawn; and this had been enough to allow for reasonable delays. But this fresh delay of two hours would bring the tunneling into daylight, and there would be no cover of darkness for the troops making the attack after the powder charge was detonated.

General Wang held a hurried council with his officers and the *laopaishing* who were going to do the digging. They decided that with a little extra effort and a little luck they *might* cut the tunneling job down to about six hours—well within the hours of darkness; and the order was given to go ahead.

We moved up to our temple observation post, within easy rifle range of the strong point. Entering the main building, we were greeted by a sight wholly in keeping with the whole weird business. At either end of the big, heavy-beamed, rectangular room sat two huge figures. These were the "Guardians of Heaven"—warriors of ancient age and fearsome expression, who looked immense on their platform pedestals. The awe-inspiring effect was enhanced by the deep, black, wavering shadows that our tiny lamp cast behind them. In sharp contrast, all along the walls were ranged—shoulder to shoulder—life-sized figures of the sages. With their grave, benign expressions, like philosophers or judges, and their long, flowing robes (skilfully pleated, though made of a mudlike plaster), they had a most impressive dignity. One felt hushed and awed in the presence of these ancients.

We had barely settled ourselves when the firing began—uncomfortably close, as we discovered when occasional bullets slapped against the thick temple walls. The Japs must have discovered the tunnelers almost as soon as they had begun. When the Paluchun answered with a volley of shots—to keep them confined to their strong point—the Japs cut loose with everything they had. They fired their rifles, machine-guns, mortars, and a cannon that threw a shell which exploded like a seventy-five. Some of these landed so close that our temple shivered. They were firing blindly, of course, since they could see nothing in the drizzly blackness. When their fire died down, the Paluchun, which husbands carefully its precious ammunition, fired just enough shots to set the Japs off again.

This kept up all through the night. We hoped they hadn't been able to radio for help—a squad had been sent in to destroy their aerial. Another unit of eleven commandos tried a surprise attack. They were discovered and showered with grenades. Ten of the eleven were wounded, though all were able to get back.

During lulls in the battle we could clearly hear Kaida and Otani shouting to the Jap garrison to surrender. They were right up close, in the line of fire from both the Japs and the Paluchun. They certainly took their work seriously.

Shortly before dawn, General Wang ordered us back to a mountain village about two miles to the rear. Something seemed to have gone wrong. With the dawn a report came in that the tunnelers had run into some unexpected obstructions which held them up; and with daylight coming on they had had to quit.

With powerful forces of Japs moving in our direction, it would perhaps have been prudent to abandon the whole project and withdraw. The General held conference with the others. In the midst of this a field telephone jangled—a report on the Jap columns to the east and northeast: they were not on the move; apparently they knew nothing of our presence or of the attack on Lofan.

"That settles it," announced the General. "We'll finish the tunnel tonight and blow them up as planned."

We blew them up.

Appendix

DRAFT PROGRAM OF THE JAPANESE PEOPLE'S EMANCIPATION LEAGUE

(Drafted by the Standing Committee of the Anti-War League of the Japanese People, North China Branch, During its Session in January 1944, at Yenan, China.)

TO END THE WAR

As a consequence of the "Manchuria Incident," the Sino-Japanese War, and the "War of Greater East Asia," the militarists and the big munition-capitalists in Japan have greatly profited, while the Japanese and Asiatic people have suffered immeasurable sacrifices. The longer the war lasts, the greater and the severer will be the difficulties facing our nation. Therefore we demand:

a. That the war be ended at once.

b. That the Japanese troops and fleet be withdrawn from all the territories and waters occupied by them.

c. That a just peace be negotiated with the belligerents.

The above measures aim at helping our people to secure a peaceful life.

A LASTING PEACE

As it has been universally known that nearly all the wars in Asia during the past fifty years have been waged by the militarists of our country, we demand:

a. That those responsible for the "Manchuria Incident," the

239

Sino-Japanese War, and the "War of Greater East Asia" be severely punished.

b. That the influence of the militarists on Japanese politics be ended.

c. That the conscript system be replaced by a volunteer system, and that present armaments be reduced to a size sufficient only for Japan's territorial protection.

d. That a thorough peace policy be adopted in our foreign relations.

e. That Japan join a new international peace organization in the postwar era (a new League of Nations).

The above demands aim at averting another war and at setting up the most satisfactory relationship with foreign nations on the basis of the principle of existence and true co-prosperity.

AN ECONOMIC POLICY OF PROSPERITY

As a result of the prolonged and devastating war, the economic condition of our country has fallen into the utmost depression. We therefore demand:

a. That military expenditure be reduced to the minimum, and that the bulk of the national budget be devoted to reconstruction works and to the economic development and prosperity of the people.

b. That a highly developed machine-tool industry be established as a basis for heavy industries.

c. That a very efficient agrarian system be adopted, and mechanization of agriculture be carried out.

d. That external trade be developed in harmony with international relations.

The above demands aim at insuring the independence and prosperity of our nation.

DESTROYING THE MILITARY AUTOCRACY

As the militarists have been the most autocratic and most notorious force in Japanese politics, we demand:

a. That all privileges possessed by the militarists be abolished.

b. That the militarists' interference in political, economic, educational, and cultural affairs be forbidden.

c. That all organizations inspired by the militarists be disbanded.

The above aim at purifying Japanese politics.

A FREE DEMOCRATIC POLITICAL SYSTEM

As the freedom and rights of the Japanese people have long been under the heel of the militarists, we should demand:

a. That all such notorious decrees as the Act of Confiscations, the Act of General Mobilization, and that of Security Maintenance, be cancelled.

b. That political prisoners accused and sentenced for being anti-war, anti-militarist, or against social injustices, be set free.

c. That restriction of residence and of political affiliation be removed.

d. That full freedom of speech, press, meeting, and organization be granted to the people.

e. That men and women above the age of twenty shall have the right to vote.

f. That a democratic system of government be set up.

g. That in order to establish a democratic system a people's conference be called to recast the constitution.

The above aim at the building up of a free and democratic new Japan.

IMPROVING THE PEOPLE'S LIVING

Our people, long suffering under the exploitation of the militarists, have been living a third-class life. The hopeless war has again thrown them into hunger and poverty. We therefore demand:

a. That the prices of commodities and the taxation imposed upon laborers be lowered, and that all unreasonable and compulsory economic or labor burdens be abolished.

b. That the restrictions on wages and salaries of workers and laborers be abolished, and replaced by a just system of wages and salaries; that working hours be shortened, and that working-class quarters be improved; and that a Trade Union system be set up.

c. That the system of compulsory purchase of peasants' crops, and other unjust agrarian or agricultural decrees, be abolished, and that the peasants' union be permitted to exist.

d. That compulsory labor and military drill imposed on students be abolished, and that the progressive students' organizations be legalized, and freedom of research insured.

e. That effective relief be given to the middle-class merchants.

f. That all possible means be adopted to improve and raise the living conditions and culture of the Japanese people.

SAFEGUARDING THE LIVELIHOOD OF SOLDIERS, SAILORS, AND THEIR FAMILIES

As the living conditions of the presently conscripted soldiers, as well as those retired, are most miserable, we demand:

a. That a living standard for the families of presently conscripted soldiers be guaranteed.

b. That the living standard of all those maimed in the war be safeguarded.

c. That the living standard of soldiers and sailors in service be improved, and the rights of reading, meeting, and voting be granted to them.

The above aim at the improvement of the living conditions of those who have suffered most in the war.

Index

243

CHINA

U.

Kysylkhoto
TANNU-TUVA

Due

M N G

Tikwa

S I N K I A N G

NINGSI.

K A N

CHINGHAI

T I B E T

Lhasa

S I K A N G

Brahmaputra River

Ganges River

I N D I A

YUNNAN

B U R M A

THAILAND INDO-

① Shensi-Kansu-Ningsia
② Shansi-Suiyuan
③ Shansi-Charhar-Hopei
④ Shansi-Hopei-Honan
⑤ Hopei-Shantung-Honan
⑥ Shantung
⑦ Hwaipei
⑧ Northern Kiangsu
⑨ Central Kiangsu
⑩ Hwainan
⑪ Southern Kiangsu
⑫ Central Anhwei
⑬ Eastern Chekiang
⑭ Hupeh-Hunan-Anhwei
⑮ Kwangtung
⑯ Hainan